Paddy and the Republic

Dale T. Knobel

Paddy and the Republic

Ethnicity and Nationality in Antebellum America

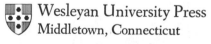 Wesleyan University Press
Middletown, Connecticut

1986

Brief portions of this book appeared in the following
articles by the author: "Know-Nothings and Indians:
Strange Bedfellows" in *The Western Historical Quarterly*, April 1984; "A Vocabulary of Ethnic Perception:
Content Analysis of the American Stage Irishman,
1820–1860" in *Journal of American Studies*, April
1981; and "Native Soil": Nativists, Colonizationists,
and the Rhetoric of Nationality" in *Civil War History*,
December 1981.

All inquiries and permission requests should be
addressed to the Publisher, Wesleyan University Press,
110 Mt. Vernon Street, Middletown, Connecticut
06457.

Distributed by Harper & Row Publishers, Keystone
Industrial Park, Scranton, Pennsylvania 18512.

LIBRARY OF CONGRESS CATALOGING IN
PUBLICATION DATA
Knobel, Dale T., 1949–
    Paddy and the republic.

    Bibliography: p.
    Includes index.
    1. Irish Americans—Public opinion—History—19th
century.   2. Public opinion—United States—History—
19th century.   3. United States—Ethnic relations.
4. Nativism—History—19th century.   1. Title.
E184.16K57 1986   973'.049162   85–8554
ISBN 0–8195–5117–1 (alk. paper)

Manufactured in the United States of America

First Edition

For my mother and father

Contents

Illustrations

NURTURE *(following p. 76)*

"The Lament of the Irish Emigrant": title page of popular 1840s ballad
A "flood" of Paddies: cartoon, *Harper's Monthly*, 1856
The stage Irishman: Tyrone Power's 1847 farce, *How to Pay the Rent*
Counting the Irish: Federal Manuscript Census, Hudson, Ohio, 1850
"Here and There; or Emigration the Remedy": English woodcut, 1848
"By industry and economy I am become prosperous": lithograph, 1843
"Popery Undermining Free Schools": woodcut, *The Papal Conspiracy Exposed*, 1855
"Jamie and the Bishop": cartoon from the election campaign of 1844
Anti-Catholic newspaper: *The Protestant Vindicator*, 1841
Protestant martyrs: illustration from *A Pictorial History of England*, 1845
Philadelphia "Bible Riots": broadside, 1844
Philadelphia "Bible Riots": lithograph 1844

NATURE *(following p. 156)*

New clothes, same old Paddy: cartoon, *Harper's Monthly*, 1854
"Celtic" physiognomy: cartoon of New York cabmen, *Harper's Weekly*, 1860
Lantern-jawed and low-browed Irish threaten the public schools: cartoon, *Harper's Monthly*, 1852
"Wanted—Protestant Girls": advertisement, *The New York Times*, 1852
A half-human Irish family: cartoon, *Harper's Monthly*, 1855
"Hans", comic and benign caricature of the German immigrant: *Harper's Monthly*, 1856

TABLES

The following tables appear in Appendix A:

The following tables appear in the Notes:

Preface

What did ethnicity mean to antebellum Americans? This is no little question to ask about the people of a comparatively small, new nation that, between 1820 and 1860, received over five million immigrants, overwhelmingly from outside the ancestral island of Britain. We know reasonably well what race meant to mid-nineteenth century Americans. But ethnicity is problematic. Doubtless this is because even more than race, ethnicity is a social classification. It is neither strictly biological nor precisely cultural. Ethnicity is a category of ascription and self-identification with boundaries defined by custom. What ethnicity means and who belongs to any particular ethnic group cannot be established objectively. One has to ask the participants in a society themselves, and the answers they give change with time. This makes studying the meaning of ethnicity in antebellum America—or in any other society—difficult and also important, for the construction a people gives to ethnicity, the way in which its members establish ethnic boundaries, and the relations they maintain with members of other ethnic groups reveal their interests and anxieties and their perception of themselves.

In attempting to recapture the antebellum image of the immigrant Irish and to place it in relation to Anglo-Americans' groping for satisfactory criteria of republican nationality, this book is guided by certain premises about ethnicity, interethnic relationships, and ethnic stereotypes. It adopts a social-psychological rather than an anthropological definition of ethnicity, taking ethnicity to be subjective and ascribed rather than objective and ideal. It treats ethnic groups as perceptual categories, with undoubted roots in linguistic, cultural, and ancestral consistencies, but perpetuated when populations set boundaries around themselves meant to define who belongs and who does not. Looked at this way, "ethnicity" has a verbal as well as a nominative quality; it is a process of giving identity to others and thereby to self. Thus ethnic diversity can endure in a society long after original differences between ethnic groups have begun to dissipate.[1] Moreover, I concur with social-psychologist Herbert Blumer that interethnic (and interracial, which was Blumer's original concern) image-making is collective rather than individual; it takes place, as Blumer put it, "in the remote rather than the near . . . the collective image of the abstract [i.e., other] group grows up not by generalization from experience gained in close, first hand contact but through the transcending characterizations that are made of the group as an entity."[2] Stereotyping transpires in public and has a prescriptive impact upon individual perception.

This outlook upon ethnicity and interethnic perceptions rationalizes the study at hand and guides its prosecution. It suggests, obviously, that ethnic interaction is channeled as much by how groups see one another as by what they are and what they do. It indicates that ethnic stereotypes grow and spread—and change—as the members of one group speak to each other through public media about members of another. That is, stereotypes reside in language; they are matters of words or, more to the point, patterns of words that become idiomatic for one people conversing about another. Consequently, to locate an ethnic stereotype is to study language, language in public media which played a prescriptive role in culture. Of necessity, this study which sets out to interpret antebellum Anglo-Americans' image of the Irish devotes a good deal of attention to simply finding it.

If insights taken from social science suggest where to look for the popular image of the Irish in antebellum America, the disciplines of the craft of intellectual history indicate how to look for it. Some of these disciplines have been changing recently, and several of the changes are particularly relevant to my enterprise. The first is intellectual historians' increasing sensitivity to the ubiquity of shared cultural symbols—among which I would include ethnic and racial stereotypes—which, as Gordon Wood describes them, "give meaning to behavior," and to the likelihood of finding them in many different layers of cultural alluvia.[3] Thus my surmise that the symbol/stereotype of the Irish in antebellum America showed up elsewhere than among articulate, direct, and self-consciously polemic disquisitions on the Irish. Instead, it subsisted primarily in *inciden-*

tal public conversation touching upon the Irish—on the popular melodramatic stage, in the literature of the schoolroom, among the columns of daily newspapers and monthly magazines, in best-selling fiction and travelogues or published reminiscences, and in the paperwork of government.

In the United States, the mid-nineteenth century introduced the age of the printed word. There had, of course, previously been a world of print in colonial and early national America, but one which involved most people indirectly, reaching them through the mediation of speech. But antebellum Americans waged their political battles in newspapers, sought domestic advice from magazines, taught their children from primers, and evangelized with tracts. They shared understanding and experience in essays and reminiscences, governed themselves with commission reports and legislative journals, and sought amusement in the first pulp novels and serialized fiction. Unlike the private, *written* word, the public, *printed* word not only reflected prevailing language patterns (and thus thought) but also prescribed. Foreign observers were especially impressed by the dependence of the large American reading population upon newspapers—for their information and also for their verbal style. Natives themselves expressed astonishment at the "immense number" (and influence) of other periodicals—religious, reformist, literary, scientific, political—that appeared and disappeared during the decades preceding the Civil War. Today's students of the period note the emergence of the first "best-selling" fiction, which began to supplement the traditional spoken literature of popular melodrama.[4] Bearers of the printed word like these were mechanisms of socialization. They propagated, authenticated, and legitimized patterns of language use. If the words applied to specific ethnic groups in routine antebellum "conversation" became culturally normative, that is, became stereotypes, we would expect to find them here.

Intellectual historians' growing evidentiary eclecticism, however, is matched by their aroused suspicion about how sources can be used—especially verbal sources such as the ones that carried forth the antebellum image of the Irish. "If Fourth of July orations are one's principal source," Lawrence Veysey warns, "one is entitled to talk about the views of the speakers as a collective entity, not about Americans as a whole. If school texts are used, one may discuss the views of their overwhelmingly Whiggish New England authors, not those of Americans at large."[5] Such caution proves salutary to the extent that it encourages historians to look for evidence sufficient to sustain broad conclusions. It may do disservice, however, when it discourages scholars from asking big questions at all, making the more limited research projects which examine only a class, a community, or an interest seem safer.

This inquiry into the relation of ethnicity to nationality through the medium of verbal stereotypes is not confined to a class or a community but is concerned with an interethnic image that was by its very nature societal. It tries to guarantee that the images in language that it locates in diverse sources cut across narrow interests and subcultures by turning to techniques of "content analysis." Broadly speaking, any study of verbal media is a content analysis, but in its more technical sense the term "content analysis" refers to the use of a particular array of research tools for uncovering, measuring, and comparing word patterns in text. Since these are techniques which probe beneath the surface of rhetoric, they extend the range of verbal evidence available to the researcher. Moreover, the systematic nature of content analytic research makes it possible to compare source materials to one another, allowing us to determine whether word patterns common to one kind of source were representative of word patterns in all. The content analyst spells out beforehand exactly what he is looking for in sources, making more difficult evidentiary sleight of hand.

As patterns in language, stereotypes are systematic—regular and repetitious. It requires system to locate system, especially when the patterns lie sufficiently beneath the surface of language to be obscured even from its users. Social psychologists study stereotypes by creating special opportunities for the display of language. They perform interviews, ask people to respond to scales, and administer questionnaires. But historians looking for past stereotypes have to deal with language as they find it. They cannot control the context or quality of the communications that descend to them from the past, but they can, nonetheless, ask questions of these communications as they might ask them of living interviewees. Thus "content analysis," described by one of its theorists, Philip Stone, as embracing "any research technique for making inferences by systematically and objectively identifying specified characteristics within . . . text." Fundamentally, content analysis involves identifying patterns of words.[6]

Modern content analysis traces its origins to Harold Lasswell. Lasswell, inspired by cryptographers at the University of Chicago, during the First World War, developed a systematic study of the "language of politics." Lasswell was concerned that the social scientific study of attitude lagged well behind the study of behavior. Inevitably, attitudes are only subject to indirect measurement. It is impossible to get inside the mind and observe attitude as one might observe conduct. Yet Lasswell suspected that indirect research could be rendered less intuitive and more concrete and objective. "Words," he decided, "provide us with clues [to attitudinal states] . . . we obtain insight into the world of the other person when we are fully aware of what has come to his attention." But it is well for the student of attitude to take language at less than face value, for words, of course, are liable to deceive. So the quantitative techniques of content analysis pioneered by Lasswell and his associates attempt to measure the building blocks of language—words and grammatical structure—rather than the surface of rhetoric.[7] The ultimate goal of such techniques, obviously, is to discover what people *mean* by studying but not quite believing what they *say*.

The quantitative nature of content analysis gives it power; it also provides grist for critics. Its power is the capacity to discern patterns, to compare, to be verified. Yet quantification is an inducement to over-simplification. Lasswell was inclined to measure absolute quantities. What rendered a word or phrase or a theme important in analyzed text was raw frequency or, perhaps, frequency beyond some arbitrary threshold. Edmund Ions, author of *Against Behavioralism: A Critique of Behavioral Science,* has identified as a serious fault in content analytic research the naive "presumption that communication patterns . . . follow normal curves or other frequency distributions encountered in statistical theory." This is a troubling charge, not only because it seems to fit Lasswell's early work but because it appears applicable to many modern content analytic studies—in history as in other disciplines. Morris Janowitz complained in the late 1960s that there had been an "intellectual stagnation" in content analysis for nearly twenty years.[8] There is not much evidence that things have changed since. Too many applications of content analysis to historical problems have failed to move beyond the absolute frequency count. The big question for most practitioners of content analysis seems to be "How many?" How many "statements about Domestic Communism as a percentage of all relevant statements" appeared in the speeches of President Harry S. Truman from 1945 to 1950?[9] How many laudatory articles on the Soviet Union appeared in American magazines during the Second World War? How often did United States senators show the proper rhetorical courtesies to colleagues during the decade preceding the Civil War? Content analysis in historical research frequently does read overmuch into sheer quantity.[10]

The present study of a popular verbal stereotype is not concerned in any way with absolute frequencies; it is not an effort to discern how often the Irish surfaced in the "conversation" of antebellum America but to identify *how* they were mentioned whenever they were represented in words. It is satisfied with the testimony of contemporaries that the Irish were a recurrent, if incidental, topic of conversation in the mid-nineteenth century. What is important to this study is relative frequency. Which sorts of words predominated in conversation touching upon the Irish at a particular point in time? Which sorts were few and far between? I have tried to discern the vocabulary of ethnic description applied to the Irish in antebellum America, to determine whether it changed over time, to establish whether it was uniquely American or the extension of a traditional English stereotype, and to compare it to the rhetoric of vituperative nativist critics of Irishmen, Catholics, and immigrants. The arithmetic answers (how many, how few) that content analytic techniques provide are not of much intrinsic interest, but the inferences one can make from them are—inferences about the growth and elaboration of a stereotype in relation to stereotyper needs and interest, to developments in interethnic relations, and to the actual characteristics of the stereotyped. (For a thorough discussion of content analysis and its applications to this study, see Appendix A.)

This is not, in any event, a book about content analysis, and readers will find little enough of it in the text. Content analysis only provides an evidentiary foundation for the story of an evolving ethnic stereotype, suggesting the kinds of illustrations that, at different junctures in the mid-nineteenth century, authentically represented word imagery. The unobtrusiveness of content analysis in the text is a product of accident as well as of calculation.

I first came to this study fresh from an immersion in the research literature of social psychology and—temporarily outrunning my historian's sense of the complexity of human nature—expected to find a rather mechanistic relationship between ethnic interaction and ethnic stereotypes in antebellum America. I naively anticipated that for every upsurge in Irish immigration, downturn in the American economy, highly publicized sectarian debate between Catholics and Protestants, and fiercely contested election in which foreign-born voters held the balance there would be a corresponding, albeit masked, shift in popular images of the Irish. Content analysis, I expected, would reveal every twist and turn.

As it turned out, I was right to think that the Irish stereotype had more flexibility in it than the corpus of scholarship would lead us to suspect, especially that it was more than a recrudescence of traditional English stereotypy. But I did not quite imagine that the most important conditioning agent was ideological rather than sociological, that it was a fluid conception of American nationality. I did not originally intend that this would be a book about antebellum nationalism. That the evolving Irish stereotype captured Anglo-Americans' growing interest in a nationality by descent was equally unpredictable. As this study progressed, I learned more than I would have imagined about the way in which the faddish phrenological pseudosciences helped create a cultural environment that might encourage such a nationalism. And I discovered the essential irrelevance to this process of nativist attitudes toward the Irish and toward American nationalism. Both pseudoscience and nativism emerged from this study more fascinating to me, the former because of its success in affecting popular thought, the latter because of its failure.

The plan of this book observes the sequence of my developing understanding of the Irish stereotype's character and significance in antebellum America. An introductory essay raises the question of just what ethnicity (and ethnic diversity) might have meant to mid-nineteenth century Anglo-Americans, suggests why existing scholarship fails to provide a satisfactory answer, and explains that this is an issue of some moment. Chapter One indicates how a study of antebellum public "conversation" may be able to capture popular dispositions toward ethnicity by identifying the changing content characteristics of the verbal image of the Irish. Chapters Two and Three develop the early and later antebellum Irish stereotype, adding the architecture of illustration to the framework of content analysis. They examine particularly the sources of changing interethnic descriptive idioms—sources within changing constructions of American nationality and without. Chapter Four, "Science and the Celt," describes the role played by popular pseudosciences in propagating the idea that interior human character was readily discernible in exterior aspect, encouraging the public to take seriously a nationalism attached to a particular ethnic descent. The most vocal critics of European immigration—devotees of antebellum America's several nativist clubs, lodges, and political parties—are scrutinized in Chapter Five. Nativist rhetoric bore its own distinctive image of the Irish and its own distinctive disposition toward ethnicity and nationality. Burdened by these, nativists were unable to prolong the lives of their organizations by taking full advantage of popular ethnic prejudices. But, then, neither could the image of the Irish in late antebellum verbal culture be sustained. One by one, the ideological props that supported it gave way. As the last chapter of this book tries to show, however, the attitudes toward American nationality exposed by the changing image of the Irish before the Civil War had enduring consequences, helping to set conditions for Americans' handling of racial and ethnic diversity in the concluding decades of the nineteenth century.

Acknowledgments

In preparing this book, I have accumulated many obligations, some old, others more recent. George M. Fredrickson—whom I claim as teacher, colleague, collaborator, and friend—saw value in my enterprise at its inception and has been loyal since in offering advice and encouragement. At an early stage in the project, Robert H. Wiebe proved a valuable advisor, discouraging me from thinking too small. Over a period of years I have received one or all of the following—encouragement, advice, and criticism—from Stephen A. Innes, Harry L. Watson, John H. Lenihan, James C. Bradford, and James M. Rosenheim.

I wish to acknowledge assistance rendered by the staffs of Northwestern University's libraries and the Sterling Evans Library of Texas A&M University. Additionally, I derived particular benefit from the research collections of the University of Chicago, the University of Texas at Austin, Rice University, Kent State University, and Sterling and Beinecke Libraries of Yale University, as well as the Library of Congress and the public libraries of Chicago, New York, and Cleveland. I am grateful for financial support provided by the College of Liberal Arts Research Committee and the Fund for Eminence in the Humanities and Social Sciences of Texas A&M University. Carole Knapp of the Department of History at Texas A&M typed—and retyped—the manuscript with speed and intelligence.

I am particularly appreciative of the editorial guidance provided by Jeannette Hopkins, Director of the Wesleyan University Press. She did not let me off easily, always pressing me to clarify, simplify, and explain.

It is my great pleasure to acknowledge Professor Robert B. Boehm, my uncle, for having placed me in the way of writing this book by—

long ago—encouraging a fascination with American history in general and the history of antebellum America in particular. My wife, Tina Jamieson Knobel, and our children, Allison and Matthew, were impatient supporters, wishing me well in this venture but insistent that I set it aside from time to time to share their lives. I thank them for offering the proper perspective.

Paddy and the Republic

Paddy and the Republic

"Maybe, those among ye, that's half a mind to make a bit thrial o'
Ameriky, fears it's all strangers ye's going to find there. Jist the contrary it
is. Whin the ship we wint over in hault in to the wharf, ye'd thought, an
y'd bin there, that ye was in Cork or Dublin, for all the world; sich powers
o' Irish men an Irish women were crowding down, to saa oult acquaintances,
an haar news fro' the Emerald Isle, an to tinder their sarvices. Our paple
are growing fast i' that country, depind. What with their own incrase an the
constant immigritting fro' all parts o' Ireland, there's na dout, in the minds
o' sinsible calkillaters, but we may possiss the hull country one dee."
      Lucius Manlius Sargent, "An Irish Heart," in *The Temperance Tales*
                                                            (Boston, 1848)

THIS IS NOT a book about the Irish in antebellum America; it is
a book about the popular image of the Irish in antebellum America,
which was quite another thing. It suggests that serial images of the
Irish were closely related to evolving notions about ethnicity and,
especially, the nature of American nationality.

   In 1965, when his revised study of white Americans' image of
the Indian was published as *Savagism and Civilization*, Roy Harvey Pearce's disarmingly commonsensical conclusion that most of
the public discourse about aboriginal Americans from the seven-
teenth century to the mid-nineteenth had been, in the final analysis, only Euro-Americans "talking to themselves about themselves"
still seemed remarkably innovative.[1] Within half a dozen years,
Pearce's equation of interracial perception with self-perception be-

3

came one of the orthodoxies of American historiography, bolstered and extended by admirable new studies of white Americans' images of the Chinese by Stuart Creighton Miller and of Afro-Americans by Winthrop D. Jordan and George M. Fredrickson. Dissimilar in many respects, *Savagism and Civilization, The Unwelcome Immigrant, White Over Black,* and *The Black Image in the White Mind* nevertheless all demonstrated that at critical junctures in the development of an American society, "outsiders" had been popularly portrayed in ways that helped the "insiders" make sense of themselves.[2] As Jordan's vivid description of interracial relations in the colonial period made plain, Anglo-Americans discovered at an early date how to use minority groups as points of reference for a metaphorical surveyors' "triangulation" that placed the whites just where they wished to be.[3]

Historians know well that the ranks of "outsiders" in America's past have been filled out by more than racial minorities only. Among these were elements from the great wave of non-English European immigrants—principally from Ireland and Germany—that arose and crested during the four decades before the Civil War. Although the antebellum era—originating less than half a century after union and concluding with disunion—was one in which the Anglo-American ethnic majority was preoccupied with self-perception and self-definition, with defining American nationality, there is no substantial literature which places antebellum interethnic imagery in relation to self-imagery. Perhaps this helps explain why—in light of Pearce, Miller, Jordan, and Fredrickson—historians no longer talk about *the* nineteenth century's image of Indians, Asians, or blacks, having learned that interracial perceptions changed along with self-perceptions, but (as the guilty accomplices of folklorists and students of literature) persist in talking about *the* American image of the Irish before the Civil War, as if the perception of the United States' largest white ethnic minority was quite unaffected by Anglo-Americans' pursuit of self-identity.

The mid-nineteenth century was a crucible of American national identity. Antebellum Americans eagerly sought a distinctive national character that might provide them with a usable past, with a unifying present, and with a predictable future. Many of the great extended debates over the nature of American nationality during the four decades preceding the Civil War revolved about the issues of race, religion, and what contemporaries called "political character." Blacks, slave and free, were not properly Americans, though native-born, but "aliens—political—moral—social aliens," Henry Clay thundered in the Congress of the United States. "We are decidedly more exclusively 'American' than many of our white brethren," the editor of New York City's *Colored American* roared in rebuttal.[4] "Puritanism, Protestantism, and True Americanism are only different terms to designate the same set of principles," said Presbyterian evangelist Charles Boynton from his Cincinnati pulpit. Roman Catholic convert Orestes Brownson taunted back, "Protestantism is not and cannot be the religion to sustain democracy."[5] "No man educated under one system of government can ever become thoroughly inbred with the essence and spirit of another," read the immigration plank of the American party platform in 1854. But "if not an American, pray what is he?" asked a contributor to *Putnam's Monthly*. "An Englishman, a German, an Irishman he can no longer be; he has cast the slough of his old political relations forever."[6]

Race, religion, and political character were primary sources of national identity for antebellum Americans; they were means by which Americans distinguished themselves from others. Other identities were treated as contingent, popularly regarded as inevitably related to—even dependent upon—these three. As the bases for making categorical judgments about people, they were the root-stock of virulent prejudices. White, Protestant, and "republican" seemed to many contemporaries to be necessary indicators of nationality. Were they regarded as sufficient too? Strenuous efforts to institutionalize racial, religious, and ideological prejudices demonstrated the importance mid-nineteenth century Americans invested in the three criteria of nationality. In the case of race, of course, institutionalization was both extensive and devastatingly effective. Slave codes in the Southern states, whites-only franchises in most of the Northern states, State Department passport policy, and, ultimately, the U.S. Supreme Court's Dred Scott ruling of 1857 built racism into the forms and practices of antebellum society.[7] Concurrently, anti-Catholic zealots sought to institutionalize religious prejudice by rewriting the nation's naturalization oaths and by requiring religious tests of candidates for public office. Immigration "reformers" sought to build standards of political conformity into the naturalization procedures and proposed excluding the foreign-born from all positions of public trust. In Massachusetts, during the mid-1850s, "reform" legislation temporarily tightened the standards of state citizenship along these lines.[8]

Although institutionalized racism operated primarily to keep blacks from the full privileges of American nationality, efforts to formalize religious and political prejudices largely worked against white European immigrants, the larger number of whom were Irish and German. Did religious and political prejudices mask underlying *ethnic* prejudices? Was ethnicity also a primary identity for antebellum Americans, a definite criterion of nationality? Did Irish, German, or English descent qualify or disqualify someone for inclusion in the family of Americans? If ethnicity—like race, religion, and political character—was one of those "national" identities, then it, too, would provide a source of categorical judgment about both individuals and groups.

A modest historical literature, scarcely a decade old, suggests that the confidence of Oscar Handlin that "Americans of the first half of the [nineteenth] century had assumed that any man who subjected himself to the American environment was being Americanized" or of Merle Curti that all expressions of antebellum ethnic nationalism constituted mere Fourth of July puffery was excessive.[9] Paul Nagel's *This Sacred Trust: American Nationality, 1798–1898* demonstrated that there were more than enough reasons for Americans of the 1830s and 1840s to begin to define themselves as an endurant people, a "Volk" in the language of contemporaneous German romanticism, and not simply as self-selected participants in a contractual republic. These included desires to render the increasingly friable Union more than a "unity" of interest or even of principle; to overcome the divisiveness of the "miserable trammels of party"; to "harmonize lofty calling and meager attainment" as the age of the founding fathers receded; and to project a glorious national destiny. Members of the majority Anglo-American descent group were well-conditioned to adopt an ethnic nationalism that transcended holiday oratory.[10] Suggestive recent studies produced during the American Revolution bicentennial lent at least tacit support to such a suspicion. Gilbert Osofsky wrote about the breakdown of the "romantic nationalist tradition" before the Civil War, the tradition which connected national independence with personal freedom and accounted being *in* the free land sufficient qualification for being fully *of* it. And Kenneth Stampp noted that in the 1830s anxiety about the fragility of a union based upon mere utility to the participants began to produce the first systematic efforts to justify perpetual union.[11] Many citizens would be looking for some source of perpetuity under these circumstances.

Historians tend to agree that before the Civil War, at least, ethnicity did not become bound up with nationality in any way equivalent to the popular connection of nationality with race, religion, or political character. The bellweather case has been the most conspicuous and aggressive manifestation of antebellum American nationalism, the nativist enthusiasm of the 1830s–1850s. If the extreme nationalists who formed the core of what eventually came to be called the "Know-Nothing" movement did not make specific white ethnicity a criterion of American identity then no one did. The presumption here is that Abraham Lincoln was exactly right when he identified the nativist secret societies and political clubs of mid-century as running ahead of the general public in enthusiasm for a highly exclusive nationality. Lincoln's famous critique of Know-Nothingism was that whereas Americans had already fairly watered down the principle of human equality enunciated in the Declaration of Independence by compounding nationality and race, the nativists would also exclude Catholics and the foreign-born from true Americanism—and might, if permitted, add further qualifications.[12] About twenty years ago, historian Yehoshua Arieli, in *Individualism and Nationalism in American Ideology,* suggested that, indeed, by the middle decades of the nineteenth century there were accumulating pressures in the United States for "a new type of nationalism . . . a nationalism of the Old World type based upon common descent" and that "Know-Nothings" were their chief representatives.[13] But most students of the period observe that nativists rarely appealed to specifically ethnic prejudices. For nativist ideologues, ethnicity seemed to be a contingent, not a primary, identity. Irish "papists" and German "radicals" were the typical objects of nativist scorn, the emphasis of nativist denunciations falling upon religions and political character rather than ethnicity. Historians with otherwise diverse understandings about the sources and character of antebellum nativism agree that nativists' ethnologic theory was rudimentary and that without an ideology that could connect nationality with heredity, there was no effective way of establishing ethnicity as a primary identity that could not be sloughed off easily.[14]

Although a few historians hazard that there were some notable expressions of Anglo-Saxonist or Anglo-Americanist ethnic nationalism outside nativist circles during the mid-nineteenth century, they have been hesitant to attribute such sentiments to more than literati in immediate touch with the currents of European romanticism. Even historians' increasing application of "ethnocultural political analysis" to antebellum voting behavior has not caused the larger number to take ethnicity per se much more seriously. Instead, they treat ethnicity as a cipher for religion and describe ethnocultural tribes rather vaguely as "pietist" or "liturgical" in character such that the labels spill over strictly ethnic boundaries.[15]

Historians regularly point out that there were no successful efforts, at least, to institutionalize ethnic prejudice in antebellum life or to place strictures upon the rights available to persons of Irish, German, or other particular European descent strictly because of putative ethnicity.[16] Despite the plethora of "No Irish Need Apply" notices in newspaper advertisements and shop windows, ethnicity itself never became an effective basis for wholesale economic discrimination. And without this there could be few barriers to social mobility in an age that increasingly linked status and wealth. Religious and ideological prejudices, of course, cut across ethnicity. The physical and cultural similarities among the main components of the antebellum white population—British, Irish, German—would seem to make ethnic boundaries indistinct and any form of purely ethnic discrimination difficult to enforce. Perhaps because of this failure, James Kettner did not address the question of ethnicity and nationality in his recent study, *The Development of American Citizenship, 1608–1870*. The only serious questions that developed about birthright to American nationality and its privileges before the Civil War, Kettner indicates, involved racial minorities.[17]

This book grows out of my discomfort with conventional wisdom about mid-nineteenth century Americans' self-identity, antebellum nationalism, and the social significance of ethnicity before the Civil War. In an era when many citizens seemed desperate for a unique and useful national character, when the dominant element in the population was so thoroughly British in descent, and the customs and language decidedly English, ethnicity would seem a distinction far too convenient to be ignored. At the very least, the extraordinary vituperation directed specifically at the Irish in America, compared to the more equivocal reception accorded other ethnic components of the Atlantic migration recognized by contemporaries and moderns alike, points toward considerable ethnic sensitivity among the public at large. This was after all a time, as J. R. Pole puts it, when there was the greatest popular interest in distinguishing between who was *of* the republic and who was only *in* it.[18] The larger portion of the white population, for whom French commentator Alexis de Tocqueville had found an ethnic label—"Anglo-American"—overlooked few opportunities to set themselves apart from others.[19]

Historians may well be asking their questions about ethnicity and nationality in antebellum America of the wrong sources. The organized and aggressive anti-Catholic and xenophobic nativist movement (even considered very broadly) is scarcely a suitable index to the parameters of antebellum nationalism and the nature of Anglo-American ethnic attitudes. It seems extremely hazardous to rely upon the rhetoric of a distinctive and particularly strident minority as a gauge of the dispositions toward ethnicity of the majority of white Americans. The antebellum nativist can be rather clearly identified; he was a member of a nationalistic secret society like the Order of the Star-Spangled Banner or, alternatively, an anti-Catholic enthusiast identified with the American Protestant Society or the American and Foreign Christian Union. He can be singled out as someone who voted for the candidates advanced by political groups such as New York City's Native American Democratic Association in 1835, Philadelphia's American Republican party, which flourished a decade later, or the American party, which operated more or less nationally during the mid-1850s. Thanks to a new generation of voting studies, these individuals are not nearly as anonymous as they once were; we know many of their characteristics. They were not so very numerous—at the peak of nativist activity we would be hard-pressed to call them typical voters, even if their concerns were symptomatic of a larger public's. Their motivations were extraordinarily varied.

As problematic is historians' expectation that they can read inter-ethnic attitudes out of collective behavior, that the action of mobs or other forms of overt public hostility to immigrants and Catholics accurately measures popular dispositions toward ethnicity, race, religion, and political character. Such behavior, of course, is channeled by environment and opportunity. Under certain circumstances (particularly in mobs), people do what they may not feel and feel what they dare not do. At best, only a small number of Americans participated in the dramatic instances of anti-immigrant hostility recorded for history and it is troublesome to extrapolate from these extraordinary events to ordinary ethnic attitudes of a societal character.

The present study relies upon a systematic examination of American language as a measure of the breadth and depth of specifically ethnic prejudice in the United States during the four decades preceding the sectional fracture of 1860. It observes the treatment of the Irish—the antebellum United States' largest white ethnic minority—in the patterns of everyday communication. It connects language with the nature, sources, and functions of popular ethnic attitudes. It presumes that language captures the way in which ethnic groups "see" one another, hence that language prescribes, as well as reflects, popular interethnic attitudes.

This is a book about an ethnic stereotype, a popular image that even contemporaries routinely called "Paddy" (and "Bridget"), propagated in commonly spoken and written discourse. "The symbol for the Irish," immigration historian Thomas Curran has written of the antebellum period, "was Paddy." Paddy, he said, represented Popery, poverty, and political corruption; Paddy was synonymous with "foreign." Other scholars have other lists of synonyms for Paddy. Adrienne Siegel, author of a recent study of cities and city people as represented in nineteenth-century American literature, suggests that the "Paddies" were tagged as dirty, unruly, mercurial, and improvident: attributes allegedly fixed to "minority groups in many periods of American history."[20]

Historians like to think of Paddy in symbolic terms. They examine the rhetoric of nativist politicians or observe the conduct of anti-Catholic mobs and extrapolate from that what they take to be popular perceptions of the Irish, combining the most salient descriptions into a caricature. The resulting array of words becomes Paddy. One historian's Paddy is likely to differ somewhat from every other historian's, although historiographical fashion has given Paddy a rough appearance and the core of a personality.

But Paddy is, properly speaking, not a scholarly invention. Research need not create Paddy, only locate him. For Americans before the Civil War, Paddy was a word portrait, a collection of adjectives applied over and over again to the Irish in Americans' ordinary conversation. This is the authentic definition of a stereotype. The words did not merely represent attitudes; they shaped attitudes. They reflected experience with the Irish; they also directed interethnic experience. And the words—or pattern of words—evolved as the nature and context of interethnic relationships evolved. As a stereotype, Paddy simultaneously captured the needs, interests, and self-perceptions of Anglo-Americans as they came into contact with the Irish, and also, in turn, adapted to the results (or at least the perceptions) of contact. Paddy was certainly not a Know-Nothing invention foisted on a gullible public. For the larger number of white Americans, Paddy *was* the Irish: men, women, and children.

This book's goal is to discover Paddy's actual constituents, to locate the words that were the stereotype and from the words to infer what Paddy meant to speakers, auditors, readers, and writers—to the mass of antebellum Americans. Historical inference is more art than science, but the collection and organization of data—of words—can be pursued in a systematic, scientific way. A well-conceived poll of representative language might allow us to offer some holistic observations about the treatment of the Irish in Anglo-American culture with confidence that what is captured is more than the outlook of an unrepresentative minority. Such a poll demands breadth as much as depth. The temptation to read deeply in a single literature such as explicitly anti-immigrant nativist literature is great. Most Americans, however, encountered the Irish stereotype in diverse doses, in school books and newspapers, in magazines, novels, and travel literature, in politicians' speeches and public oratory, and even in the spoken literature of the popular stage. A search for Paddy necessarily begins with these.

Paddy was in motion. There was at any particular point during the antebellum period a consensual image of the Irish in the patterns of language, but over the course of time the image changed. What this motion shows is that the popular sense of American nationality was changing, too. The answer to what J. R. Pole identified as the big antebellum question—who was really of the republic?—was in flux. The verbal image of the Irish "hardened" perceptibly between 1820 and 1860. During the 1820s and 1830s the popular Irish stereotype made a close connection between environment, nurture, character, and behavior. There was a character/conduct matrix linked to ethnicity but subject to reform. Americans, by implication, could be made of Irish stock, with difficulty perhaps, but still made. By the end of the 1840s, the stereotype had become considerably less forgiving, drawing a tighter connection between behavior and birth, suggesting that it was more difficult for the immigrant Irish to shake off their background and become acceptable republicans. During the last decade before the Civil War, the verbal image of the Irish virtually merged ethnicity and nationality, implying that authentic republicans could only be born and not made. As the image of the Irish evolved, it captured a growing tendency among Anglo-Americans to try to define their nation as a people or "Volk" rather than as a contractual union.

The metamorphosis of the verbal image of the Irish gives us new reason to take more seriously the popular impact of the ethnological pseudo-sciences that swept over antebellum America. Reginald Horsman, in *Race and Manifest Destiny: The Origins of American Racial Anglo-Saxonism,* has suggested that the paucity of "ethnologic" arguments in nativist rhetoric is no indication that racialist nationalism failed to win public interest.[21] The contrast between Paddy and the decidedly different word portrait of the Irish employed by nativist pamphleteers and rhetoricians at once underscores the scant role of Anglo-Saxonist thought in nativist ideology and suggests that historians have characteristically underestimated public receptivity to an ethnic nationalism. Not only might this shed new light on what Stephen Thernstrom has called nativism's "striking" failure to generate more than ephemeral mass support, but it also suggests that the evolution of American nationalism in the nineteenth century, which ultimately issued in the elaborate racism of the Progressive era, was far from a simple lineal process.

This book documents the gradual institutionalization of ethnic prejudice in antebellum American language. There it became a powerful criterion of American nationality, as capable of influencing social structure and behavior directed at maintaining that structure as if it had been institutionalized in statute. The institutionalization of a specifically ethnic prejudice directed at the Irish suggests that ethnicity became another primary identity for antebellum Americans. Americans drew self-identity from their attitude toward an ethnic minority they characterized as un-American. Ethnicity became an identity to which other characteristics—such as religion and political character—became contingent. Recognition that ethnicity was, at least for a time, an important source of American self-identity is critical to an understanding of the nature of antebellum nationalism as well as of the limits to the popular appeal of nativism and of the reception accorded to European immigrants before the Civil War.

"In everyday conversation, in politics, and in business, how often do we hear of emigration," observed the editor of New York's monthly *Knickerbocker* magazine in December, 1840. No wonder. Seventeen years earlier a contributor to the *North American Review*, discovering that Germans were landing in the United States at the rate of one thousand per year, called the flow of immigrants "prodigious."[22] What cause for comment, then, must the 100,000 European arrivals in American ports during 1842 have created—or 1854's 406,000. Ethnic diversity was not altogether new to American experience but the newcomers' numbers were. "Emigrants" as contemporaries called them—or immigrants, as we would say now— were the subject of talk from the early 1820s up to the Civil War.

With only two exceptional years, the Irish—even discounting the Ulster Scots-Irish and migrants of Anglo-Irish descent—constituted the largest single ethnic component of European immigration between 1820 and 1854. Thereafter, until the Civil War, they were outnumbered only by German arrivals. Few other nationalities were sufficiently represented in the mid-nineteenth century phase of the transatlantic migration to distract much of the attention of the Anglo-American ethnic majority from the Irish. Together with newcomers from Britain and the German principalities, the Irish made up virtually the entire flow.[23] The British—English, Scots, Welsh, and Scots-Irish—were more or less easily overlooked by Anglo-Americans. Although Germans inevitably excited comment from native observers, the Irish featured more prominently in

American conversation during the four decades preceding the sectional fracture.

Mid-nineteenth-century Anglo-Americans worried the "problem" of European immigration. It was debated in the popular press, documented in the journals of legislatures, and made the subject of nativist thunderings; whole volumes were devoted to proving that immigration was either the nation's fortune or its ruin. This discourse was blatantly didactic; its object was to persuade. Necessarily, it focussed on the Irish.

But more often—and more significantly—the Irish were mentioned *incidentally* in the ordinary, everyday verbal exchanges of antebellum Americans. These nondidactic, even subconscious, references to the Irish descend to us through all kinds of "conversation" preserved in print. In 1855 *Harper's* magazine thanked its readers for "all the 'good stories' they send us of our brethren and sisters of the Emerald Isle." The "Musical Soiree of the Ladies of the Methodist Protestant Fair" for 1844 treated its patrons from the District of Columbia to the strains of "Erin is My Home" and "Lament of the Irish Emigrant." Nathaniel Huntington's widely-used *System of Modern Geography for Schools* (1836) taught, "Notwithstanding the natural fertility and beauty of Ireland, poverty and misery prevail . . . the spirit of industry is discouraged," and, thereafter, admonished its impressionable readers to "Describe the general condition of the Irish." Henry Bidleman Bascom, bishop of the Methodist Episcopal Church, South, reported in the pages of his travel diary—published with his biography in 1847—that in western New York State he "dined on fat middling and fried eggs and passed the night at a tavern where I was annoyed by the noise and ubiquity of a parcel of Irish waggoners, half-beast-half-devil, from whom I was relieved only by their getting too drunk to continue their revel."[24] Over and over, the Irish surfaced in such "conversation," as well as in that preserved in antebellum melodrama, novels, essays and addresses, published reminiscences, and government documents: the alluvia of verbal culture. Some of these references were to the Irish in America, others to the Irish in their homeland. Because Irish immigration to the United States was an ongoing phenomenon with no end in sight, the distinction was blurred. This year's Galway cottager might be standing next year on the docks of Manhattan.

That incidental references to the Irish in antebellum "conversation" were frequent, and hence important, was recognized by perceptive contemporaries who understood the power of words—especially repeated words which become a style in language—to mold popular attitudes. As Francis Bowen put it in a discussion of "The Irish in America" for *The North American Review*, "Sympathies and antipathies as to men and things, depending upon temperament or chance association, are more potent than the sober results of judgment." The chance associations of Anglo-Americans with the Irish in everyday conversation—in ordinary language—were many. Their influence was strong. How strong was suggested by Delaware's Senator James Bayard, who justified a request to the U.S. Department of State for a report on the character of Irish immigrants in 1855 with the remark that "It is to obtain in an official form, which we all of us may have attained, but probably imperfectly, in a variety of modes, through newspapers and otherwise."[25] Most Americans never received any information in more "official form" that either contradicted or corroborated what they received incidentally as the auditors and readers of words. In fact, the more often the Irish were encountered in language, the stronger the influence of words. "Official" confirmation, ultimately, might seem irrelevant and contradiction errant. Abolitionist Lydia Maria Child sensed that the words neither had to be very numerous nor sophisticated to have power. "I never hear an Irishman called Paddy, a colored person called nigger, or the contemptuous epithet 'old beggar man,' without a pang at my heart," Child wrote in 1841, "for I know that such epithets, inadvertantly used, are doing more to form the moral sentiments of the nation, than all the teachings of the schools."[26]

Antislavery activists, who had considerable experience with the relationship between words and attitudes, were quick to grasp the implications of popular conversation. The "poor Irish emigrant," a subscriber wrote in to William Lloyd Garrison's antislavery *Liberator*, was, like the black American, a victim of the "fiend prejudice." For the words that treated the Irish in everyday conversation were not random; there was pattern to them—as there was pattern in the words applied to blacks.[27] Words propagated an image of the Irish, and thus an attitude (for all such intergroup images are value-laden) able to substitute for real personal experience with Americans of Irish birth or descent and, hence, to become a source of undifferentiated judgment. "Certain propositions are assumed gratuitously . . . not because they are true, but because we have been accustomed to believe them," explained Ohio magazinist James Hall in a discussion of anti-immigrant sentiment for his readers.[28] The undifferentiating quality of the image rendered even gender distinctions irrelevant. "Bridget" was only Paddy with skirts.

"Irish is a word of most composite signification with us," wrote a contributor to an 1848 number of a widely-circulated monthly magazine, Boston's *The Christian Examiner*. There was truth enough in that, and not only because the Irish were so often topics of both speech and print at a time when their increasing numbers seemed to many contemporaries to be virtually synonymous with white ethnic diversity in the United States. It was certainly right on the mark to call the object of significance a "word." During the mid-nineteenth century, the word "Irish" mobilized an entire sub-language that defined and evaluated all to whom the term was deemed to apply. "Irish" was a word with "composite" meaning. A composition of words is what gave it sense—descriptive adjectives, nicknames, and predicate complements of several kinds put to work in ordinary talk and writing. In any period, the words had a central tendency. Their use was idiomatic. Accordingly, so laden with value was the word "Irish" that Horace Greeley remembered it as an expression of torment among his childhood playmates.[29] No matter how many immigrants landed on the republic's shores between 1820 and 1860, the larger number of Anglo-Americans would have no sustained personal experience with Irish men and women of the first generation nor perhaps even with their offspring of the second. Geography or residence or occupation or class kept them apart. But they did encounter the Irish constantly through words— they read about them, heard about them, talked about them, and sometimes even wrote about them. Thus they "learned" about the Irish and pretended that they understood them through and through. Even those who would gain more immediate experience of Irish-Americans found that exposure shaped by their previous and sustained contact with the Irish in language. To locate the composite idiom (the words) mobilized by the word "Irish" in the common repositories of language is to locate an ethnic stereotype.

To call Paddy a stereotype is to make it clear that the word image was more than the sum of its parts, no mere accumulation of random references. The word image was societal rather than personal, consensual, a style in language. Not all references to the Irish shared the same words but they drew from a common vocabulary and had particular descriptive emphases. The idiom—Paddy—was not confined to any particular interest group or subculture, just as it was no nativist invention. And the image could change as verbal habits changed—but usually at a rather deliberate pace. There is an inertia in language.[30]

On the other hand, to call this ethnic stereotype a composition of words is to demystify an expression that is too often an example of social scientific jargon. This ethnic imagery is not accessible to us only through the most speculative exercise in psychohistory. Paddy was a literary and rhetorical phenomenon that is still available for immediate inspection if we know how to look for it. Of course, antebellum illustrators and caricaturists sometimes tried to represent Paddy in pictures and actors attempted to portray the image with makeup, costume, and gesture, but at best they were giving abbreviated alternative form to an image pervasive in common language.

What did "Irish," then, signify among antebellum Anglo-Americans? Was it primarily a religious stereotype, associating the American Irish with particular ecclesiastical forms and theological principles? Or a political stereotype—also focusing on belief connecting the Irish with particular dispositions toward or capacities for government? Or was it a cultural stereotype, stressing behavior and role and highlighting the customs, characteristic occupations, and social institutions of the Irish in the United States? Or strictly an ethnic (or, perhaps, ethno-racial) stereotype, suggesting that Irish descent conferred physical and psychological character and lay at the root of all other manifestations of group distinctiveness?

At a time when Americans were trying to establish a national self-identity, these are potentially revealing questions. Likewise, at a time when the nation was about to struggle (militarily and intellectually) over the place of blacks in American life, how Anglo-Americans would react to white immigrant ethnic minorities was no small matter. It involved the question of what made a person an American—birthplace, race, specific ethnicity, religion, political principle, shared experience? Could one not born an American become one? The understanding Anglo-Americans had of the nature of their nationality would have the greatest bearing upon how they would receive into American society and polity not only blacks but also the more ethnically diverse immigration of the late nineteenth century.

"The identity of the population of any country is essential to the preservation of good order, to the perpetuity of its established institutions, and to the protection of its citizens," wrote Samuel Busey in a lengthy tract on European immigration published in the late 1850s. "Identity," for Busey, not only meant "character" but also "uniformity."[31] The two went hand in hand in the minds of many mid-nineteenth century Americans. The people of the United States would have no distinctive character, no nationality, unless they were uniform in some respect.

James Kettner has recently reminded us that the antebellum establishment of "birthright" citizenship in law—ostensibly confirmed by the Civil War—by no means indicated that the public mind was cleared of all "questions about the extent, the shape, and the exclusiveness of the community of citizens." The continued inequality of black citizens in fact, if not in statute, demonstrated the terms of full inclusion into the ranks of Americans had not yet been entirely settled. And if not settled for blacks, were they completely settled for others?[32] At mid-century, Americans were still working out exactly what nationality meant.

So, too, students of antebellum social reform note the waning, as mid-century approached, of early nineteenth century reformers' "environmental optimism," which had affirmed that human nature was plastic and reformable. Michael Katz, historian of antebellum education; David Rothman, observer of the asylum—prisons, orphanages, poor houses, and mental hospitals; and John Kasson, who has examined the model paternalist factory towns of early industrial New England, among others, all suggest that pessimism about the redeemability of human character accompanied the reformers' increasingly frequent encounters with European immigrants.[33] This also reflected developing ideas about self and others among Anglo-Americans, about the nature of human capacities and incapacities. National character, if a matter of nature, could safely be conferred upon a far less diverse population than if nurture dictated.

Examination of verbal stereotypes ought to emancipate the study

of antebellum nationalism from the stifling embrace of nativism—
the loud, sometimes violent, and intermittently political criticism of
European immigration in general and Roman Catholic immigrants
in particular. The noisy advocates of "America for Americans!" en-
joy high visibility among professional historians for their part (still
much disputed) in the reshuffling of political parties that preceded
the Civil War, and among laypeople for the quaintness of their organizations (e.g., Order of the Star-Spangled Banner), their hon-
orific titles (e.g., Grand Sachem), and their ceremonies (e.g., The
Third Degree of Brotherhood), as well as for the apparent extrava-
gance of their bigotry. "Know Nothings" (the 1850s nomenclature
which has become generically descriptive of antebellum nativists)
are objects of the same kind of fascination often displayed for the
mummeries and excesses of the Ku Klux Klan. In 1970 Oscar Handlin wrote, "The attitudes of various ethnic groups toward one another have been almost entirely unexplored. While the historians
of the past three decades were more sophisticated than such earlier
scholars as Gustavus Myers and R. A. Billington, who brought together under a vague rubric, such as nativism or anti-Catholicism,
a variety of manifestations of hostility, the treatment of group prejudice and conflict was nevertheless inadequate."[34] The study of antebellum nativism has become more sophisticated since that time;
still, this has seldom been the study of ethnic prejudice of a societal
nature. Handlin's criticism retains much of its original force. Any
inferences about Anglo-Americans' ethnic prejudices from the rhetoric, forms, or practices of organized nativism require extrapolation
from anti-foreign hostilities that were rarely specifically ethnic and
a leap of faith from the loudly articulated dispositions of a minority
to the almost inarticulate ones of a majority (roughly equivalent to
reading the nature of popular interracial attitudes in, say, the 1970s
out of the activities of a small but visible Klan). John Higham's
popular and widely-circulated definition of nativism—"intense opposition to an internal minority on the grounds of its foreign (i.e.,
un-American) connections"—suggests why the historical literature
devoted to this subject contains so few direct treatments of ethnic
attitudes.[35] To many antebellum Americans, Roman Catholicism
was foreign; monarchy was un-American, as were Illuminism and
Free Masonry. To some, cities were foreign, even factories and machines. "Demon rum," crime, and poverty were also alien. Aboli-

tionism was denounced as a foreign device and remarkably, even something as thoroughly Americanized as racial slavery was, too. It is possible to say much about anti-foreign sentiment in mid-nineteenth century America and still say little about the agency of ethnicity and ethnic prejudice.

A study of societal stereotypes embedded in language is an effort to grasp more directly widespread ethnic attitudes—even those, especially those, held subconsciously—without going through the mediation of nativism. We ask too much of the nativist phenomenon in antebellum America when we ask it to speak for Anglo-American society as a whole. And we give back too little. Doubtless the flourishing of anti-immigrant and anti-Catholic hostility in the middle decades of the nineteenth century was a revelatory cultural episode, but we would certainly understand it better if we knew the environment of ethnic attitudes in which it subsisted. We could assess a good deal more accurately both the sources and limits of nativism's appeal.

Another advantage of studying ethnic attitudes through verbal stereotypes is that the approach does not confuse prejudice with discrimination. This is not a study of actions, of assaults, verbal or corporal, which are frequently related to enduring attitudinal states indirectly. It attempts as much as possible to capture attitudes expressed in their least intentional and therefore least manipulated form—ordinarily, reflexive verbal stereotypes. As American philosopher Charles Sanders Pierce once said, "It is the belief men *betray* and not which they *parade* which has to be studied."[36]

A delegate's query to his colleagues at the United States Anti-Masonic party convention in 1830—"What constitutes an American citizen?"—was an important one for contemporaries and remains crucial for students of the antebellum period.[37] The definition that Anglo-Americans gave to the nation's most populous white ethnic minority, the Irish, captured in language, reveals much about the way in which they conceived of American national identity.

CHAPTER ONE

Finding Paddy

" 'Your stories of Irish blunders,' writes an Ohio friend, 'are vastly amusing; but did mortal man ever hear of anything more Erinical than this, which a friend of mine vouches for?' "
"Editor's Drawer," *Harper's Monthly* (August 1855)

RESCRIPTED AND staged for American audiences, *The Omnibus*, an English comic melodrama, was a hit when it opened in Philadelphia in 1833. The chief instigator of fun was an Irish houseboy, one Pat Rooney, of whom his indulgent mistress offered: "I grant he is a little too familiar, but he does not mean to be impertinent; he's as simple and unsophisticated as a child, and honest as he is light-hearted."

A year later, and not far from Philadelphia, when Irish immigrant laborers on the Baltimore and Ohio Canal demonstrated against their employers, *Niles' Weekly Register* traced the "riots" source to the character of the participants: "The origin of these outrages lies much deeper than whiskey. They come from ignorance and prejudice, with superstitious adherence to unholy combinations, and accustomed resorts to force in their own land."[1] "Familiar," "simple," "unsophisticated," "honest," "light-hearted," "ignorant," "prejudiced," "superstitious": here was feedstock for an ethnic stereotype. Was it only accidental or quite characteristic that in *Niles'* and *The Power Omnibus* alike description of Irish subjects fastened upon

21

what might be called "character" rather than upon appearance or behavior and that both particularly drew attention to alleged qualities of the mind? Or mere idiosyncrasy that both implied that character was an artifact of nurture and education—and coincidence that they shared this implication with a contemporaneous school geography's account of the Irish: "If education be the formation of character, and if circumstances are the instruments of education, we can see in the history of the Irish nation, at least in part, the sources of the tenacious pride, the poetic temperament, the rich mosaic imagination, the quick feeling, the intense nationality of the Irish people"?[2]

An 1850 article written by the liberal Unitarian minister Theodore Parker of Boston for the *Massachusetts Quarterly Review* expressed a strikingly different view of the Irish, one which betrayed little optimism that what had become habitual in nature could ever be nurtured out: "Is it to be expected that an ignorant, idle, turbulent, and vicious population will, by a mere repeal of bad laws, become industrious, provident, moral, and intelligent?" If these were words typically employed to describe the Irish in the years around mid-century, then styles of language had been much altered since the time of the great Philadelphia Bible Riots (1844) and the onset of the famine-era immigration from Ireland. The *New York Times'* account of mob violence in Brooklyn half a decade later, in the mid-1850s, was different yet: "It was the old hatred of the Saxon and the Celt. They may crush down the Irish until they become the servile and degraded class they are in the Old World. . . . With a struggle of races, the Saxon must carry all before it."[3] This seemed to capture another version of Paddy, a word portrait that neither looked to a bad education nor to ineradicable habits but to the imperatives of "blood" to describe the Irish. If each of these were typical of the verbal image of the Irish at somewhat different junctures, then there could not have been anything like *an* ethnic stereotype called Paddy but, instead, several, and the kind of confident summary statements concerning *the* perception of the Irish in antebellum America so common in the historical literature must be considered suspect.

The only answers we can have much confidence in would come from actually taking a poll of language as it is preserved for us from the forty years of American popular "conversation" that preceded the Civil War. And the answers may well defy our expectations of what Paddy was and what Paddy meant. Of necessity, such a poll must draw upon sources representing what Richard M. Dorson calls popular, mass, and elite cultures.[4] We seek, after all, a *societal* stereotype. Although the language of popular culture originates in word of mouth, it readily takes to print. Antebellum oral culture, for example, was preserved in the scripting for melodrama, not only among the most widely-patronized entertainments but also a responsive channel for public emotions. Popular culture circulated in the antebellum newspapers, which clipped and shared one another's stories and anecdotes, relying heavily upon the contributions of amateur correspondents and letterwriters. It passes down to us through the sporting and entertainment magazines, which filled their pages with jokes, tales, and chronicles of race course and gaming table.

Dorson calls the organs of "mass" culture repositories for "centrally directed signals."[5] Today, of course, the metropolitan newspaper, national newsmagazine, or electronic media have this character. But before the Civil War, it was represented by the literature of the schoolroom, the publications of churches and "benevolent" enterprises, political magazines like *Niles' Weekly* or the *Whig Review,* the literature of legislatures and other government agencies, as well as didactic novels, essays, and biographies that grew out of the era's reformist enthusiasms: temperance, African colonization, the antislavery movement. These materials more nearly captured the United States' "official" culture, emanating from bureaucratic sources and national in their distribution. A high—although not uniformly distributed—literacy rate for native-born white Americans, the growing ubiquity of the public school (at least in the North), and the increasing interest and participation in political contest ensured a large audience.

Not only "elite" culture, circulating in the literary, philosophical, and professional journals, novels and essays of literary merit, addresses and scholarly treatises—the bearers of systematic thought or "intellectual discourse"[6]—but also fully amalgamated antebellum common culture conveyed the popular verbal image—the stereotype—of the Irish. Shared symbols betrayed a cultural reflex.

Paddy had both size and shape. Although we can never discover *all* the words that antebellum Americans used to describe the Irish, the number was finite. A modern student of ethnic stereotypes cogently explains why: "communication is a social process and word usage is highly regulated. Thus, there appears only a relatively small number of words incorporated from the natural language for the description of ethnic groups." Social psychologist Howard Ehrlich, working with questionnaires, compiled a list of just one hundred and twenty-three words which seem to function as modern-day Americans' core vocabulary of ethnic adjectives.[7] But questionnaires inevitably impose some structure upon the responses. Polling language found in the cultural alluvium of a historical period is almost bound to produce a larger number of words appropriated to the purpose of interethnic description. But not so large as one might think. Among 2,255 descriptive references to the Irish, Germans, "immigrants," and Anglo-Americans in antebellum printed text consulted for this study, just 392 different descriptive terms recur. (See Appendix A for a list of these.)[8]

But Paddy's shape is more important to us. By shape, I simply mean the pattern of word use. A vocabulary of a few hundred words was the raw material of conversation about ethnic groups. But the preference that speakers and writers displayed for particular words is what gave the stereotype a distinctive character, is what made it an idiom. Nor is it just words that are important, but the *kinds* of words. "Pugnacious" and "quarrelsome" are different words, but they have exactly the same descriptive emphasis. So too with "impudent" and "impertinent." "Friendly" and "generous" are, to be sure, not synonyms, but they also point to a single dimension of personality or character—just as "ragged" and "low-browed" are both descriptions of physical appearance. One of the more effective modern efforts to classify *kinds* of ethnic adjectives hypothesizes that there are really just fourteen different types. After the experience of working with language in historical sources, I would add one more to make it fifteen.[9] The heart of this quest for Paddy is based upon analysis of about 1,600 references to the Irish in antebellum conversation.[10] If the descriptive terms in these were randomly distributed among the fifteen categories, about one hundred and eleven words would turn up in each. But the actual distribution ranges between thirty-two words and two hundred and twenty-three, scarcely random. Nearly forty percent of all treatments of the Irish in a diverse literature culled from four decades of American "conversation" fell into just three adjective categories. Moreover, if the antebellum period is broken down into shorter time spans, the concentration of particular kinds of descriptive expressions is even more pronounced.[11]

There was, then, such a thing as Paddy, a consensual stereotype of the Irish sustained in the patterns of Anglo-American conversation. Or, rather, there were several Paddies—at the very least three. For the evidence is compelling that the treatment of the Irish in popular discourse evolved over time, crossing a couple of watersheds. And well it should have evolved if it was an authentic stereotype which helped its bearers make a certain—if extraordinarily oversimplified—sense of a complex world, which captured Anglo-Americans' view of ethnic others and of themselves. Over the course of the antebellum period, the form of the stereotype changed markedly; the way in which the Irish were described changed more than the focus upon any particular alleged trait. This is a key discovery. After all, we expected to find a stereotype in language; the testimony of antebellum Anglo-Americans themselves led us to anticipate it. An exercise in content analysis offered confirmation that it was there and some solid evidence about just how tight the word configuration that defined the Irish in Anglo-American verbal culture really was. But in the historiography of antebellum ethnic relations there is little to suggest that the Paddy in Americans' vocabulary on the eve of the Civil War was very much different from the Paddy that subsisted in their language forty years before.

The kinds of words used for interethnic description in the patterns of antebellum language were of two principal types: those treating "extrinsic" characteristics and those treating "intrinsic." Extrinsic characteristics show outwardly; they are the artifacts of inheritance, condition, or behavior: physical traits, aesthetic/cultural sensitivities, economic condition, religious and political proclivities, relative emotionality, evidence of industry and persistence, or, conversely, of unreliability and caprice, or a disposition toward aggressive and violent behavior. Interpersonal "relational" qualities, intellectual capacities, and moral traits—both positively and negatively evaluated—may be called intrinsic, in the sense of inside, literally, aspects of what we might call "character."[12]

Although the period 1820 to 1844 preceded the vast famine-induced Irish immigration of the late 1840s, the Irish ethnic minority in the United States grew steadily in both size and visibility during these years. Contemporaries saw 1844 as a turning point; that was the year of the widely publicized Kensington and Southwark riots at Philadelphia, with violence of unprecedented scale between Irish Catholics and Protestants of both Anglo-American and Orange Irish descent. From 1820 to 1844, the verbal image of the Irish was, to a remarkable extent, a stereotype dominated by intrinsic characteristics. It drew much more attention to aspects of interior character than to the full range of behavior, condition, and appearance; it focused not on Irish religious affinities or political loyalties or economic condition but on interpersonal style, fundamental morality, and intelligence.[13] This did not mean that the behavior or condition of the Irish went unrecognized in patterns of language. What it indicates is that behavior and condition were understood by the users of language to be the correlates of character and—since this was a pejorative stereotype (as systematic or unsystematic examination of the language makes plain)—that this negative behavior issued from "impudence," "ingratitude," "ignorance," "foolishness," "wickedness," "contrivance," and the like.

Still, there was bound to be a certain ambivalence, even charity, about a verbal image that associated ethnic distinctiveness with character. For character could be understood as a product of environment and of nurture and, therefore, subject to development. It was not formed and fixed for all time. New England educator and divine Timothy Dwight captured the implications of ordinary conversation in early antebellum America when he wrote in the 1820s:

From what I have read and heard, and particularly from my own observation, I am persuaded that the national character of the Irish is inferior to no other people. To me they appear not to be surpassed in native activity of mind, sprightliness, wit, good nature, generosity, affection, and gratitude. Their peculiar defects and vices, I am persuaded, are owing to the want of education, or to a bad one.[14]

This perspective did not hold up over time. Between 1845 and 1855, immigration from Ireland grew explosively (compelled by the potato famine) under the long shadow of the Philadelphia disturbances and several other subsequent, highly visible episodes of what was taken to be interethnic violence. By the mid-1840s, the verbal image of the Irish had become decidedly extrinsic and remained so until the Civil War. Direct references to condition, behavior, and physical appearance dominated, not randomly distributed among the various types of extrinsic descriptives but instead clustered in only two or three of the fifteen descriptive categories that serve as our points of reference.

The last "third" of the antebellum period, from 1853 to 1860, was a time when the Irish influx, although still very large, was gradually eclipsed in magnitude by the arrival of German immigrants. The most visible arena of interethnic relations during these years was the political. Between 1852 and 1865, anti-immigrant and anti-Catholic tickets were successful in contests for governorships, congressional seats, and representation in state legislatures; in 1856 the nativistic American party ran its own presidential candidate.

In the period 1845–1852, verbal imagery directed attention to propensities for "conflict/hostility" and "emotionality" as well as to physique. Forty percent of the perceptive units sampled from the conversation of this era featured such descriptives, with adjectives highlighting an alleged propensity for conflict and hostility making up fully 15 percent of the whole, the most overworked adjectives of all.[15] For the period 1853–1860, physical descriptions of the Irish took their place. Along with descriptions appropriately labeled "emotional" (adjectives like *frisky, enthusiastic,* and *temperamental*), "conflict/hostility" (*dangerous, quarrelsome, vicious*), and "insubstantial" (*idle, improvident, reckless*), they made up one half of the total.[16] This scarcely suggested that Anglo-Americans no longer gave attention to Irish "character" but that, increasingly over time, they found character revealed in conduct and, ultimately (in a fairly dramatic way), in physique, for the words of this type most often used were not descriptions of dress but of bodily conformation.

What had changed was a style of perception itself—Anglo-Americans' way of understanding ethnic others and presumably themselves. One could argue that the stereotype was hardening, becoming less tolerant. There is little hint of the early antebellum optimism about the plasticity of ethnic character in the comment of a mid-century diarist, which captures quite well the drift of conversation as a whole, that "More incongruous elements it would be difficult to bring together than the jolly, reckless, good-natured, passionate, priest-ridden, whiskey-loving, thriftless Paddy, and the cold, shrewd, frugal, correct, meeting-going Yankee."[17] To be sure, there was still a certain compliment paid to the Irish in such observations as these, but the characteristics praised—as well as those denounced—seemed much more deeply embedded, were perhaps even immutable, and scarcely products of an education, good or bad. Nonetheless, it was not such a "hard" stereotype as that which conversation captured a little later, deeper into the 1850s. "Big-fisted, double-jointed shoulder hitters who pride themselves on travelling through life 'on their muscle,'" one writer appraised the denizens of New York City's Irish slum, "demi-savages of civilization, and far more dangerous than the real, inasmuch as they possess greater scope for evil."[18] In this vivid illustration—as in the tenor of ordinary conversation itself—character and physique became intertwined; the implication was that Paddy was born, not made.

A sizeable historical literature suggests that antebellum Americans sought to validate their claim to be an inherently republican people by defining themselves as a white people. By connecting the qualities they thought requisite in a self-governing citizenry with race, they created a comforting auto-stereotype. Racial minorities, of course, were the foils of this stereotype. In popular images of blacks and Indians appeared all the qualities that were deemed ill-suited to republicanism. In recent years, a few scholars have ventured that similar stereotyped characteristics were applied to Irish immigrants; nevertheless, they have been almost uniformly reluctant to take the next step and acknowledge that antebellum perceptions of the Irish—like perceptions of blacks and Indians may—have fallen under the influence of what Marvin Harris has called the nineteenth century's "biologization of history," the association of a cultural hierarchy with heritable physical distinctions. Explicit Anglo-Saxonist rhetoric has seemed too rare outside intellectual circles and nativist Anglo-Saxonism too half-hearted to recommend the idea that Anglo-Americans might have found comfort before the Civil War in identifying themselves as a natural "people," a descent group, despite the acknowledged incentives for them to do so.[19] But the existence of a Paddy in the language of antebellum Americans that redefined what had once been taken as the fruit of education, first as habitual behavior and, subsequently, as physiological imperative suggests that neither a search of elitist rhetoric nor of nativist invective can tell the whole story of developing attitudes toward the Irish, in particular, and ethnicity and nationality, in general.

As interesting as what was in the stereotype is what was left out. Adjectives having anything immediately to do with religious and political proclivity or economic condition were uniformly rare in ordinary conversation touching upon the Irish. "Immediately," of course, is an important qualification, for the patterns of everyday language may have contained other word matrices which effectively associated the Irish with particular religious, political, and economic conditions or tendencies, though such indirection itself is doubtless suggestive. Still, at a time when anti-Catholic clerics, societies for home missions, and not a few politicians were clamoring about the "Jesuitical" Irish with their "papish" beliefs and irrepressible Old World "nationalism," the infrequency of such adjectives in most media is, in and of itself, noteworthy. So is the fact that, at a time when the Order of United American Mechanics and—a little later—the American party were denouncing the drain of the "vagrant" Irish upon the public purse and the threat posed to native Americans' jobs by "distressed" Paddies willing to work for the lowest wages, there were so few immediate references to the economic condition of the Irish in popular discourse.

Apparently the noisy and visible nativist movement had little direct effect upon the primary vehicle of interethnic perception in antebellum America—language. Understanding why requires an exploration of nativist parlance itself. But it also propels us right into the middle of a long-tailed debate over the principal sources of interethnic perception in antebellum America—whether culture, experience, or psyche was more important. Though it commenced nearly half a century ago, it is a decidedly modern debate, beginning only after historians had given up on the idea that Americans' perceptions of immigrants were likely to be products of clear, objective vision. Ray Allen Billington's *Protestant Crusade* still holds up as the most thoroughly-documented exposition of the view that Anglo-Americans inevitably looked—and looked askance—at the immigrant Irish through the heavily tinctured lenses of an inherited, culturally-normative anti-Catholicism. By the same token, Oscar Handlin's *Boston's Immigrants* remains the most direct representation of the argument that it was the actual "conflict" of economic interests, lifestyles, and political ambitions that most colored the view natives acquired of newcomers. Revised by John Higham and, more recently, by Michael F. Holt, this interpretation now takes the form that if the "conflict" was not always face to face between the native and the foreign-born, Anglo-Americans at least found it convenient to take immigrant minorities to be the causes of their distress during times of economic, political, or cultural anxiety.[20] The actual verbal image of the Irish—the words themselves—gives us some reason to doubt the adequacy of either approach to explain the Anglo-American perception of particular immigrant minorities before the Civil War (though each contributes to the understanding of *organized* nativism). The record of antebellum "conversation" suggests neither that the general public assimilated the militant anti-Catholic rhetoric of nativist ideologues nor that material ambitions and "status rivalries" can fully account for the forms assumed by Paddy.

Some might conclude from the paucity of direct references to religious identity or political and economic interest that a superior understanding of antebellum stereotype is offered by David Brion Davis's argument that images of immigrants were projective caricatures, that citizens invented the "enemies" that they needed to confirm a comforting self-perception and that Irish Catholics, or Mormons, or Masons would serve this purpose equally well.[21] The poll of American conversation will not sustain this conclusion. There *was*—at any given time—a word-portrait of Paddy that was rather narrow and specific. It was *not* a stereotype interchangeable with the popular images of immigrant Germans or of "immigrants" generically, much less of Mormons and Masons. Nor could Paddy have been entirely cooked up in the collective psyche of Anglo-Americans; it was demonstrably capable of responding to objective experiences in interethnic relations. Just consider which descriptives stood out in the word portrait of the Irish for the half dozen years or so after the mid-1840s: treatments of alleged violence, hostility, criminality, and disorderliness. Coming immediately in the aftermath of the widely-publicized Philadelphia riots of the spring and summer of 1844, which were popularly understood (to some extent misunderstood) to have pitted Irishman against Anglo-American as well as Protestant against Catholic, there can be little question of the responsiveness of language to social circumstances.[22] Doubtless the attention paid to this episode was magnified by its coincidence with the upsurge of Irish immigration occasioned by Ireland's starving time, and few other developments in interethnic relations were capable of having so dramatic an impact upon the public consciousness. But even this one instance is enough to show that no stereotype is wholly manufactured in the mind. The frequency of such adjectives as "turbulent," "pugnacious," and "vengeful" fell off as

the Philadelphia riots and, for that matter, the Great Migration receded into history.

While the evidence seems compelling that there *was* a distinctive sublanguage of ethnic description for the Irish in antebellum
conversation, in order to be assured that this language was specific
and not simply a pattern of words applied to white ethnic minorities
generally, we need some indication of cultural consensus that this
idiom was peculiarly appropriate for the Irish. Obviously, the same
sample texts that provided numerous perceptions of the Irish also
generated descriptive statements about the other principal antebellum immigrant minority—Germans—as well as about "immigrants"
as a class. For about every eight references to the Irish in this literature, there was one mention of Germans and another of "immigrants" with no nationality specified.[23] It was, of course, just this
which made it possible to compile a vocabulary of ethnic adjectives
that might illuminate the raw material from which the conversation about ethnic groups was crafted.

Humorist Thomas Butler Gunn's portrait of the proprietors of a
New York City "Gasthaus" in the late 1850s should be recognizable to modern readers:

He is a stout, middle-sized man, with a broad, good-looking face, light,
curly hair, short beard, and shaved upper lip, always in his shirt sleeves,
and seldom out of temper. . . . She is equally bulky in appearance but
dark-haired and very talkative. . . . As industrious and painstaking as
her husband, she is a hearty woman, with a proportionately large appe-
tite, a laugh and a joke for male boarders, and a ten-widow power
tongue. . . . Altogether, they are . . . hard-working, honest, good-
humored, solid.[24]

It was typical of the times. The verbal portrait of German-Americans exhibited in a modest sample of antebellum language reveals
the distinctive features of this stereotype: its relative favorableness,
its pronounced emphasis upon economic condition and aptitude, its
marked departure from the contemporaneous image of the immigrant Irish. Despite voluminous evidence of popular fears about the
dangers of ethnic diversity in the abstract, the verbal stereotype of
Germans, in particular, was actually rather complimentary. In text
published before 1845, half of all descriptive terms applied to German subjects praised moral character or substantial, industrious be-

havior. By contrast, among contemporaneous treatments of the Irish, such favorable descriptions constituted a mere 5 percent of adjective usages. The most frequently used descriptives for Irish subjects, those denoting demeanor or disposition problematic to social relationships, such as "impudent" or "ungrateful," were virtually absent from treatments of Germans. These notable differences in the language employed to deal with German and Irish subjects in antebellum conversation were sustained over time. Between 1845 and 1860, the adjectives *most* frequently applied to Germans—those suggesting industriousness and economic substance—were almost entirely absent from discourse about the Irish. But that characteristic appearing least often in discussion of Germans—"conflict/hostility"— was second in frequency among references to the Irish. While treatments of alleged Irish physical attributes were much more frequent after 1844 than before, no comparable tendency is evident in the discussion of Germans; physical description remained relatively rare. Actually, for the whole period 1820–1860, the most pronounced emphasis was upon qualities representing industry, continuity, and persistence.[25]

The antebellum German stereotype had more in common with the contemporaneous Anglo-American self-image than with the popular image of the Irish. As noted above, the word portrait of Germans was not simply neutral but actually positive. Anglo-Americans did distinguish themselves from the German population. An Anglo-American "norm image" also turns up in incidental sampling of antebellum conversation; predictably, it is almost wholly self-congratulatory. To describe their own qualities of mind, Anglo-Americans were inclined to use words like "ingenious," "versatile," and "shrewd"; to describe German intellectual character they employed the much more restrained "learned," "judicious," and "educated." Anglo-American behavioral traits included "energy," "enterprise," and "self-reliance," but Germans could better be described as "industrious," "persevering," and "thrifty." Not surprisingly, each stereotype contained physical analogues to these traits. Americans were "tall," "thin," and "agile," Germans "stout" and "short." Such is ethnocentrism.[26] The portrait of Germans in antebellum conversation was less unreservedly glowing than that Anglo-Americans crafted in words about themselves, but, still, close enough to raise the question of what kind of kinship Anglo-

Americans perceived between themselves and the German population and the further question of why they seemed to feel a closer kinship with the Germans than with the English-speaking Irish.

"Immigrants"—with no particular ethnicity specified—were the subjects of another sublanguage altogether. This was an idiom that changed little at all over the course of the antebellum period. It was insistently critical. It especially fastened attention upon its targets' purportedly negative "relational," intellectual, and moral characteristics. For the whole antebellum period, nearly 60 percent of all references to "immigrants" included in this study mentioned these traits, most of the remainder fastening upon alleged immigrant violence and poverty. Any species of favorable description was virtually absent.[27] The term "immigrant" had been employed since the earliest years of the republic as a pejorative reference to those who would not "harmonize" with the mainstream of Anglo-American society. This, for example, was how Thomas Jefferson treated "emigration" in his *Notes on the State of Virginia* (1785). American homogeneity, and thus happiness, would be disturbed by introducing into the bosom of the republic any very great "heterogeneous, incoherent, distracted mass" of immigrants.[28] The foreigner who "harmonized" with the native-born was no immigrant at all. "Immigrant," in other words, was a symbol, not a person. "Immigrants" were treated as the source of most national ills. "Our cities and towns swarm with this class of population," wrote the editors of the *New England Magazine* in 1834:

They come here ignorant and poor, without a knowledge of our institutions, that should make them prize them, and without any of that self-respect that might restrain an indulgence in vicious courses. However honest their purposes, they are proverbially creatures of passion, and, with the habits of dependence in which they have been educated, with their poverty and their propensity to drink to excess, they become a most dangerous engine in the hands of designing and bad men, to overawe and control our native citizens.[29]

The Irish in America had their champions, the Germans too. But who would speak in favor of the "immigrant"? If language is a measure, apparently very few. It was not only out-and-out nativists who chastised "immigrants." A disembodied symbol without means of self-defense, the "immigrant" was equally available to all as a scapegoat for political, social, and economic evils.[30] Antebellum America possessed a special language just for speaking of this abstraction.

If Paddy was neither principally an instrument of anti-Catholic demagogues nor the product of frustrated material ambitions, neither the creature of psychological projection nor a mere outcropping of language directed at any and all immigrant minorities, where did the word image of the Irish come from? To some extent, it descended, of course, from language itself—from styles of "conversation" carried forward from earlier generations and passed along by others who shared the English tongue. In 1819, when Matthew Carey, Dublin-born Philadelphia bookseller and publicist, released his celebrated historical apology, *Vindicae Hibernicae; or Ireland Vindicated,* he took pains to justify the exercise:

> To most readers it will probably appear extraordinary, and a work of supererogation, that, in a country and age so remote from the scene and era of the events which are discussed in this vindication, it should be deemed necessary to investigate the subject it embraces. The reasons are powerful, and fully justify the undertaking.
> The history of Ireland . . . is almost one solid mass of falsehood and imposture, erected . . . on the basis of fraud and perjury. . . .
> Nevertheless, from such foul and polluted sources alone, the knowledge of Irish history is derived . . . and, though it may appear extravagant, it is nevertheless a serious truth, that a large portion even of those who pride themselves on their literary acquirements, are almost as ignorant of the affairs of Ireland . . . as they are of those of the Arabians or Japanese.[31]

Though Carey's immediate objective was to counteract prejudices which he believed delayed Catholic emancipation in Great Britain, there is no doubt in these words of introduction that he was addressing Anglo-Americans, too. Through cultural tradition and, moreover, sustained literary contact, they were recipients of the same "terrific tales" about the Irish that helped prescribe the interethnic perceptions of Englishmen. And they were heirs to a word portrait of the Irish locked up in the English language itself. Carey demonstrated an intuition needing no social-psychologists' empirical proof that there is reciprocity between words and sentiments. But it would be quite wrong to conclude that the antebellum American Paddy was nothing more than a borrowed English one. For the most part, the kinds of transatlantic literature that Carey was talking about only reached a small, sophisticated audience in the United States. They were primarily written in the first place by and for gentlefolk. This was equally true of English novels and short stories and a nonfiction made up in large measure of histories, geographies, and travel accounts. The latter were especially popular among Americans, still working out their destiny as a nation and as a people, for they provided useful comparisons between themselves and others. Novels and stories, dominated in the early nineteenth century by character and local-color sketches featuring a pseudorealistic style, were the travelogue's natural companion. Only English popular drama, perhaps, was without a pronounced elitist bias, although a large number of early nineteenth century scripts were adaptations of contemporary novels.[32] That this was, in origin, largely an elitist literature is important for, as L. Perry Curtis, Jr., has pointed out, nineteenth century English gentlefolk had a definite stereotype of the Irish that effectively met class needs. Essentially projective, as Curtis describes it, this stereotype ascribed to the Irish all of the weaknesses "respectable" Englishmen feared they might find in themselves that would be incompatible with the burdens of imperial leadership. Likely, this was the stereotype that showed up in transatlantic literature.[33]

The point here is not that transatlantic literary styles accurately captured an English societal stereotype of the Irish, or that such literature was read by most Americans, but that if contemporaneous English habits in language influenced American conversation about the Irish at all, they must have done so through print. And it is demonstrable that while this literature carried a word image of the Irish that bore some notable similarities to the early antebellum American version of Paddy, it was not the identical stereotype. Analysis of a sample of English literature that circulated in the United States before 1845 indicates that the verbal image of the Irish in this material was, like its American contemporary, dominated by "intrinsic" descriptives, by the portrayal of "character" rather than condition, conduct, or appearance.[34] Both word images displayed a certain forgivingness, a willingness to account the alleged features of the Irish environmental in origin and subject to modification. But a much greater ambivalence was displayed in the portrait borne by transatlantic literature than in the early antebellum American equivalent. The American image of the Irish was nearly censorious, with very great agreement among many sources; the image in English literature circulating in America was only mildly critical, with considerable disagreement among sources and a much higher proportion of favorable descriptive statements about the Irish.[35] Both word images focused attention upon character, but American materials more often chose negative descriptives.

The verbal portrait of the Irish in early nineteenth century English literature should be instantly recognizable, for it is a close approximation of what is often represented to us as the stereotypical stage Irishman of drama, joke, and story. Here is the Irishman of contrasting parts: "Restless yet indolent, shrewd and indiscreet, impetuous, impatient, and improvident, instinctively brave, thoughtlessly generous, quick to resent and forgive offenses, to form and renounce friendships."[36] During the first four decades of the nineteenth century, the verbal image of the Irish captured in English literature comprised equal portions of praise and damnation. It was riven with contradiction. The aspects of character praised most often were also those laid open to the most frequent condemnation. On the one hand, the stereotype ran to a vocabulary which portrayed a people easy to get along with, to deal with in personal transactions: respectful, friendly, sociable, generous, good-hearted. On the other, it almost equally imputed to the Irish just the character that would render them the most difficult partners in any face-to-face exchange: clannish, distrustful, inconsiderate, impudent, selfish. Likewise, the Irish were credited with being witty, shrewd, and ingenious but simultaneously silly, careless, childish, and dependent.

Relatively speaking, the first forty-five years of the nineteenth century were a period of redirection in Anglo-Irish relations. Except for intensified rural unrest toward the end of the Napoleonic Wars, anti-English violence in Ireland was temporarily muted after the abortive revolt of 1798. Instead, Irish reformers maneuvered within the limited political space offered by the Act of Union in 1801. In England there was creeping acceptance of the need for some measure of Catholic emancipation, and a legislative breakthrough was achieved during the late 1820s. This was not accompanied by any acknowledgment of Catholics and Irishmen as social, political, or religious equals, but it did encourage a certain optimism that the Irish—at least the "respectable" Irish—could grow into the political responsibilities accorded them and that Anglo-Irish disputes could be resolved within conventional political channels.[37] English writing about the Irish reflected this sanguine temper. Authors of Irish history, geography, travelogue, and fictive folk narrative alike overwhelmingly agreed that of all the peoples of greater Britain, the native Irish were the least civilized, the most troublesome, and altogether decidedly un-English. Few seemed to doubt that the distinctive character of the indigenous population of Ireland could be easily traced back for centuries; but if they called Irish character unusual and often labeled it undesirable, they also took pains to show that it was redeemable. Almost gone were the extravagant assertions of an earlier period rekindled by the rebellion of 1798 that the "wild Irish" were incurable savages.[38] The fashion of the early nineteenth century was to treat Irish "national character" as environmental in origin.

Some of the cruder efforts to explain Irish uniqueness to English (and American) audiences stressed how accidents of climate and geography affected lifestyle. Robert Bell's *Description of the Conditions and Manner of the Peasantry of Ireland,* for example, attributed the "strange peculiarity" of Irish behavior strictly to diet. "Living for the most part on vegetable food and with scarcely any other beverage than water or milk," Bell wrote, "these people have a flow of animal spirits and a vivacity of temper unknown in countries whose inhabitants constantly feed on flesh and strong drink."[39] Other analysts of the Irish condition, especially progressive Anglo-Irishmen, traced the distinctive features of an ethnic culture to ubiquitous poverty. Proverbially Irish folk traits like generosity and wit could be understood as products of the peasant's struggle against a forbidding environment. "In Ireland," Richard and Maria Edgeworth explained, "the countenance and heart expand at the approach of wit and humor; the poorest laborer forgets his poverty and toil in the pleasure of a joke." Customarily, though, it was English authors who took the bolder step and indicted British misrule for the alleged perversities of Irish character. In an authoritative tone, John Pinkerton, author of the widely-used school text *Modern Geography,* wrote that among the ordinary Irish "the blunt honesty, the bold independence of the English yeomen are wanting; and in their place, the servility and artifice of the slave." "Oppression . . . originated with the native chieftains, and was continued by the English colonists, and to it many of the leading traits in the preceding character may easily be traced," Pinkerton explained to impressionable young readers.[40] The implication, of course, was that modern English government was more enlightened, that with oppression removed the Irish would progress. Either way, to Englishmen the stereotype was self-congratulatory. Its critical elements validated their own superiority and right to rule over Ireland; its positive environmental aspects demonstrated a conviction that progressive government would elevate the Irish. No wonder that Curtis has found that a pronounced "hardening" of middle and upper class Englishmen's image of the Irish did not occur until rather late in the nineteenth century, when a more militant Irish nationalism seemed unwilling to operate any longer within the bounds of the Union of 1801.[41]

Anglo-American perceptions of the Irish doubtless owed something to traditions in language derived from their English cultural inheritance and reinforced by the continued passage of literature and language from Britain to America. But the Irishman of transatlantic literature could not be quite that of American conversation.[42] Even in the first decades of the nineteenth century there was difference enough in the two Paddies to suggest that the conditioning agents of culture, experience, and psyche were dissimilar. The differences would become even more apparent as the American stereotype moved off in some new directions in the mid-1840s. English visitors to the United States quickly became aware of that. "The mere fact of being an Irishman," Francis Wyse disclosed to the readers of his lengthy American travel narrative in 1846, "is all but considered a crime in American belief."[43] Wyse—no particular sympathizer with the Irish—could see that the words Americans used about the Irish had a different "composite signification" from the ones he was used to. This should be no surprise to us. The Irish population that Wyse observed in America was neither the Irish in their native setting nor precisely equivalent to the immigrant serving and laboring community in Britain. They occupied new contexts, roles, and relationships within a new environing society. Moreover, the antebellum United States was a new nation, eager to define itself and its destiny, and still working out how to identify its nationality. Over time, this would have the greatest impact upon the forms that Paddy assumed.

CHAPTER TWO

"The Sin of the
Irishman Is Ignorance—
The Cure Is Liberty"

"The diffusion of knowledge, and especially moral and religious knowledge . . . is the only foundation of national virtue. . . . On the other
hand, general ignorance is almost invariably attended with general corruption, as is fully exhibited in . . . the Catholic countries of Europe."
W. C. Woodbridge and E. Willard, *Universal Geography* . . . *For the
Use of the Higher Classes in Schools* (Boston, 1835)

ALEXIS DE TOCQUEVILLE, the famed observer of early antebellum America, thought it easy to distinguish between American patriotism and European. In the Old World, love of country was "instinctive," a birthright refined by "a taste for ancient customs and
a reverence for traditions of the past." But in the United States, it
was a product of personal experience and calculated self-interest, of
participation in shared political life.[1]

In making this distinction, Tocqueville underscored the two
meanings of the word which the French and English languages
alike render as "nation." On the one hand, nation refers to a people
or descent group. On the other, it describes a political unit, a state.
According to Tocqueville, European nationality was of the first
type, American of the second. In contrast to the "historical" na-

tional peoples of the Old World, what made the Americans a nation at all was the republican polity, its laws, and the shared rights and benefits citizens derived from it. In America, no real nation existed prior to the state. In the words of a modern student of American nationality, Yehoshua Arieli, "National identity was not a natural fact but an ideological structure."[2] Citizenship, not membership in what might be denominated a "Volk," was the basis for inclusion in the nation. Loyalty to nation was one and the same with loyalty to Constitution. This decidedly anti-romantic construction of nationality, which placed little stock in blood or hoary tradition, was extraordinarily consequential for the early republic. It made possible a self-limited popular sovereignty in which individual and minority rights could be protected by law against majority will; after all, the nation—having no existence before the state—could scarcely claim primacy for itself over the statutory framework that gave the state life. At the same time, it offered encouragement to anyone who would give authority to individual conscience over social convention; and ultimately it could be used as a rationale for secession and the dissolution of the nation-state. The state was, after all, a temporal convenience, not the will of an historical "people" in any organic sense.[3]

Historians disagree over the intentions that lay behind such a construction of American nationality—whether they were only the product of a desire to differentiate New World nationality from Old (especially English) and in so doing legitimize the revolt of the thirteen colonies, or whether they reflected an effort to sever Americans from ethnocultural obligation to England, or, on the contrary, were a palpable necessity to differentiate American from Englishman in order to create a nation out of a colonial population already substantially non-English.[4] Historians agree that this conception of nationality rendered citizenship, as James Kettner puts it, "contractual, volitional, and legal rather than natural and immutable."[5] By education and predilection, the founding fathers found such citizenship as natural for a republic as they found it hazardous. Arthur M. Schlesinger, Jr., reminded scholars during the Bicentennial era that the first generation of Americans was convinced of the improbability of their experiment in self-government and of the absence of any exceptional qualities innate to the American people that might allow them to pull it off more easily than their precursors in Florence, Athens, or Rome. History and theory alike persuaded them of the cyclical mortality of states and the special vulnerability of republics to corruption. European contemporaries reminded them of the hopelessness of their venture in ways they did not appreciate but could not ignore. The latent Calvinism of their culture suggested that judgment fell on the just as well as the unjust and warned them against reliance upon a manifest destiny (that would come later). If there was any hope for the republic it was in environment—in the happy circumstances of geography and demography or in the incentives for popular virtue and intelligence that prudent men could create.[6]

The implications were at once that while citizenship was volitional the republic could ill afford to accept every volunteer and that there was nothing outside of nurture that rendered a man suitable or unsuitable for republican citizenship. Evidence of this outlook showed up in the form of the earliest federal naturalization acts, those of 1790, 1795, and 1802 (the politically charged act of 1798 was exceptional). All required a period of residence before admission as a citizen during which the probationer could discharge the effects of a prior environment and take on those of the new.[7] A Maryland congressman argued in the debates on the 1795 act that such a probation was demanded of immigrants so that "prejudices which the aliens had imbibed under the Government from whence they came might be effaced, and that they might, by communication and observance of our laws and government, have just ideas of our Constitution and the excellence of its institutions before they were admitted to the rights of a citizen."[8] Moreover, they might come to feel a part of society, share the interests of their neighbors, and take on local habits. The act of 1802 reinforced this thrust by calling for a declaration of intent to naturalize three years before finalization which would both ensure continuous residence and focus community scrutiny upon an applicant's character.

To the first generations of republic citizens, then, the American was made, not born. The beneficent influences of nature in North America which permitted—encouraged, they would have it—material and intellectual independence, the mutual familiarity and obligation occasioned by being born into the midst of a national community, or the assimilation of republican ideas, interests, and ways through acclimation prior to naturalization—these were what made the American. These were the hallmarks of nationality. Notably, they did not include blood membership in a Volk, in other words, ethnicity. (That the act of 1790 made *race* a qualification for naturalization, few contemporaries would have found contradictory.)

The way in which Americans viewed themselves went a long way toward conditioning the way in which they viewed others. That their nation did not have, officially, a specifically ethnic basis by no means made the early antebellum Americans that Tocqueville reported upon insensitive to ethnicity; it simply placed a certain construction upon it. Ethnicity denoted environment of origin and the institutionalization of environment in character. Republican theory held that character was critical to citizenship, hence to nationality. Any tendency to scrutinize character was a stimulus to examine ethnicity. This is exactly what stood out about the early antebellum word image of the United States' principal ethnic minority—the Irish. The Irish were clearly treated in language as a distinctive ethnic category, associated with particular environmental influences and a certain resultant character matrix. This stereotype did not suggest that character was fixed and changeless. But it did imply that some conscious effort was necessary to dispel the associations of ethnicity. And it suggested that the environment of Ireland was particularly ill-suited for the generation of republican character.

Samuel Griswold Goodrich, author of numerous popular geographies for home and school—books sometimes praised and sometimes damned for offering "knowledge made easy"—warned the readers of his *Ireland and the Irish* to "be especially guarded against two sources of prejudice to which we are particularly liable." One, as Goodrich explained it, was this: "We read English books, papers, and pamphlets. We read them under the inspiring influence of Britain's great name. . . . We see in the English people . . . exclusive love of country . . . which leads them to vindicate the tyranny of the government in Ireland, by portraying the Irish as an untamable race, deaf to reason, and only to be ruled by the harsh inflictions of power." Books, "tales," language, words crossed the Atlantic easily. These had the capacity to take the place of—or at least supplement—real observations, serving as the basis for social evaluation. But Goodrich also saw a second source of American "prejudice" toward the Irish outside of words and tales: "in our personal experience, we are familiar with the most ignorant and unfortunate of the Irish nation. We see, in servile employments, those who have been exposed to all the debasing influences that degrade mankind. Is it fair to draw from these a standard by which to judge a whole people?"[9] Interethnic contact, "experience" in Goodrich's words, affected perceptions which took expression in language. Such experience neither had to be extensive nor accurately and objectively interpreted in order to influence belief. For antebellum Anglo-Americans, then, words were both generators and couriers of interethnic perceptions—of stereotypes, the raw material for the undifferentiated group judgments we call prejudices.

The verbal image of the Irish in American culture during the early part of the antebellum period—the two and one-half decades beginning with 1820—reflected the dual function of words with respect to interethnic perceptions. Compared to the treatment of the Irish in American language after the mid-1840s, this was a recognizably "English" stereotype, suggesting how cultural styles passed from Old World to New in words. It was, of three successive variants of Paddy in American "conversation" the most "intrinsic," devoting more attention to the alleged interior character of the Irish (their moral, intellectual, and social "relational" character) than to what was taken by contemporaries as the externally visible record of character in conduct, condition, or appearance. By contrast with subsequent developments in American language, it was little concerned with the physical depiction of its targets. And it offered the most balanced—if somewhat incongruous—mixture of praise and condemnation in its treatment of Irish subjects. In all these ways the American stereotype of the Irish located in antebellum "conversation" prior to 1845 was like the language of ethnic description that pervaded the literature of English gentility—a transatlantic literature, as we have seen—and as such is testimony to the prescriptive power of words. But while the early antebellum treatment of the Irish in words was *like* the contemporaneous British stereotype it was not the British stereotype—not quite. It was decidedly *more* critical of the Irish; and more consistently critical, too. The transmission of traditional English verbal culture cannot be held wholly responsible for Anglo-American ethnic perceptions.

As Goodrich seemed aware, American experience had the capacity to alter traditions of perception—and thus alter language. Anglo-

Americans, after all, confronted a set of objective circumstances different from that of their British cousins. As observed earlier on, Anglo-Americans encountered the Irish in new contexts, roles, and relationships. And they had different *self*-perceptions which had much to do with their perceptions of others. From both the debt owed by Anglo-American language circa 1820–1844 to inherited British idioms and its departure from that traditional rhetoric we can learn more about the construction placed upon ethnicity in antebellum culture. Word patterns have directed us to the emphases of popular stereotypes. But we have to examine words themselves—words in phrases, sentences, and paragraphs that are the stuff of conversation—to make out what these emphases mean.

Throughout the first three quarters of the eighteenth century, the English North American colonies had become progressively less English. By the end of the Revolutionary era, only about two-thirds of the population of the thirteen rebellious dominions traced birth or descent to the ancestral island of Britain. Even including the Ulster Scots-Irish, no more than 75 percent of the new republican citizenry could really be called "British." The other quarter was composed of substantial concentrations of "native" Irish, Germans, and the Dutch and smaller but statistically significant communities of Frenchmen and Swedes. This pattern was roughly sustained through the War of 1812. But during the 1820s, 1830s, and early 1840s, the United States' ethnic patchwork began to assume a new design that it would bear until nearly the end of the century. The great Atlantic migration that accelerated after 1820 did not so much add variety to the existing population pattern through the introduction of new ethnic groups as selectively embolden it by dramatically increasing the size of several already represented.[10]

As early as 1828, the first year in which European immigration to the United States neared 25,000 persons, it was apparent that the gradually rising flood of population transfer had three primary tributaries: the British (Scots-Irish included), the German, and the "native" Irish. Within a short time German arrivals doubled British and the Irish almost equaled the sum of the two. After the 1820s, in fact, Irish and German immigrants consistently made up 70 percent or more of the full complement of European landings in a single year. Of these the Irish represented the larger number. While European immigration was scarcely unprecedented before 1820 and while Irish immigration in particular would grow much larger after the mid-1840s—to be followed by German a few years later—it was during the construction of a new ethnic geography between 1820 and 1845 that the visibility of the Irish in America increased. This made the backdrop for interethnic contact and perception unique. The early antebellum immigration to the United States from Ireland was mostly a migration of Roman Catholics but was not as denominationally uniform as later. Until the mid-1830s, at least, a considerable proportion of Irish arrivals remained Anglicized Protestants.[11] The newcomers were often quite poor, but they were not, in the aggregate, as impoverished as the distressed peasants and smallholders who would land in such large numbers after the Potato Famine commenced. The Irish were concentrated heavily in cities and in the Northeast, but the flurry of canal construction that spread to the Old Northwest and even to the upper South during the late 1820s and 1830s temporarily, anyway, gave them multi-regional representation and a substantial presence in the countryside.

Before 1845 there was no well-organized or powerful nativistic political movement. But anti-Catholicism—an Anglo-American tradition—flourished. During the 1820s, Charleston, Baltimore, and Philadelphia all experienced prolonged "trustee" controversies (over the investiture of Catholic church property in lay or clerical hands) that focused and invigorated Protestant hostility to the Catholic episcopacy and Roman centralism. Public debate over required Bible reading in tax-supported schools stirred up Cincinnati during the 1830s and Philadelphia and New York City in the '40s. In 1834 a Protestant mob incinerated a Catholic girls' seminary outside Boston, and two years later the publication of Maria Monk's sensational *Awful Disclosures of the Hotel Dieu Nunnery of Montreal* stimulated a succession of lurid exposés which fanned suspicions of both Catholic women's orders and the celibate priesthood. During the 1820s and '30s organs of Protestant militancy—publications like New York's *Observer* and *Protestant Magazine* and Philadelphia's *Downfall of Babylon*—noticeably increased in number. New organizations growing out of the evangelical fervor of the Second Great Awakening, including the Protestant Association, the American Protestant Reformation Society, and the Christian Alliance, provided both readership and financial support for enterprises of this character.[12]

Before the 1840s the eruption of anti-immigrant and anti-Catholic rhetoric into politics was largely restricted to the New York City Native American Democratic Association's campaign to "reform" municipal government in 1835 by turning Catholics, immigrants, and their sympathizers out of the Common Council. During the public school controversies in New York and Philadelphia several years later political nativism began to attract more enthusiasts. In 1843 both cities acquired branches of an American Republican Party which joined with anti-Catholic organizations in neighboring states during 1845 to form the Native American Party. At the very end of 1844 New Yorkers created the American Brotherhood and Philadelphians the Order of Sons of America, the first of the nativistic secret societies that would flourish for a decade.[13] These parties and partisans would be an important element of a new backdrop for interethnic relationships after 1844. Would they have much impact upon popular ethnic perceptions (or vice versa)?

"The Irish in general are quick of apprehension, active, brave, and hospitable, but passionate, ignorant, vain and superstitious," wrote American textbook author Jesse Olney in a widely-circulated school geography, first published in 1828.[14] Intermixture of praise and censure like this was entirely typical of Anglo-Americans' conversation about the stock for the United States' fastest-growing immigrant minority during the early antebellum period. So was the concentration of words upon "character," upon the capacity of the Irish for intelligence, morality, and social amicability. These not only turned up when Anglo-Americans like Olney were specifically groping for words to capture the essence of the Irish but also made a pattern in incidental references to Irish men and women, individually and generically, preserved for us in many forms of print. In this they were precedented by English stereotypes. But, as noted, unlike the ambivalence that seemed to characterize the verbal portrait of the Irish among genteel Englishmen during the first part of the nineteenth century, the summary assessment implicit in the American idiom was unmistakably pejorative. The less admirable attributes of the Irish fully checked their better qualities. Goodrich explained to readers of his popular "family library" that there was simply no question that the "improvident restlessness" of Irish character "about canceled out the patriotism," its chief merit. Likewise, wrote Francis Bowen for the *North American Review,* "in the same degree in which they are originally warm and social, they become morose and gloomy."[15] Virtue and vice, wit, and blunder, good-temper and ill coexisted in this word portraiture but vice, blunder, and bad-humor usually prevailed.

It is scarcely surprising that the words that came to Anglo-American lips (and pens) when "conversation" turned to the Irish directed attention to "character" rather than to conduct, condition, or physical appearance. For "character" was central to Anglo-Americans' perception of themselves and had been since the Revolution. Though the English descent of a substantial majority was undeniable, after their departure from the British empire most citizens of the fledgling United States were far more interested in authenticating themselves as "Americans" than in identifying with an inherited ethnicity. But what was distinctively "American" about this people if not its Englishness? The United States possessed an untried political philosophy, infant governmental institutions, brief traditions, a potentially fluid social order, and—even at the time of the Revolution—something less than cultural homogeneity.

The problem of giving meaning to "American" seemed particularly acute when it was agreed upon both sides of the Atlantic that every durable nation-state required some uniformity, either of experience or inheritance. It was impossible to predict anything of a nation's future without some sustained history, or, barring that, widely-shared human character attributes to support a forecast. During the early nineteenth century, Americans were still suffering the barbs of Europeans on this matter. Michael Chevalier, a visitor to the United States during the presidency of Martin Van Buren, tweaked his hosts by describing their country as "a body not yet in a state of consistency; it has no definable character, no fixed destination, it is incapable of anything great." As much as they resented these taunts, Americans were inclined to agree that they had some merit and offered similar self-criticism. Displaying typical concern, an antebellum correspondent of the *Southern Literary Messenger* said that "every people should have a *national character;* that is, the people of the nation should have some particular trait of character common to all, and, at the same time, differing from other nations."[16] Americans were especially concerned with forecasting their nation's future for the simple reason that, as the *Western Monthly*

Magazine's James Hall put it, "every previous attempt to maintain a free government upon a large scale had failed."[17] Furthermore, no one—certainly not the founding fathers—suspected that a republic could be dropped among just any people and survive. Despite their elaborate scheme of institutional checks and balances, none of the nation's architects—not even James Madison, the chief advocate of safety in diversity—anticipated that self-government would work among any but a united people. "It is for the happiness of those united in society to harmonize as much as possible in matters they must of necessity transact together. Civil government being the sole object of forming societies, its administration must be conducted by common consent," Jefferson had written in his wartime *Notes on the State of Virginia*.[18] Common "character," it was widely understood among both first generation United States citizens and third, could offer both unity and predictability.

Besides, republican ideology seemed to demand that a self-governing citizenry display particular character traits. "We live under republican institutions," editor Hall wrote in an article titled "On the Formation of National Character," "where the whole power of the government is in the hands of the people, where every act of sovereignty is but an emanation of the public will." This was both the genius and the pitfall of republican government. What was the danger? Hall's successor at the helm of the Cincinnati magazine, Joseph Reese Fry, supplied the answer: "Ignorance is the poison of a republic and no citizens are really desirable save those who are well informed. . . . Republics always tend strongly to radicalism—they always have their demagogues who excite the passions and prejudices of the ignorant, that they may mislead them for their own advantage. . . . One man of bad moral character, no matter how ingenious he may be, will do more injury to a country than a thousand spinning jennies will do good."[19] Virtue and intelligence—sound character—that was the sustenance of the American state. This is hardly a revelation. Gordon Wood and Bernard Bailyn, among others, have written extensively upon the opinions of the founding fathers in this regard. To serve as the working principle of a society, liberty required more self-discipline and restraint, more selflessness and community spirit than the inhabitants of European monarchies—where the state provided heavy-handed discipline—customarily were called upon to display. Without benevolence, the product of sound moral nurture, and intelligence, the consequence of education, popular self-government—even of the kind restricted to white male property-holders that characterized the early American republic—would not work.[20] Thus the writings of the founding fathers are rife with insistent calls for virtue and intelligence in the people. "This virtue; morality and religion; is the armor, my friend, and this alone, that renders us invincible," Patrick Henry counseled a correspondent in the last year of his life. Less confident in religion, perhaps, as a guardian of morality, Thomas Jefferson recommended education. The important truths, he wrote George Ticknor in 1817, are "that knowledge is power, that knowledge is safety, that knowledge is happiness."[21]

What is significant here is not that "virtue" and "intelligence" were well-represented in the rhetoric of first generation republicans but that they were sustained in the vocabularies of the second and the third. In fact, they became cultural dogma. "To borrow a cant phrase of the day," historian William Hickling Prescott wrote in 1841, "we shall be true to our *mission*—the most momentous ever intrusted to a nation; that there is sufficient intelligence and moral principle in the people . . . to choose the right rulers."[22] We can, in fact, find this verbiage just about anywhere in early antebellum culture; we do not need to limit our attention to intellectuals—to semi-official keepers of patriotic rhetoric—like Prescott. When voters of Washington County, New York petitioned the United States House of Representatives in 1838, they prefaced their memorial: "Experience has proved the weakness of all human institutions under the attacks of corrupt principles, and has made the fact evident that the material of their strength lies in the intelligence, sound principles, and good morals of the people." It even seemed that the republic not only needed to sustain intelligence and good morals to survive but also owed its origins to these very commodities. "Governments are not formed but grow," declared New England essayist Frederick Henry Hedge in 1838; they "have their origin with the character and habits of the people governed." The republican form of American government was a direct outgrowth of the character and habits of Americans of the Revolutionary generation. But, as Thomas Paine had warned those very rebels in *Common Sense,* virtue was neither hereditary nor perpetual. The sustenance of sound character demanded the people's constant attention.[23] In the

1820s, 1830s, and 1840s, the survival of the nation still seemed to hinge upon virtue and intelligence—upon good character, that is. An authentic American was one who demonstrated the moral and intellectual character requisite to participate in the American experiment in popular sovereignty.

Did native-born Americans or Anglo-Americans generally have a monopoly upon good character? Contemporaries doubted it. When the question of what constituted American nationality came up at the Anti-Masonic party national convention in 1830, the key speakers roundly denounced the proposition that Americanness naturally attached to those "born within certain boundaries." Rather, nationality was a matter of "inner strength or character," of "heart."[24] To a considerable extent, then, American nationality was volitional. One proved one was a genuine American by loyalty, of course, to the laws and government of the United States. But, more fundamentally, one assumed nationality by guarding one's virtue and cultivating one's intelligence. Character was assumed to be a product of nurture rather than nature. "We owe all this prosperity, under Providence, to the intelligence that planted, to the intelligence that maintains, our republican institutions. We owe it to education," offered the *Western Monthly Magazine*. "The virtue of the people has heretofore saved our country; and if we would perpetuate its freedom, we must cherish religion, cultivate sound morals, and disseminate knowledge."[25] Virtue was not inborn but was something to "cultivate." Intelligence did not run in the blood but was the product of "education." In part, then, the attainment of appropriate republican character required some activity, some nurture. But it was also popularly assumed that virtue and intelligence had become habitual among the American people and to some extent were absorbed by socialization. "As the flavor of the grape depends greatly on the soil by which it is nourished," Cincinnati physician-essayist Daniel Drake enthused, "so the temperament of individuals is modified by the intellectual 'aliment' in which their minds subsist in childhood and youth." The American "aliment" was regarded as especially conducive to character development. American liberty "frees the spirit, improves the condition, and raises the character," preached an enraptured patriot in 1835.[26]

What did all of this have to do with the perception of European immigrants—particularly the Irish—by those who accounted themselves truly "American"? It meant, of course, that newcomers would be primarily scrutinized for their character. What were their moral values, their intellectual capacities, their amicability in social relations? Since Americans regarded themselves as having certain attainments in these respects, they would focus their attention upon them in others. Would the moral and intellectual fiber of the foreign-born be suspect? Of course it would, since to a great degree morality and intelligence were understood to be products of environment. And the American environment was deemed peculiar. "What can he know of these [the "sympathies," "feelings," and "ways of thinking which form the idiosyncrasy of the nation"], who has never been warmed by the same sun, lingered among the same scenes, listened to the same tales in childhood, been pledged to the same interests in manhood by which these fancies are nourished; the loves, the hates, the hopes, the fears that go to form national character?" asked the historian Prescott.[27] National character—*uniform* national character—involved virtue and intelligence and was heavily dependent upon environment. In nationality, blood availed little but birth and nurture much. Thus in the early years of the republic even English immigrants would be suspect. We remember how quickly Anglo-Americans were to manipulate the United States' naturalization laws to exclude the French and their alleged confederates from citizenship during the 1790s, but we forget the alacrity with which such laws were turned against newcomers from England at the time of the War of 1812.[28] If even English character was subject to scrutiny—and rejection—how predictable was the close Anglo-American inspection of the Irish. And how predictable it was too that treatment of the Irish in language was especially a treatment of Irish "character."

Anglo-Americans shared with the English a tradition of referring to the Irish in terms of "intrinsic" character, but it was, I think, guaranteed that the American treatment of the Irish character would be more critical than its English progenitor because Anglo-Americans not only absorbed the stigmas placed upon the Irish in traditional English verbal culture but also attached to them the perceived ills of Great Britain and the Old World that they themselves had lately struggled to escape. Irish moral, intellectual, and "relational" characteristics—major emphases of the early antebellum ethnic stereotype—were, in fact, usually deemed natural products of European (especially British) political, social, and religious arrangements—of environment.

Models for early antebellum censure of the Irish were already in place before the 1820s—before the American Irish had either become very numerous or very much an issue in everyday conversation. One of these was the idiomatic denunciation of European decadence, license, and excess which originated with conservatives and Anglophiles during the French Revolution. When war with France seemed imminent in the 1790s this indictment became more widespread, finding sustenance—paradoxically—both in suspicions of French Catholicism and Enlightenment rationalism. Later, Napoleonic imperialism—while it muted cries that the French had gone to democratic extremes—reinforced popular notions about French degeneracy and made them seem applicable to the Europeans generally. At least the French and their confederates seemed particularly vulnerable to demagoguery and despotism.

The War of 1812, of course, diverted attention from the Continent and directed it at Britain. The British were not charged with libertinism but with tyranny. Purportedly unreconciled to the loss of the flower of their American empire a generation earlier, the British were understood to be up to their old anti-republican tricks. A corrupt and unrepresentative parliament and a despotic prince were trying to snuff the torch of liberty that had been lighted in the New World and to restore the discredited social and political forms of the Old. As the instant mythologizing of Andrew Jackson's lopsided victory over the British at New Orleans in 1815 proved, Anglo-Americans readily saw the war as a struggle between republican simplicity and virtue and monarchical avarice, venality, and intrigue.

As they became more numerous and more visible in America, the Irish were, incongruously, heirs to the censures previously directed at both the French and the British. Guilt by association brought upon them much of the criticism previously aimed at the French. The religious heritage of France was Roman Catholic; so was the heritage of Ireland. The French had staged a bloody revolution in 1789. The Irish—no matter that it was a small cell of bourgeois Protestant Irish—had launched an abortive one less than a decade later. When England had faced the upstart Napoleon almost alone, Ireland had seemed the British Isles' vulnerable Achilles' heel, a center for continental agents and radical plots. Thus the Irish were readily connected to the charges of decadence, license, and democratic radicalism that it had seemed appropriate to level at France. This libertinism and excess, it was suspected, the Irish would bring with them to America. "Why," asked the editors of Cincinnati's *Daily Gazette* in 1844, "are they so insolent, or lawless, or revolutionary in spirit?"[29] The traditional English image of the rude and undisciplined "wild Irish" nicely supplemented the notion that the immigrants were frightfully continental in their debauchery and self-indulgence. Notwithstanding that Irish "wildness" was allegedly due to a lack of civilization while French decadence was presumably a product of civilization gone to hedonistic excess, the two characters were compounded into one all the more terrifying.[30] A peculiar feature of such descriptions of the immigrants, however, was that they were not really commentaries upon Irish political principles, though they had obvious political implications, but rather treated alleged "lawlessness," "rebelliousness," and "turbulence" as moral failings.

But the Irish in America were also—paradoxically—heirs to aspersions Anglo-Americans cast upon Great Britain. This, of course, is one of the things that made early antebellum characterizations of the Irish somewhat different from contemporaneous British ones. Anglo-Americans saw the seed of Irish character deficiencies not just in continental infection but in the effects of British rule. Surveying recent books about Ireland and the Irish, the *North American Review* of July 1840 declared that the general view was that those leaving the island for the United States overwhelmingly seemed to be the "worn down, servile victims of licentiousness and poverty." They were products—in their moral, intellectual, and social character alike—of their condition. That condition was created largely by others. "The Irish peasantry," wrote W. C. Willard and E. Woodbridge in what may have been the most influential American school geography of the mid-nineteenth century, "are in the most wretched ignorance and poverty. They are degraded by the oppression of the landlords; and their stewards or 'middlemen.' " Combined with the absence of "free and tolerant laws," noted another contemporary textbook writer, such oppression inevitably "discourages the spirit of industry."[31] The consequences of these conditions, as this author suggested, were deemed to be as much spiritual as material. In an age which linked material success directly to character, what was really important was the impact that condition had upon the mental and moral faculties. For the Irish, that condition was held by many to be characteristically British. In a popular exercise book in elocution, American children read:

By the fruits of it I will judge your system. What has it done for Ireland? New Zealand is emerging—Otaheite [Tahiti] is emerging—Ireland is not emerging—she is still veiled in darkness—her children safe under no law, live in the very shadow of death. . . . How is the wealth of Ireland proved? Is it by the naked, idle, suffering savages who are slumbering on the mud floors of their cabins?[32]

Bad government was a principal source of that environment which enfeebled the Irish character. Worse, the fruits of British maladministration in Ireland seemed to be gathered to an alarming extent in America. "We are persuaded that there is nothing which has operated, and is operating, so unfavorably upon the peace and prosperity of the Union, as the irruption of these hordes of vicious and ignorant vassals from Great Britain and Ireland, who pour in upon us like the Goths upon Rome," shrilled the usually temperate editors of the *New England Magazine* late in 1834, combining the traditional English representation of the Irish as "wild" barbarians with an unambiguous declaration that the distinctive Irish character ought to be considered the responsibility of Britain itself.[33] Once again, the immediate consequences of Britain's benighted governance were treated as moral and intellectual. They were "viciousness" and "ignorance." These, of course, might well have social and political ramifications, but they were derivative of flawed character, not ideology.

What made this imputed character seem worse, however, was a perception that American society was ill-equipped to tame it. An open society emphasizing voluntary deference rather than rank and privilege, self-restraint rather than discipline, America was susceptible to ruin from vices which blossomed under the conditions of liberty. "What is to become of a poor, wretched population, ignorant in the extreme, naturally passionate, very mistaken in their views of American freedom, thousands of them too superstitious to seek wisdom from their neighbors, and almost always under the influence of strong drink?" a correspondent enquired in a letter to the *New York Morning Herald*. The question was rhetorical; the writer anticipated that most Anglo-Americans would respond with the same answer. The newcomers would mistake freedom for license; they would become, in the words of a New York City magistrate, "mischievous strangers."[34] The repressions and frustrations they faced in their homeland were genuine, but the consequences were all too likely to be realized in America. "Foreigners," a Philadelphia judge charged the jury in the trial of an Irish-American during 1844, "used at home to a military police, taught by long oppression to regard all laws as tyranny and all officers of the law as enemies, and feeling none of the American interest in self-government, are a constant element of disorder." The immigrants' failings were of a moral kind and these were bound to be a source of apprehension in a nation which had learned to "trust the execution of the laws to the voluntary obedience of the offender or the casual support of the citizen." A United States House of Representatives report on immigration issued a few years earlier stated the case this way: "The character of our free institutions was not adapted for such citizens; nor did the framers of those institutions contemplate the nature and mental character of the bulk of those who have since blotted our country."[35]

If the Irish in America were problematic enough when left to their own devices, they were intolerably burdensome to the republic when they fell into the hands of designing and unscrupulous Americans. The rude and unlettered Irish immigrant, it was often predicted, would all too easily become a tool of unethical and over-competitive native politicians and their supporters, turning American politics into a contest of sheer numbers rather than principles. "Look at the New York *Courier and Enquirer*," charged newspaperman (and future abolitionist martyr) Elijah Lovejoy in an 1835 editorial for his *St. Louis Observer*. "Two or three years ago it was the champion of the Irishmen; it would not suffer a word to be used in derogation of them or their priests. And why? Simply because it was then attached to that party to which most of these ignorant foreigners belonged. . . . And though we believe it is now on the right side, so far as Popery is concerned, yet have we any confidence in such a coadjutor?"[36] Servile, uneducated, unaccustomed to self-government or the rule of law itself, prone to take liberty as an excuse of cast off inhibition, the Irish in America were a substantial danger to a self-governing republic which welcomed all to citizenship. Criticism of the Irish on this score, however, was again not precisely criticism of their political ideology or practices. It was criticism of the moral and intellectual aptitudes which made them unsafe repositories for political privilege.

No wonder, then, that the specifically political characteristics of the Irish were so infrequently a part of early antebellum conversation. Political character was merely symptomatic of a disease of a moral or intellectual nature. Might this also explain the relative infrequency of treatments of the religious character of the Irish in everyday American discourse, that is, the explicit identification of Irish and Catholic? The evidence suggests so. In 1835 a Cincinnati magazine editor, commenting on sectarian violence that had lately rocked the city, noted that even the most intemperate Protestant zealots seemed not to object directly to Irish Catholics' "religious tenets, but [to] their moral character." Irish Romanism was no more than a natural blight upon minds cramped by poverty, ill-education, and bad government. "No man, in his senses, ever believed fully and fairly, the [Roman Catholic] doctrine of transubstantiation," wrote a Protestant minister in the mid-1830s. "Let us not be misunderstood; there have, doubtless, been many men who *thought* they believed it, but owing to the prejudice of education, their minds, in this point, were dark, and saw things that were not as they thought they were. So often do we see individuals inflicted with mental imbecility on some particular subject."[37] Such was the plight, he thought, of the Irish. But the implication was that once freed from the yoke of British tyranny and priestly domination and accorded a proper republican public school education, even the Irish could be rendered receptive to the truths of Protestant faith.

All of this is testimony to the fact that the early antebellum stereotype of the Irish was environmental. The Irish were a distinctive people, but their distinctiveness derived from nurture rather than nature. Poverty, oppression, misgovernment all set the conditions for life in Ireland. These affected not only lifestyle and outlook, but, more important, character. The Irish took to drink and emotional excess to escape their misery. They confused liberty with license from reaction to tyranny. They were misled by Catholicism because their minds were contracted by ill-education and dependence. At the same time these conditions might bring out the best in the Irish character: joviality, neighborliness, goodheartedness, and loyalty. Shared trials encouraged such personality traits. These would not be dominant, however, and would at best share time with the less attractive qualities. And that in itself would take a toll on Irish character. It would render the Irish—in the popular Anglo-American perception—unpredictable, mercurial, moody, vacillating between selflessness and selfishness. But this character was not understood by Anglo-Americans to be innate. Wrote Timothy Dwight, cleric and educator, of his observations of the Irish in New England: "The evils which I have specified are not, however, derived from the native character of these people. . . . Give them the same advantages which are enjoyed by others, and they will stand upon a level with any of their neighbors."[38] If the Irish were products of condition, why, change the condition, and the Irish would be changed.

Such environmentalism accounted for both the incongruous mixture of praise and censure in the early antebellum verbal image of the Irish (reconciled by calling them "mercurial") and the extraordinary attention paid to inner traits rather than to physique or even behavior. Condition made character and character, in turn, issued in certain predictable behaviors. Among these, naturally, were political or religious inclinations. No need, then, to harp upon political or religious predilections directly; these were simply derivative. This is what we would expect of the evangelical anti-Catholicism of the 1820s and '30s. The emphasis of the American and Foreign Christian Union or the Home Missionary Society was not upon the exclusion of Catholics from political rights and responsibilities but on conversion. Catholicism would not, obviously, be regarded by the evangelicals as a fixed characteristic of the Irish. It would be seen as an intellectual aberration that had captured untrained minds. One prominent anti-Catholic cleric counseled the Irish immigrant in 1834, "Break the chains of priestcraft and be free!" He and most of his contemporaries exhibited few doubts that it was possible in an improved New World environment. William Orne White, a young Harvard graduate who offered an address on "The Irish Character" at the college commencement of 1840, put this view succinctly: "The sin of the Irishman is ignorance—the cure is Liberty."[39] I do not think it would be stretching the point to argue that this persistent environmentalism kept excessive representation of violence or hostility out of the early verbal image of the Irish in America. While the publicity accorded periodic unrest in canal labor camps or wild affrays between immigrant and native fire companies and militia units was extraordinary (British travelers in the United States regularly commented on this) and might have provided the basis for a perception of the Irish as incurably violent, the Anglo-American stereotype of the Irish placed no more emphasis here than the traditional British perception did.[40] Violence—even if believed typical of the Irish—could easily be written off to the moral imperfections growing out of an Old World background (and perpetuated through imported Catholicism) and to an intemperate response to the lifting of Old World restraints. Anglo-Americans may well have believed that it would dissipate under the more humane conditions of the New. In fact, since Old World conditions were thought to encourage outrage and unruliness among all people, it might seem inappropriate to make it peculiarly a part of the Irish character.

A thoroughgoing conviction that character, including Irish character, was environmental, did not relieve Anglo-Americans from all anxiety about the immigrants. The Irish were a cause for concern precisely because condition did not produce conduct directly but only as mediated by character. And character, while it could be changed, was durable. Probably it would survive a simple change of scenery and could only be altered by some definite activity. This would be difficult since malformed character would doubtless resist improvement. Ignorance bred by environment would merely reproduce the conditions that nurtured it if left alone. Despotism and papism had produced a climate of ill-education in Ireland. Transported to America, darkened minds would fall into old habits. Consider religion. Immigrants brought with them not so much fixed religious convictions as "deplorable ignorance." "Here is a sort very favorable to the luxurient growth of papal error," the editors of the *American Quarterly Review* suggested. "The whole ceremonial of the Romish church, the doctrine, and gorgeous ritual, are adapted precisely to meet the inclinations and circumstances of all the ignorant men and women in our land."[41] There was nothing special about the attachment of so many of the Irish to the church of Rome. Other untutored intellects might be dupes to it also. But the environment of Ireland, many Anglo-Americans believed, was bound to produce an exceptionally large number of untrained minds. If this environment—even in part—was recreated in America, ignorance might be sustained through an American-born generation or two, as well. The popular image of the Irish in early antebellum America captured this. These ideas turn up everywhere, even in the most unlikely places, as in the representation of the stage Irishman in popular melodrama.

"The Americans," observed a European expatriate in 1837, "do not laugh at honest bluntness, or good-natured simplicity. . . . If Jonathan is to laugh, he must have a point given to him, or, in other words, he must laugh to some purpose." To Vienna-born Francis Grund, contemporary comic melodrama and its first cousin minstrelsy demonstrated beyond all doubt that his adoptive countrymen were decidedly "fond of laughing at the expense of their neighbors." "English, French, Dutch, and German," he noted, "are in turn made to suffer the stings of American wit. . . . The Irish, of late, has [sic] become very popular."[42] Grund's commentary reflected both the frequency with which ethnic characters of all sorts were portrayed upon the mid-nineteenth century American stage and, in particular, the emerging public taste for the stage Irishman. The mid-nineteenth century American stage Irishman was a popular figure in this popular medium. Despite the acclaim heaped upon such serious contemporary tragedians as Edwin Forrest and Junius Brutus Booth, "romance," "farce," and "domestic drama" characterized the kinds of plays patronized by most Yankees. Populated with one-dimensional stock characters (customarily a "suffering hero or heroine, a persecuting villain, and a benevolent comic," according to one student of this entertainment), prone to make black and white contrasts between personalities and motives, and more than likely to conclude "happily with virtue rewarded after many trials and vice punished," melodrama carved easily through life's social and moral ambiguities. Its effectiveness in providing simplified portraits of life, in summarizing, categorizing, and evaluating people and events, made it especially attractive entertainment in an environment of change and uncertainty. No doubt this helps explain the origins of modern melodrama in late eighteenth century Britain at a time when the island was undergoing rapid industrialization and urbanization with their attendant occupational, status, and residential dislocations. Likewise, it suggests why the medium was transported to the United States and flourished there during the first three quarters of the nineteenth century, a time of rapid popu-

lation growth, geographical expansion, and technological and economic development. Antebellum society was a society of new people, new "neighbors," to use Grund's terminology, the consequence
of accelerating European immigration.[43] These neighbors exhibited
new habits, new customs, new institutions, and new activities, sometimes imported but as often acquired in the process of adaptation to
a new home. Immigrants not only added more unfamiliarity to an
already changing environment but seemed actual or potential competitors for jobs, residences, and cultural or political hegemony. If
melodrama helped Americans make sense of a changing environment by simplifying it and captured their anxieties, it very likely mirrored their perception of the immigrant Irish. No wonder then that
the stage Irishman was so familiar to antebellum Anglo-Americans!

The antebellum public took popular drama seriously enough that
theatergoers were insistent upon stage "authenticity," even in the
portrayal of stock characters. Both plot and personality—in comedy,
pageant, and morality play alike—were expected to reveal useful insights into the human condition. Audiences volubly disapproved
when minor playwrights offered up hastily-sketched Irish characters
with little relevance to the ongoing story merely to enliven a dull
script. A critic wrote with disdain of one such product: "Terrence
O'Cutter is evidently a fellow trying to ape the Irishman, and not a
genuine personage. His love of fighting is all affectation and bluster
and his Hibernicisms are forced and far-fetched." Even the editor
of a nativist journal warned that the Irishman sometimes observed
on the American stage was so distorted a caricature as to be an inappropriate standard by which to judge a whole people. Implicit in
such comments was the assumption that a properly rendered stage
Irishman revealed important truths about ethnic character.[44]

Although a good deal of the melodrama that appeared upon
American stages had been written abroad, especially in England,
the originals frequently underwent extensive modification to suit
American audiences. More important, the only foreign-originated
pieces that became standard in the American repertoire and were
reissued by American theatrical publishing houses were those that
captured American tastes. The stock American stage Irishman was
a composite of the Irish characters that appeared in the several
dozen scripts that made up this conventional fare. These characters, of course, had a visual impact, but the antebellum stage Irish-

man was primarily a collection of words—a vocabulary, if you will. The words spoken about Irish characters in melodramatic scripts and minstrel shows composed the vocabulary that was the stage Irishman. The treatment of the stage Irishman in language thoroughly mirrored the verbal image of the Irish that appeared in other contemporaneous repositories of American speech. It captured the popular Irish stereotype.[45] The way in which the alleged lights and shadows of Irish character were treated on the stage was an index of popular perception.

Overwhelmingly, Irish characters appeared in comic melodrama, in plays described by their authors as farce or burlesque. Rarely were they central figures. Instead, they usually performed the parts of bumbling, shuffling, stuttering intermediaries between hero and villain. Typically, they were woeful creatures, always bumping, dropping, or breaking something, getting lost, misunderstanding or mistaking someone. The stage Irishman's speech was characterized by the "bull," an incongruity or confusion of ideas. To some extent, these characteristics were treated with much sympathy in the popular melodramas of the early antebellum period. "Unlucky" and "unfortunate" were the kinds of words typically used to describe Irish characters. The Irishman's errors were products of an ill-educated, dependent peasant background. This was the molder of character and the character of the Irish (Anglo-Americans liked to think) was well understood. As the narrator of Hugh Henry Brackenridge's *The Modern Chivalry*, a turn-of-the-century novel turned into a melodrama during the early 1840s, put it in his description of Teague O'Regan: "I shall say nothing of the character of this man, because the very name imports what he was." Condition created character and none doubted what Irish peasant character amounted to. Said O'Grady, the principal stage Irishman in the farce *The Irish Post*, of his constant blunders: "Sure I've got a right to make 'em, an't I an Irishman? I stand up for my national privileges." Conduct was a product of character. The blunderer deserved pity.[46]

But the blundering stage Irishman was also an object of anxiety. Character was reformable if the victim was willing; still, a bad character frequently resisted reformation. Ignorance might become cultivated ignorance. As the sinister Irish highwayman put it in the sanguinary melodrama *Jonathan Bradford*: "larning's one of dem effeminate superfluities that I despise, beyond signing my own name." Who could help such a man? Moreover, the blunderer was as dangerous to others as to himself. Usually the innocent suffered along with him. In half of fifty-five Irish character scripts examined in detail for the present study, this was a prevailing theme. In the most lighthearted comedies the stage Irishman usually blundered himself and his unwitting victims out of trouble after he had blundered them in. But even in these were hints that flawed character could do more than temporary damage. "He's so devilish saucy, and so provoking," *The Power Omnibus's* Mr. Ledger said of his mistake-prone servant Pat Rooney; "he does mischief without end, and tells me I'm the cause of all his blunders."[47] The peasant blunderer might not only do harm to others but deny responsibility for his errors as well. What incentive then to improve? These did not seem appropriate qualities for prospective republican citizens. Melodrama captured the fact that an environmental view of personal character was fully compatible with deep apprehensions about immigrants.

The early nineteenth century stage Irishman was a relatively tolerant stereotype, the implication being that at least the properly motivated immigrant could cultivate a suitably republican character. This not only was captured in the word portrait of the Irish in popular drama but also made explicit in much stage dialogue. Thus Captain O'Brien O'Flanagan of C. E. Grice's *The Battle of New Orleans* recognized that he had made the right bargain in trading the inferior environment of "oppressed, insulated Ireland" for the superior one of "the land of liberty and justice." In doing so, he escaped the constraints of his nativity: "I am an Irishman—that is to say, by birth; but I am an Irish-American—that is, the adopted child of humanity."[48] Such unambiguous challenges to a "volkish" conception of American nationality were, in fact, repetitious in contemporaneous melodrama. When Patrick, Shelty, and Cockney—an Irishman, a Scot, and a Yorkshireman—assembled to declare jointly their fealty to the American republic in John Minshull's *Rural Felicity,* they did not even bother to hyphenate their new nationality but called themselves "citizens of the world" who had attached themselves not to a "historical" nation but to the "government where the laws correspond with the general good of our citizens." Phelim O'Flinn, a contemporaneous stage Irish-American, attacked ethnic particularism itself: "but sure isn't all one, Irishman, Englishman, American, or Scot—all of the same family?"[49]

"The studies of the man," an early antebellum magazinist editorialized, "receive a tinge from the prejudices of the child, and certain propositions are assumed gratuitously by each party against the other, not because they are true, but because we have been accustomed to believe them." James Hall was referring to the transmission of intergroup attitudes, but he might just as well have been discussing the effect produced by the bearers of attitudes—words—themselves. He was perhaps clearer than the modern psychologist who, trying to express the same thing, wrote that "verbal stimuli potentiate hierarchies of possible responses out of which the speaker draws the response to be uttered."[50] Antebellum Anglo-Americans did not, strictly speaking, *create* a stereotype of the Irish which captured popular interethnic perceptions. The words that constituted the stereotype were heavily responsible for those perceptions in the first place. The words had that effect, to paraphrase Hall, because Anglo-Americans had become accustomed to using them.

The words most frequently associated with the Irish in the English verbal tradition did *not*, significantly, draw as much attention to Irish religious or political practices, to their economic aptitudes or circumstances, to their cultural traditions, their inclination toward passivity or violence, or their physical aspect. This is not to say that these were not matters of interest or concern to Englishmen and Anglo-Americans. That they were objects of conversation at all suggests that they reflected genuine perceptions of the Irish. But *character* descriptives were so much more common in the language of early antebellum Americans that they were actually capable of exerting an autonomous influence (autonomous to any real experience with the Irish, that is) *upon* perception. They directed attention *to* Irish intelligence, morality, and sociability.

The direction of Anglo-Americans to Irish "intrinsic" character was reinforced by their inclination to define themselves in these terms. They defined their nationality by "virtue" and "intelligence." Therefore, "virtue" and "intelligence" would describe the boundary between Americans and others. The Irish in America, increasing rapidly in visibility after 1820, figured prominently among these others.

Early antebellum Anglo-Americans, as noted, traced character to environment rather than to inheritance. And if we were to doubt it, the words that they chiefly employed to describe themselves and others—words which treated nurtured intelligence and morality rather than natural physique—offer confirmation. This was a palpable necessity if Anglo-Americans were to distinguish themselves as a nationality from their English progenitors. Especially, they grasped at authentic nationality by contrasting the American "aliment" (an archaic but expressive way of referring to a nurturing environment) to the conditions of Europe and Great Britain itself. As *Anglo*-Americans and (predominantly) Protestants, they had a long tradition of suspecting the aliment of continental Europe. As Anglo-*Americans* and republicans, they had come to suspect Britain's, too. The Irish could be connected with both. Irish character was placed in double jeopardy. No wonder that the treatment of intrinsic attributes among the Irish in early antebellum conversation was more uniformly censorious than in contemporaneous English discourse. Irish character scarcely had a chance.

The verbal image of the Irish that surfaced in the United States during the 1820s and '30s was not, however, a nationality stereotype. It was an ethnic stereotype. It applied without distinction to the Irish in Ireland, Irish immigrants to America, and native-born Americans of Irish descent. This representation of "the Irishman" in words was not, I think, a matter of design symptomatic of what Conor Cruise O'Brien later described as the tendency of the English to speak of their island neighbors in the "pejorative singular." Instead it was a by-product of the categorical nature of words. In routine "conversation," Anglo-Americans rarely distinguished carefully between the "native" Irish and Irish-Americans. The original referent of descriptive adjectives used often enough to become normative in language was eventually lost to memory, and the words became prescriptive for references to any subject that could even remotely qualify for the appellation "Irish." The stereotype of the Irish in early antebellum language, then, did not just distinguish citizens from aliens or the native from the foreign-born but separated native-born citizens too into communities of identity, into ethnic groups.

But if it was character that defined the boundary between Anglo-Americans and the Irish, the implication was that ethnicity itself was temporal and volitional. It was this, in fact, that prevented the early antebellum conception of American nationality from being absolutely exclusionary. For the Irish, like others, could buy into American nationality and ethnicity together by buying into the environment that produced American character. Without that character, neither native birth nor naturalization oath nor protestations of republican orthodoxy could produce an authentic American. That the Irish were deemed capable of adapting was evident in the words of the popular Irish stereotype. Irish intelligence was suspect, not because the Irish were inherently "stupid," but because they were "slumbering," "ignorant," "confused," and "unlettered." The Irish were not "immoral" but "degraded" and "debased"; they were not so much "arrogant" and "discourteous" in their social relations as "peculiar," "curious," and "detached." These words said nothing if not that character was environmental. To acquire an American character demanded that un-American environments be shed. In part, this could be accomplished by geographical transplantation. The Irish, for example, escaped from Great Britain's benighted governance by escaping the British Isles. But could habits of servility, dependence, and illiteracy be sloughed off in the same fashion? Anglo-Americans suspected that movement across space alone could not accomplish it. Some other activity was required, submersion in the "American" environment. What was the "American" environment? It was, of course, a republican environment. But it was also a Protestant environment. And an environment which honored Old World customs and lifestyles as little as institutions. Under these conditions, there could be no such thing as an Irish-American, Irish in ethnicity and American in nationality. A resident of the United States was either one or the other, participated in one environment and reaped its character or was nurtured by the other.

"Character" was another source of primary identity to early antebellum Americans. It told them who they were. Because American character was traced to a specifically American environment, it distinguished them from others who they did not believe had benefited from the nurture that environment provided. It defined not only their nationality but also what we would have to call their ethnicity, separating them both from Englishmen with whom they shared blood and non-English immigrants or the offspring of immigrants with whom they shared residence and sometimes birth. A self-identity wrapped around "character," of course, could be a powerful stimulus for the categorical judgment of others, for prejudice, especially when ideas about the character of particular ethnic groups became stereotyped in language.

We have been repeatedly informed—quite rightly—by students of the antebellum period that as the Irish increased in number they were regarded by many who came into direct contact with them as economic competitors. We are instructed by others—doubtless correct in their interpretation, too—that they were taken by the most intense Anglo-American Protestants as the minions of the Antichrist at Rome. Still other historians stress the terror provoked among the most traditionalist republicans that the Irish bore the odor of French radicalism.[51] But, of course, many Anglo-Americans never personally encountered Irish immigrants or even Americans of Irish descent for any sustained period at all, but they did encounter their reputation—in conversation, in words. And even those who had more immediate contact would engage the Irish under the influence of language. To all, the words would imply that the Irish were different, that they were not part of the Anglo-American community of self-identity. The foreign-born would not share American character because they did not have the advantages of an American upbringing. The native-born would also be tagged as outsiders to the extent that they could be identified by reputation, custom, or religion as Irish. For if the label seemed applicable it was prima facie evidence that the possessor had not fully shed the imported vestiges of an un-American environment and thus could not have acquired an authentically American character. To the Anglo-American worried about losing his job to an immigrant, the thought that the Irish were distinguished primarily by character was doubtless little solace. But for the anxious Protestant it was an invitation to view the Irish not as agents of Roman Catholicism but as victims and immigration as an opportunity for mission. Likewise, conservatives might take some comfort that the Irish bore not so much flawed political ideology as flawed character for politics, and that character might be changed.

We need not look only at beleaguered Anglo-American workmen or aggressive anti-Catholics or demagogic politicians in order to locate suspicions of the Irish (specifically the Irish, not "immigrants,"

"Catholics," or "radicals") in early antebellum society. Suspicion was institutionalized in the language of Anglo-Americans itself. Granted, it was a suspicion tempered by a post-Enlightenment optimism about the plasticity of human nature. The Irish, after all, could become Americans by ceasing to be Irish, by eradicating every last trace of religion, custom, or relationship that marked them as Irish. But such optimism hardly prevented skepticism about the Irish character from serving as justification for subtle and not-so-subtle acts of discrimination perpetrated against the Irish during the early antebellum years. Disregard of Irish character was obviously a powerful stimulus for a kind of evangelical anti-Catholicism aimed at Americanizing the Irish through Protestantizing them, winning the converts away from a religious environment which allegedly enfeebled both their virtue and their minds. And it was, of course, a fertile field for early antebellum political nativists who insisted that it was necessary to lengthen the period of probationary residence for immigrants before admitting them to citizenship— long enough to acquire the rudiments of an American character— and exclude entirely from positions of public trust those who manifestly lacked an American character, particularly Catholics. And the very optimism of the verbal image of the Irish was likely, in the long run, to produce discouragement with the immigrants and their children. For if character was environmental, the American "aliment" ought to work changes in the Irish. If the Irish, nonetheless, retained distinctive customs, communal loyalties, and religious preferences, the whole association of nationality and character would be called into question.

CHAPTER THREE

"An Irishman by Nature"

"The originally Celtic race is less mixed. . . . The common classes are
strongly marked with the national peculiarity of features, and by this they
are readily recognized in other countries."
Samuel Griswold Goodrich, *A Pictorial Geography of the World*
(Boston, 1856)

ADDRESSING THE American Historical Association on the occasion of the United States Bicentennial, Timothy L. Smith laid a
blanket charge: "historians continue to believe that ethnicity is a
synonym for nationality." In fact, Smith chided, "nationality is established by citizenship. . . . The sense of peoplehood . . . [is]
the essence of ethnicity."[1] This was both too broad an indictment
and too simple a correction. For some historians were certain that
it was entirely appropriate to uphold this distinction in theory and
utterly impossible to find that generations of Americans had consistently adhered to it in fact. For example, antebellum Americans.
Paul Nagel had already published the observation that whereas the
founding fathers had gone out of their way to dissociate American
nationality from any sort of peoplehood, their descendants just half
a century later were beginning to account not only race but also a
specific white ethnicity ("Anglo-Saxon," Nagel called it) among
the qualifications for republican citizenship. This development Nagel—and, subsequently, some others—argued, was encouraged by

accumulating anxieties about destiny, Union, and community as well as by the Jacksonian passion to identify a supreme popular "will."[2]

The way in which Anglo-Americans spoke of the immigrant Irish at the *beginning* of the antebellum period confirms that the original republican distinction between nationality and ethnicity was not confined to elite rhetoric. By and large, before the mid-1840s Americans saw in others what they took to be critical to defining themselves—"character." They perceived the Irish, in particular, as lacking the intelligence and virtue that denoted the authentic republican. But the cause was a disadvantaged environment, no more. Irish ethnicity, per se, was no greater qualification or disqualification for republicanism than Anglo-American ethnicity. Still, nativity on Irish soil (or perhaps even in an Irish-American home) was grounds for suspicion of personal suitability, without corrective nurture, for American citizenship and, hence, nationality.

Paddy—the verbal image of the Irish—captures the compounding of nationality and ethnicity in popular thought as the nineteenth century advanced into its middle decades. And in doing so, it confounds a traditional historical wisdom that no really ethnic construction of American nationality enjoyed much currency before the end of the century. At the same time, it challenges more modern concessions that a "volkish" construction of nationality did circulate in America before the Civil War—but could not have circulated much beyond intellectuals with continuing overseas contacts.[3]

The patterns of American language confirm that confusion of nation and people was becoming habitual well outside intellectual circles as early as the 1840s and 1850s. The evolution of Paddy captured changes in Anglo-American self-perception and in the perception of others. For by the middle of the forties, Paddy was no longer principally a portrait of "character," nor were the Irish men and women Paddy represented assumed to be conformable to republican ways by environmental conditioning. Instead the word image was dominated by descriptives which associated its referents with particular conduct and condition. By the mid-fifties these were joined by an increasing number of references to physical appearance. The unmistakable implication was that such characteristics were the very hard and quite fast correlates of being Irish. Of course it was a different matter if status and behavior were functions of habit or of biological imperative. Between 1845 and 1860, the verbal image of the Irish moved decidedly in that direction. During the mid-1840s American conversation treated as established fact the existence of something contemporaries had begun to call "Irishism"—an alleged condition of depravity and degradation habitual to immigrants and maybe even their children.[4] A decade later, Americans were beginning to talk about "Celticism." Conversation about the Irish disclosed that many had come to believe that character and conduct alike were connected with physical conformation and that the qualification for American nationality had something to do with what they called—albeit imprecisely—"blood."

In 1805 citizens of New York City established a "New England Society" to perpetuate the memory of their Calvinist forebearers; it was open to native-born New Englanders or their sons who lived in the metropolis. The society was commemorative, fraternal, and charitable; it supported a lending library and a relief fund for distressed New Yorkers of New England origin. Each year a prominent scion of New England was asked to address the membership, and the oration was subsequently published with the annual report. Throughout the 1830s, 1840s, and 1850s the repeated subject of these lectures was American "national character."

National character was also a favored theme among the speakers invited to commence what one of them, Ralph Waldo Emerson, called the "literary year" at Phi Beta Kappa chapters attached to select colleges. This was, perhaps, no coincidence, for the orators were often New Englanders speaking to largely New England audiences and as mindful of the "virtuous deeds of their ancestors" as those who addressed the filiopietists at New York City.[5] No more typical representations of what Richard Dorson has called "elite culture" can be sifted out of the documentary alluvium of mid-nineteenth century America.

Horace Bushnell, who delivered the Phi Beta Kappa lecture at Yale in 1837, had no doubt that every successful polity sooner or later discovered that it had a "sense of character to sustain." Bushnell meant by character "just principles, high sentiments, intelligence." The quality of a people's character was what lent any government its particular genius, and preservation of that character

was an appropriate object of public pursuit. The state bore an obligation to preserve and also to "ennoble" the interior qualities of its
citizens, to create an environment which would cultivate morals
and intellect. The chief threat to any society was, logically, flawed
character, what Bushnell called "vices and degraded manners."
Hartford's illustrious Congregational divine was convinced that
the principal danger to American manners and morals was the accumulation of European immigrants (including, but not limited to,
arrivals from Ireland) whose character was distorted by "low-bred
associations." Two years later, Robert Charles Winthrop told the
audience at New York's New England Society that the blessed domicile of their ancestors had, in its early years, successfully guarded
its character by "repelling from its culture the idle, the ignorant,
and the enslaved."[6] These were perfect rationalizations for the prevailing verbal stereotype of the Irish. The orators affirmed—with
particular eloquence—that "character" was the source of nationhood, that environment was the foundation of character, and that
anyone nurtured in a suspect alien environment was at best a field
for mission and at worst a presumptive threat to the republic. Anglo-Americans had inherited, through language, a decided tendency
to *speak* of the Irish in terms of character—and thus to *think* of
them in terms of character. And, simultaneously, an inclination to
regard themselves as unique in character gave rise to notions about
environment, character, and nationhood that required no explicit
elitist rationale to be put to use in the perception and evaluation of
others.

Treatment of the Irish in early antebellum conversation had portrayed newcomers not as morally and intellectually incapacitated
but only as misled. Elite rhetoric—what the historian Prescott had
called cultural "dogma"—captured this temper as well. Dartmouth
College professor Charles Brickett Haddock, on the occasion of the
1841 New England Society annual meeting, in a lecture on "The
Elements of National Greatness," advanced the argument that
American national character was made, not inherited. "Our mi-
gratory habits, the easy and frequent intercourse of all parts of the
country, our common institutions of government and education,"
Haddock observed, were the things most responsible for creating the
uniform character that antebellum Americans craved. Class, religion, and subculture would all eventually disintegrate in the face

of such powerful agents, both natural and institutional. George Cheever, the New England Society speaker for 1842, apparently felt that not enough had been said on this matter, for he adopted Haddock's title and carried on the same theme. Whence came good character and its inevitable consequence, national greatness? "In the first place, a *good parentage* is requisite," Cheever answered. By this did he mean that character came of blood? By no means; it came of the "discipline" and "habits" inbred by sound domestic nurture. Thus the nation could welcome, and even be strengthened by, accretions of "intelligent and virtuous foreigners" who had—despite unfavorable odds—received a proper upbringing. These might claim American nationality almost as a matter of right. Perhaps even the ill-bred could be reformed by American conditions in time. Cheever thought that ten years might do.[7]

"Common conscience," that is, "generally received ideas of morality, religion and law," Job Durfee told the Phi Beta Kappa chapter of Rhode Island's Brown College at the beginning of another "literary year," 1843, was the basis for a distinctive government and a distinctive people. Durfee was particularly interested in science and society, and science, he believed, was revealing the source of the American conscience. It was "blood," blood which "circulated warm through the Anglo-American heart." This was no symbolic blood representing kinship of mind or morals, either. It was the blood of hereditary descent, "traced through centuries of light and shadow, of triumph and trials, in the Anglo-Saxon," Durfee alleged. The American "mind," the American "philosophy," the American "idea of liberty and law" itself were inherited more or less intact from what Durfee took to be a pure-bred ancestral European tribe.[8] Genuine Americanness could not be claimed—ever—by those descended from other stocks, Asian, African, or even European. The national character of Americans might still involve "character," but character that was produced by nature, not nurture, a character that was distinctively *Anglo*-American. At the New England Society, similar ideas were percolating in the mid-1840s. To commemorate their ancestors in 1844, the membership invited a discourse by historian George Perkins Marsh. Marsh's message was pessimistic: "It may indeed be doubted, whether it be possible now to construct a harmonious type of national character out of the discordant materials which have been assembled." The nation was in

danger of losing its grip upon its "hereditary principles." Nations—
great nations—were homogeneous nations designed by Providence
and endowed by the Creator not only with physiological peculiarities but also with particular moral and intellectual faculties. The
United States' ancestry was "Gothic": "the great race." The nation
would retain its historical character only so long as it repelled ethnically inharmonious elements. "A nation," Marsh concluded, "like
an organic being, must grow, not by accretion, but by development,
and should receive into its system nothing incapable of assimilation."[9]

In the halls of the New England Society a decade later, Williams
College president Mark Hopkins addressed the self-satisfied gathering of New York bourgeoisie. The citizens of the United States,
Hopkins insisted, must not be allowed to degenerate into a mere
"populace," a rag-tag collection of incompatible types. They must
instead be a homogeneous "people." Only a united people could possess the sense of collective responsibility that makes self-government
possible. In 1857 another academician, Richard Salter Storrs of
Ohio's Western Reserve College, came to New York to educate
the same audience. He offered the same advice: "We aggregate
men from all climes and tongues, and call that a nation which is
only a casual human sandbar, accidentally heaped together, from
different soils by meeting currents, while they ought to make a nation grow up, homogeneous and compact, of shapely development,
rooted in the soil." Better the United States grow from within, relying upon the natural increase of Anglo-American stock, than look
abroad for augmentation.[10]

At the New England Society and among the brotherhood of Phi
Beta Kappa, nationality and ethnicity had been invested with new
meanings and placed in a new relationship. The connection of
American nationality with a particular ethnicity, Anglo-American,
Gothic, or Anglo-Saxon, was surfacing in at least these bastions of
Anglo-American elite culture from the mid-1840s past mid-century.
"Nation" was being confounded with "people," and ethnicity itself
was being taken less as a matter of culture than of blood—a product
of nature, not nurture. This was something more than the surrender of nationalism to the romantic impulses capturing other areas of
American intellectual life during the mid-nineteenth century. To
be sure, the romantic temper valued natural sense more than in-

tellect, intuition more than ideology, and society's heritage more than social engineering. But natural sense could derive from exposure to nature itself and the regeneration of the soul might, if widespread enough, perfect society. The early antebellum environmentalist interpretation of national character, which ranked morality above political philosophy and shared experience above institutional affiliations, was, perhaps, not *entirely* unconformable to romanticism. But there was a fragility to it that would push Anglo-Americans with an anxiety about their nationality toward a more concrete formulation. The endurance—even the proliferation—of regional, socioeconomic, and ethnic subcultures in the United States made shared experience seem a chimera and suggested that the common instincts that denoted a national people would have to be found elsewhere. To some extent the discomfiture with the traditional construction of American nationality uttered at the New England Society and elsewhere was a cumulative phenomenon. The further the United States moved from its founding, the greater the anxiety that it was not fulfilling the founders' expectations. The trial of sectionalism by civil war was only the most dramatic event in a sequence of pressures for the nationalization of law, institutions, and culture, which, for some, seemed consistent with a need for homogenization. War with Mexico and growing territorial ambitions heightened Americans' passion for internal cohesion and sense of distinction from others; a new round of confrontations with native Americans across the Mississippi had a similar effect. Finally, the attention directed at slavery, emancipation, and African colonization were liable to give any emergent sense of "peoplehood" an ethno-racial bent.

Ought we to take elitist antebellum oratory seriously, as seriously, say, as we regard the anguished rhetoric of another generation of American intellectuals at the end of the nineteenth century (often the sons and grandsons of Hopkins and Storrs) who lamented the dilution of Anglo-Saxon blood by discordant material—a rhetoric which helped prepare the way for national immigration restriction legislation in the early twentieth? It is at least clear that we cannot dismiss it as the bombast of an extreme nativist fringe. For the most part, the New England Society and Phi Beta Kappa orators had no immediate connection with the nativist secret societies and their political progeny that began to proliferate during the 1840s. There is good reason to wonder whether out-and-out nativists would equate nationality with ethnicity in this way in any event. Certainly a number of the conditions that allowed the ethno-racial nationalism of late nineteenth century intellectuals to infiltrate common culture and inform public policy were missing before the Civil War: the apparent cultural and physical distinctiveness of a growing number of southern and eastern European immigrants, anxieties about American national security and internal subversion, and domestic class strife. That none of these obtained in the mid-nineteenth century might be reason to take the pronouncements of the New England Society and Phi Beta Kappa orators lightly. But we can do better than this. If popular dispositions toward national character were capable of giving definition to ethnicity and (to a considerable extent) prescribing the perception of ethnic others, then the reverse also might hold true: interethnic perceptions rendered in verbal stereotypes serve as guides to self-perceptions and to popular understandings of nationality and ethnicity.

There is no question that the image of the Irish in American conversation after 1844 is more helpful in telling *how* Anglo-Americans saw the Irish than in *what* they saw. The word portrait of the Irish from the mid-1840s through the 1850s was appropriate for use by a people less interested in knowing the Irish than in spotting them, less committed to analysis than to identification. It was no longer devoted to depicting the interior quality of Irish men and women but to portraying their exterior aspect, their behavior, condition, and—increasingly—physical appearance. In fact, from 1845–1852 to 1853–1860 the emphasis of this "extrinsic" stereotype shifted; over time it became *more* extrinsic and *more* physically descriptive. And as it did so, it became more hostile too. During the mid to late 1840s, it actually parodied itself by focusing upon the alleged vengeance and volatility of Irish behavior.

As the special emphasis of Irish verbal portraiture between 1845 and 1853 indicates, Paddy was subject to the influences of an evolving definition of nationality, to actual developments in interethnic relations, and, for that matter, to the logic of language itself. The immigration from Ireland exploded in the mid-1840s, largely impelled by a succession of potato crop failures and subsequent starvation and displacement from the land. The sheer visibility of the Irish in America inevitably magnified their apparent distinctiveness from the majority that could be denominated Anglo-American. Moreover, the poverty and distressed circumstances of many of the famine-era immigrants were liable both to draw attention and to give them a more, alien appearance. H. Giles, who wrote several articles on Ireland and the emigration to America for the *Christian Examiner* between 1848 and 1852, understood the particular encouragement such visibility gave to stereotyping: "We, as a people, are intolerant of ragged garments and empty paunches. We are a people who have had no experience in physical tribulation. . . . As a consequence, the ill-clad and destitute Irishman is repulsive to our habits and to our tastes. We confound ill-clothing and destitution with ignorance and vice."[11] It was easy to doubt that the supposed assimilative effects of the American environment had worked; so different did many—particularly those who attracted attention— appear that it was easy to doubt that they would work in the future. Doubtless suspicion that the Irish were *bound* to be a distinctive people was reinforced by their over-representation in particular occupations—especially in those of inferior status. Giles understood that too: " 'Irish' means with us a class of human beings, whose women do our housework, and whose men dig our railroads. Judging merely by the senses, we are not too much to blame, for these are the relations in which, from infancy, we are accustomed to know them." He also recognized that notoriety attached to those immigrants, or those identified as their descendants, who most challenged the public tranquility: "The vicious Irishman always attracts attention. He is soon felt in a community of order as a disturbing character."[12] No matter such characters were unrepresentative; that is not how stereotypes are made. Anglo-Americans more often brought into material or political competition with the Irish were only too willing to regard them all as "disturbing characters."

Certain tendencies in language pushed Paddy in the direction of greater rigidity and hostility. The early antebellum stereotype had been both somewhat ambivalent in evaluation and forgiving in its environmentalism, yet it *was* nonetheless an ethnic stereotype; it portrayed the Irish as different. Once it became a habit to *speak* of the Irish as different and thus to *think* of them as different, it was not a great leap to treat them as different by nature rather than nurture. The initial formulation of Paddy may have actually facilitated

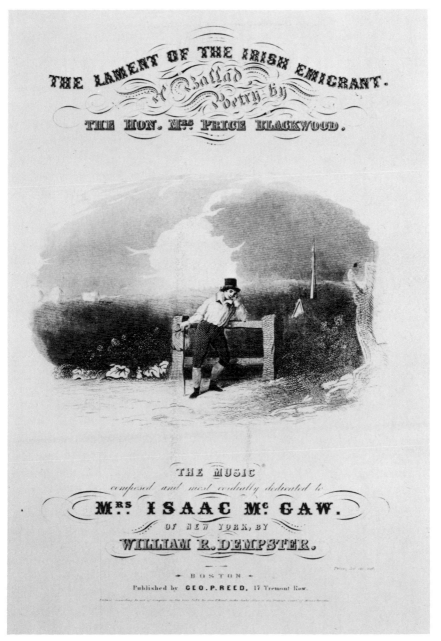

"The Lament of the Irish Emigrant": title page of a popular 1840s ballad
Courtesy, Library of Congress

"Who is them Fellows, did you say, Mum? Them Gentlemen's my Cousins, Mum, jist dropped in to kape me company, Mum!"

A "flood" of Paddies: cartoon from *Harper's Monthly*, October 1856

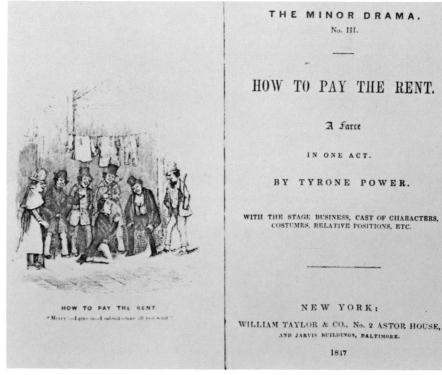

The stage Irishman: Tyrone Power's 1847 farce, *How to Pay the Rent*

Counting the Irish: roster of laborers temporarily domiciled at railroad boarding house, Federal Manuscript Census, Hudson, Ohio, 1850

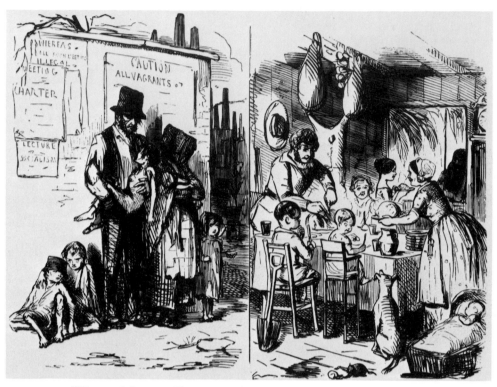

"Here and there; or Emigration the Remedy": British woodcut, 1848
Bettmann Archives

"By industry and economy I am become prosperous": 1843 lithograph depicting the promise of immigration
Courtesy, Library of Congress

POPERY UNDERMINING FREE SCHOOLS, AND OTHER AMERICAN INSTITUTIONS

"Popery Undermining Free Schools": illustration from *The Papal Conspiracy Exposed* (Boston, 1855)
Courtesy, Library of Congress

JAMIE & THE BISHOP.

"Jamie and the Bishop": cartoon from the 1844 election campaign showing James Polk trying to extinguish charges that the Democratic party pandered to the Roman Catholic church
Courtesy, American Antiquarian Society

Anti-Catholic newspaper's "Defence of civil and religious liberty against the inroads of popery": *The Protestant Vindicator*, New York, March 17, 1841

Protestant martyrs: illustration from Samuel Goodrich's popular textbook, *A Pictorial History of England* (Boston, 1845)

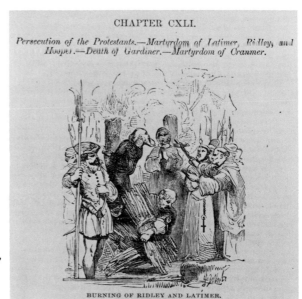

CHAPTER CXLI.

Persecution of the Protestants.—Martyrdom of Latimer, Ridley, and Hooper.—Death of Gardiner.—Martyrdom of Cranmer.

BURNING OF RIDLEY AND LATIMER.

1844 Philadelphia "Bible Riots": 1844 pamphlet, reprinted in P. S. Klein and A. Hoogenbloom, *A History of Pennsylvania* (University Park, 1980), representing the Irish as lawless and violent.
Courtesy, Pennsylvania University Press

1844 Philadelphia "Bible Riots": 1844 lithograph
Courtesy, Library of Congress

this development by encouraging overoptimism about the success of nurture on American soil in eradicating the Irish as a distinctive ethnic group. Unfulfilled expectations were capable of breeding disappointments which could be assuaged by doubting the capacity of the Irish to respond to republican nurture in the first place.

By the mid-1840s the verbal image of the Irish drew back from the description of character because ethnic distinctiveness no longer seemed a function of the nurture that produced intelligence, morality, and sociability. It increasingly featured direct treatment of conduct and condition because these seemed characteristic, habitual, and perhaps innate. It devoted little immediate attention to the poverty and destitution of the Irish but much to characteristic behavior which would not permit them to be anything but distressed. It said little directly about their religion or their politics but much about their inherent tractability and emotionality that would make them natural prey to unscrupulous politicians and a hierarchical and ritualistic church. Ultimately, it would set off the Irish by describing them more often in physical terms, as if they were a different sort of people altogether.

From the distance of London and the year 1864, American-born Dr. Thomas Nichols looked back upon forty years of Irish immigration to the United States:

Irishmen have been a great help to America in supplying the demand for rough and heavy work on canals, railways, etc., and vast numbers of Irish girls have also found employment as servants in families. They are not in all respects the best, but they were the only ones to be had in sufficient numbers. And they have their virtues. They are reasonably honest, and almost invariably chaste. Their kindness and generosity to their relations also appeal to our best sympathies.[13]

Despite the late date of these remarks, Nichols' assessment of the immigrants' role in American life and of the particular characteristics of the Irish belonged to an earlier age, to the 1820s and 1830s. Unlike the doctor, who spent his later years in the British Isles, Anglo-Americans who remained in the United States throughout the tempestuous decade and a half preceding the Civil War largely surrendered the mixture of sympathy, suspicion, and sometimes humor that characterized ethnic imagery in the first part of the antebellum period. "Necessary" was the kindest term the *National*

Intelligencer's editors could find to describe the consequences of Irish immigration in 1851. The Irish were simply "Necessary . . . to . . . the development of the vast country." Whatever contributions they made to the nation's material growth were derivative neither of intention nor of character nor of skill; they were simply products of the immigrants' most elemental brawn and brutality—directed to constructive purposes by others.[14] By the middle of the nineteenth century, it was becoming an Anglo-American habit to regard the Irish less with missionary enthusiasm and more with resignation.

During the late 1840s and the 1850s, the verbal image of the Irish in American conversation offered a decidedly pessimistic appraisal of the quality of their participation in the nation's development. Even begrudging recognition of the uses of Irish manual labor was iterated in such a way that it cast little credit upon the workers themselves. At best, the Irishman seemed to labor only under compulsion. For E. J. Sears, a contributor to the *North American Review,* the incentive for any activity whatsoever appeared to be nothing less than the threat of starvation. Unsuited to any but the crudest occupations by both ability and temperament, the Irish would not even apply themselves to these without the spectre of lingering death paraded before them.[15] Nothing could be found to depart further from the Puritan-frontier-Jacksonian entrepreneurial work ethic that Anglo-Americans attributed to themselves.

In fact, Anglo-Americans—at least judging by their conversation—found the occupational salience of the Irish in excavation and household work meaningful. "When we needed domestic servants in our towns and cities and spademen to construct our canals and railroads," J. D. B. DeBow opined in his *Review,* "Ireland furnished the full supply. . . . The Irishman rarely works on his own account, if he get employment from another." The Irish, the Southern publicist indicated, were uniquely suited to a laboring role in antebellum society. Economically inert, they were putty in the hands of ambitious, constructive Anglo-Americans.[16] Edward Everett Hale, New England author and clergyman who devoted much effort in the 1850s arguing the merits of European immigration against nativist opponents, also made it clear that the Irish were by nature the servants of a stronger, more skillful people:

As sure as water and oil each finds its level, they will find theirs. So far as they are mere handworkers, they must sustain the headworkers, or those who have any element of intellectual ability. . . . They do the manual labor. They do it most cheaply, and so leave those whom they find free to other and more agreeable walks of life. Thus practically, at this moment, our simplest drudgery of factory work and farm work comes into the hands of Irishmen.[17]

During the early antebellum period, Anglo-Americans sometimes expressed an appreciation for a few pleasing contributions of Irish character to American social life. Those favored qualities—like wit, good-naturedness, honesty, and gratitude—were all parts of the traditional English stereotype of the Irish. But by the middle years of the century, as Hale's description illustrates, American ethnic imagery fastened much more frequently upon the way in which the Irishman's body could be employed as a pack animal. Whatever the immigrant had to offer the United States was strictly a product of muscle—derivative of birth—and not of character—nurtured by environment.

The mixture of praise for Irish corporeal strength and criticism of inherent immigrant intelligence and temperament helps account for an incongruous blending of "substantial" and "insubstantial" descriptions in the ethnic stereotype prevailing in conversation after 1844, of acclaim for industriousness and damnation for carelessness and inefficiency. Anglo-Americans had to admit that the Irish added to the nation's wealth but alleged that their motivation was poor and their contributions carried out in capacities uniquely suited to their none-too-impressive abilities. Hale summarized widely-shared impressions of the Irish worker accurately by observing that "when he labors, it is in a most uneventful way, and, apparently, he is very idle most of the time."[18] Only in this fashion could many Anglo-Americans reconcile even a reluctant acknowledgment of the immigrants' economic worth with the conviction that "a more improvident, heedless, and dishonest class of people never defiled the fair face of the earth."[19] No wonder that the economic condition of the Irish was underplayed in conversation. Could such a people be anything but poor? Nor would they seem very threatening. Treatment of the Irish as economically inert doubtless comforted both the Anglo-American employer with an interest in keeping labor costs low and the native wage-earner made anxious by the accelerating flow of immigrants.

Reservations about Paddy's native capacity for work in the late antebellum period were matched by growing discouragement over the sources of immigrants' ideological attachments, both political and religious. In 1854 the *United States Review* reduced what many took to be the story of Irish participation in American political life to a fable:

One day Dunstan, an Irishman by nature, and a saint by profession, left Ireland, that is to say, the Irish immigration commenced, and with it the growth of a Catholic Church party in the United States. . . . A people of so peculiar a disposition and such narrow ways of thinking, soon became the inevitable prey of lay and clerical demagogues and every year saw them plunged deeper in the slough of ignorance where bigotry finds its appropriate atmosphere and breathes with exhaling lungs.[20]

The early antebellum verbal image of the Irish had also emphasized the susceptibility of the immigrants to political manipulation. This unfortunate prospect was deemed the product of purely environmental causes such as lack of education, misunderstanding of democratic forms, and the inheritance of British misrule. Now, in the years around mid-century, the Irish appeared corruptible by nature. The immigrants' "narrow ways of thinking" were represented in language as the consequences of birth rather than experience. Responsibility for Irish political excesses was effectively transferred from the unscrupulous native politician to the uneducable alien voter.

As long as Anglo-Americans persisted in viewing their own politicians as the culprits and immigrants as the victims of a misguided partisan zeal, criticism of naturalized voters remained the province of the political party that suffered the most from immigrant ballots in the most recent election. Hence, Federalist-Whig diatribes about Irish radicalism were typical of interparty rhetoric during the early antebellum period. But by the 1850s, castigation of the purportedly manipulable foreign vote was no longer the exclusive prerogative of any particular faction. If the Irish were constitutionally incapable of intelligent participation in the governance of the nation then all parties suffered by their inclusion in the body politic. Around mid-century, attacks upon Irish political "bossism" came from every ideological quarter, though Democratic orators were usually careful not to go too far.[21] No doubt the universality of sentiment contributed significantly to the Know-Nothings' attempt to cast themselves as a political reform party. Nativists offered to cleanse American political life for the benefit of all by removing the uneducable and tractable Irish from the rolls of qualified voters. This view of Irish political character was no nativist invention. It was a logical corollary to an emergent perception of Irish mentality and conduct as products of nature. And, in fact, if Irish political defects were really understood to be innate, then the nativist program—a twenty-one year residency requirement for naturalized citizenship—might seem to many contemporaries only a way to defer a problem, not solve it. It would do nothing at all to protect the public from voters of American birth but Irish descent.

Until nearly the middle of the nineteenth century, most Anglo-American descriptions of the Irish portrayed immigrant Roman Catholicism as no more than one of many characteristics of environmental origin contributing to an ethnic identity. In Ireland, the indigenous population had simply known no better religion. Protestantism, after all, was the faith of the hated English landlord class and the Scots of the Ulster Plantation. English religious oppression was responsible for Irish resistance to Protestant truths and helped explain the rigid, ingrown nature of Irish Catholic dogma. It presumably reinforced the anti-intellectual bias of the Roman Catholic Church, widely regarded to have kept the peasantry ignorant of any competing theologies as a matter of policy. In fact, most American Protestants assumed that, given a decent exposure to the tenets of reformed Christianity, the Irish might actually welcome proselytization. For a time they believed that the American environment would provide immigrants exactly such an opportunity. Until well into the 1840s the most common sort of "anti-Catholic" organization in the United States was the home missionary society, which concentrated upon giving the benighted minions of the Pope a beneficial dose of scripture and Protestant interpretation. Even such a skeptic of the institutional churches as Margaret Fuller had insisted that religion was a function of education and home environment, and she, for one, fully expected that "as the Irishman, or any other foreigner, becomes Americanized, he will demand a new form of religion to suit his new wants . . . and if there be Catholicism still, it will be under Protestant influences.[22]

Though sentiments like Fuller's continued to circulate right up to the Civil War, by the late 1840s they were already falling out of fashion with Anglo-Americans. More common was the attitude coarsely expressed by the New York City sidewalk evangelist, the "Angel Gabriel." Haranguing a Brooklyn crowd in 1854, he insisted, "so ignorant are the Irish—the land of potatoes and buttermilk—that they will have nothing but authority—the Priest and Pope." The Irish did not merely suffer Catholicism, they deserved it. The author of an article published in the *United States Review* the same year simply concluded, "The Irish *must* have a periodical supply of religious twaddle." This interpretation of Irish religious affinities conformed nicely with other contemporary assessments of immigrant character. All implied that the Irish lacked capacity for independent thought and action. The argument took typical form in William Bentley Fowle's school text in elocution, *The Free Speaker:* "Irish soldiers abounded in our armies, and have fought in some of our battles; but they have never led."[23] It was coming to be built into conversation that there was something in the Irish temperament that discouraged initiative and required deference to authority and dogma.

During the decade immediately preceding the Civil War it became more and more of a settled fact in American folk culture that the Irish had not chosen Catholicism but that Catholicism had chosen the Irish. It was the native character of the Irish that made them peculiarly susceptible to popish superstition. This was more than the perception of a few intolerant cranks. The sense of it permeated American conversation in the fifties, appearing in media as diverse as the Transcendentalist essays of Emerson, the sermons of Theodore Parker, Woodbridge and Willard's famous school texts, and Burton's tabloid of "gentlemen's" humor and commentary. A correspondent for the *North American Review* cast it as an ethnogeographical principle:

If at this day we look at the map of Europe, we find very generally, if not universally, that where the race is Keltish, there the religion is Catholic; where it is Teutonic, there it is Protestant. . . . We expect that the growth and strength of popery in these United States will be measured, in general, by the existence and influence among us of the Keltic blood.[24]

Other contemporaries would have found that Emerson's more compact statement in *English Traits* captured their sentiments better. In such matters as government and religion, Emerson observed after making a visit to the British Isles, "race avails much." In either case, less attention was being focused on the effects of Catholicism upon Irish mind and morals—an early antebellum theme—than upon the nature of the people who expressed allegiance to Rome.[25]

Paradoxically, as the equation of Irishness and Catholicism hardened, the proportional representation of religious description in the Irish stereotype declined. The ebbing commentary upon immigrant religious attachments in incidental "conversation" during the 1840s and 1850s suggests a growing fatalism in Anglo-American interethnic attitudes. By mid-century it was simply no longer cause for much comment that the Irish were Catholic. What else could they be? Surrender to the inevitable was the tenor of temperance enthusiast Lucius Manlius Sargent's "Irish Heart"—a short story frequently used as a reading exercise in schools—which illustrated that, in the case of immigrants from Ireland, Protestantization was ineffective in altering either moral sensibilities or conduct. The Irish character was impervious to improvement, religious or otherwise. This lent new significance to the charge that had been heard since the early part of the century and that the Methodist church's *North Western Christian Advocate* repeated in a headline in 1853: "Popery and Republicanism are incompatible."[26]

To mid-century Anglo-Americans—to the participants in "conversation"—Catholicism was not an unimportant characteristic of the Irish, simply an unremarkable one. At an earlier period, the Irishman's religious affinities appeared a particularly appropriate demonstration of the effects of environment upon human character. But when Americans began to see them as a product rather than a cause of character, religious attachments—like political ones— were rendered no more important than a number of other indicators of inherent "Irishism." It became much more relevant to talk about the sources of Irish character itself and its behavioral consequences in general than about any single character trait.

To stress the capacity of subjective factors—self-perceptions and an evolving definition of national character—to redirect the verbal image of the Irish is not to suggest that the stereotype entirely lost touch with objective circumstances. That would be nothing less than to say that the Irish in popular discourse ceased to be the Irish, that "Irish" became a cipher for "foreigners" or "immigrants" or "Catholics." But the word-portrait of the Irish in American conversation, distorted as it may have been, remained specifically a picture of the Irish (and not interchangeable with "immigrants" or other immigrant minorities) throughout the entire antebellum period and reflected ongoing developments in the nature and context of ethnic interaction. It was—as social psychologist Anthony Dworkin has pointed out all authentic stereotypes are—not *about* a group of people but derivative of a relationship *between* groups of society. That it did not mirror this relationship perfectly suggests the way in which perception stands athwart the intersection of objectivity and subjectivity. Stereotyping is neither reportorial nor inventive but rather involves selection, emphasis, and elaboration.[27]

The representation of the Irish in American "conversation" for the better part of the decade following 1844 affords a vivid example of the process by which words both perpetuate and create perception. During the late 1840s and early 1850s, in magazines and melodrama, in school texts and novels, the alleged violence of Irish conduct and disposition was central to verbal portraiture. Neither earlier, before 1845, nor later, after 1852, was this emphasis matched in the patterns of language. Nor was there anything to compare with it in the treatment of the Irish in English descriptive literature previously received in America. Doubtless words were reporters, recounting popular impressions of the incidence of interethnic violence in American life. For this was, after all, a period in which extraordinary national attention was directed toward what much of the Anglo-American public took to be examples of habitual Irish quarrelsomeness, ferocity, and lawlessness: the Kensington and Southwark riots at Philadelphia. They clearly were, as their student Michael Feldberg has called them, "among the most dramatic and violent episodes in pre-Civil War American history." Since each was followed by lengthy trials and investigations, they filled the national press for weeks on end. Pitting Protestants against Catholics and nativist societies against immigrants, the riots came to represent in the public mind the struggle between Irishman and Anglo-American (no matter that Orangemen were arrayed with the nativists).[28] In other words, they took on an interethnic aspect that encouraged the public to see other episodes of violence to which Irish-Americans might be party as fundamentally interethnic, too.

To some extent, stereotyped convictions about Irish habit and predilection actually lay at the root of the riots. The disturbances at Kensington were precipitated by evangelical Protestants' expectation that agitation to excuse Irish Catholic youth from the reading of the King James Bible in the public schools was the first step toward excluding the Bible from classrooms altogether. Inevitably the darkened minds of the Irish would move against the light of scripture order by the priests. Likewise, stereotyped ideas about Irish lawlessness and ferocity, encouraged by the first round of conflict between nativists and immigrants in May, helped set the conditions for renewed combat in July. When nativist organizations paraded during the Fourth of July weekend they so anticipated a violent reception that, not at once finding it, they took the offensive.[29]

There were, within a few short years, plenty of circumstances to which a perception of the Irish as inherently violent could be applied—from the wild affrays between fire companies and street gangs in Philadelphia to turbulence in Irish neighborhoods in New York and Boston. Like Irish susceptibility to poverty and Catholicism, Irish ferocity was understood by the mid-1840s as highly resistant to amelioration. Peter Parley pessimistically cautioned the readers of his popular geography, *Manners and Customs of Nations,* not to expect too much of Father Theobald Mathew's much-publicized efforts to cure Irish disorderliness by encouraging abstinence from alcohol: "It might seem problematic whether this will be of long continuance, as any great and sudden alteration in the habits of a people can hardly be expected to be permanent, particularly in a people so prone to act from impulse as the Irish."[30] Language that captured the perception of the Irish as naturally violent, emotional, and turbulent, once idiomatic, whether a consequence of real experience or of belief, then became prescriptive. All were expected to see the growing number of Irish in America as unruly and threatening.

Aspirations for the creation of worthy American citizens out of Irish material clearly rested upon the assumption that the apparent mental and moral deficiencies of immigrants were products of Old World environmental forces. Particularly broad-minded Englishmen had long believed this to be the case and so, apparently, did the larger number of Anglo-Americans during the first four decades of the nineteenth century. The early antebellum verbal image of the Irish blamed deficiencies upon the twin oppressions of English rule in Ireland and Catholic authoritarianism. As late as 1848 a writer for the *Southern Quarterly Review* affirmed that Irish degradation was *wholly* the responsibility of English misgovernance, and about the same time a committee of the Massachusetts legislature reviewing the state's enfranchisement requirements concluded that the "destitution and wretchedness of those armies of foreign immigrants" from the Emerald Isle were unmistakable products of previous training and condition.[31] Such attributions of Irish character to environmental influences became scarcer after 1844.

The verbal portrait of the Irish during roughly the last decade preceding the Civil War connected ethnic character with inheritance. Immigrant pauperism, wrote the editors of *Harper's Monthly* in 1858, long associated with the debilitating effects of Old World rack rents and poor laws, could more accurately be described as the consequence of "mental pauperism," an historical characteristic of the Irish people. Theodore Parker, addressing "The Causes of the Present Condition of Ireland" in the *Massachusetts Quarterly Review* a few years before, also regarded as fallacious the attribution of all Irish character deficiencies to English rule. "Is it to be expected," he asked, "that an ignorant, idle, turbulent, and vicious population will, by a mere repeal of bad laws, become industrious, provident, moral, and intelligent? The supposition is contrary to all known history and experience." Parker's words, of course, circulated only among a relatively small circle of literati, but his ideas about the inherency of ethnic traits were actually a good deal like those of a less refined but far more popular spokesman, revivalist Charles Grandison Finney. Finney summarized a common late antebellum attitude toward ethnicity and government when he offered it as a matter of principle that "God has always providentially given to mankind those forms of government that were suited to the degrees of virtue and intelligence among them."[32] Increasingly, Anglo-Americans believed that the Irish heartily deserved their despotism.

Such dispositions toward ethnic character took their most articulate form in the writings of intellectuals. Romantics like Henry David Thoreau, self-described realists like Parker, and old-fashioned Whig conservatives like George Templeton Strong all referred to the Irish during the last years of the 1840s with phrases filled with resignation—resignation to the innateness of Irish national character and its inferiority to the character of Anglo-Americans. Far from the centers of ethnic group conflict described by Hansen or Handlin or the other historians of immigration, Thoreau wrote of his Irish neighbor at Walden Pond, David Field: "With his horizon all his own, yet he, a poor man, born to be poor, with his inherited Irish poverty or poor life, his Adam's grandmother and boggy ways, not to rise in this world, he nor his posterity, till their wading webbed bog-trotting feet get talaria to their heels."[33]

Other members of New England's intellectual community, equally insulated from any actual rivalry with immigrants, agreed with Thoreau's assessment of Irish prospects in America. Not long after Thoreau completed his tenure in the woods, Parker lectured civic-minded New Englanders on the "Moral Condition of Boston," ascribing Irish criminality—which he validated with impressive police statistics—to native character:

It is not surprising . . . that the Irish are ignorant, and, as a consequence thereof, are idle, thriftless, poor, intemperate, and barbarian. . . . Of course they will violate our laws, these wild bisons leaping over the fences which easily restrain the civilized domestic cattle, will commit great crimes of violence, even capital offences, which certainly have increased rapidly of late.[34]

New York's patrician Whig, George Templeton Strong, in a diary entry for April 28, 1848, described the Irish crew sent to excavate the cellar for his new house as "twenty 'sons of toil' with prehensile paws supplied them by nature with evident reference to the handling of the spade and the wielding of the pickaxe and congenital hollows in the shoulders wonderfully adapted to make the carrying of hod a luxury instead of a labor." Given these sentiments, it is easy to understand Strong's public attacks on "Celticism" in the 1850s, especially his remarkable comment that "Our Celtic fellow citizens are almost as remote from us in temperament and constitution as the Chinese."[35] Such talk might be taken as ludicrous examples of private misanthropy were it not that they conformed to the overall drift of the late antebellum Irish stereotype in American language.

By the early 1850s, references to the Anglo-Saxon (or Anglo-American) and Celtic "races" in America and descriptions of the innate and ineradicable characteristics of each permeated the columns of newspapers, political monthlies, and literary magazines and were even filtering into schoolbooks and all sorts of government publications. When the *New York Daily Times* reported a riot in Brooklyn on June 6, 1854, as the first indication of "race war" between Saxon and Celt, it was using no hyperbole but conformed entirely to the growing popular understanding of the nature of ethnic differences. As many students of the antebellum period have observed, "race-thinking" was rarely a part of mid-nineteenth century nativist ideology, but outside of nativist rhetoric, the conversation of common culture itself took on much of the terminology previously used only by the devotees of the "ethnological" pseudosciences. It was with a justified confidence that readers would take him seriously that a contributor to a popular Southern literary magazine insisted that all future discussions of the Irish in America would have to be based upon the premise that *"they are* a different race."[36]

Physical appearance, mentioned in fewer than 10 percent of all comments on the Irish in American conversation before 1845 reviewed for this study was, by the mid to late 1850s, the most frequent object of description, constituting about one-fifth of all interethnic references. Discussion of physical character increased in frequency and changed in style. During the 1820s and 1830s, word illustrations of Irish appearance most often highlighted the effects of environment. The Irishman was typically "dirty" or "ragged" or "unkempt" and less frequently "dark," "choleric," or "carroty-headed." Later references to Irish appearance were more often somatic descriptions, referring to inherited features like eye and skin color, facial configuration, and physique. The Irishman was "low-browed," "brutish," or even "simian."

As Anglo-Americans altered the way in which they talked about the Irish (and, consequently, the way in which they "saw" the Irish), they also adjusted their explicit rationale for ethnic difference. The traditional environmentalist description of ethnic distinctiveness began to drop out of currency in the American popular

press during the last years before the Civil War. Increasingly, jour-
nalists, essayists, and the ubiquitous "correspondents" described
differences between ethnic groups as matters of "race," as immutable characteristics traceable to prehistory. In contrast to the hopes
of the United States' founding fathers that republican institutions—
political, educational, and moral—would produce an elevated common character, it was popular wisdom at mid-century that national
character constituted little more than an expression of the innate
character of the nation's dominant ethnic constituency. Thus the
editors of the *American Whig Review* could write in 1851 that
"the British North American colonies were settled almost exclusively by Anglo-Saxons, and their rapid progress was owing in a
great degree to the energy and vigor peculiar to the race to which
they belonged." Many commentators on ethnic character seemed
to work backward from the perceived or preferred characteristics of
the American nation to the alleged characteristics of Anglo-Americans as the predominant ethnic stock. A contributor to Philadelphia's *Presbyterian Quarterly Review,* for example, remarked that
Anglo-Americans shared in the "Teutonic fixed type of character"
and, therefore, that their chief attributes were "intense love of
freedom, indomitable valor, steadiness, sobriety, receptivity to culture, sagacious intellectuality." In incidental "conversation" these
were just about the same qualities Anglo-Americans regularly attributed to themselves—their auto-stereotype.[37] Once they took
them to be products of good breeding; now they claimed them as
birthright.

By 1860 the use of "ethnological" terminology in connection
with discussions of white ethnic groups was commonplace in school
texts, popular reference books, and official documents. The Civil
War era edition of William Channing Woodbridge's familiar school
geography subdivided the Caucasian "race" into Celtic and Gothic
"families." The former, American youth were informed, displayed
"strong passions and lively dispositions;" the latter were "ingenious,
but usually phlegmatic and most distinguished for patient, persevering industry." George Ripley and Charles A. Dana, compilers
of *The American Cyclopedia: A Popular Dictionary of General
Knowledge,* treated it as an accepted fact that the population of
the United States contained elements of both the northern and
southern "races" of Europe, the first represented by the English,

Scots, and Germans, and the second, by the Celtic Irish. Each "race" brought a distinctive "temperament" with it into American life.[38]

During the years immediately before the sectional fracture, public officials intent upon uncovering the sources of urban poverty, crime, and disease, began to recant openly the environmental explanations of social evils accepted for decades and to adopt an "ethnologic" approach. The Massachusetts State Board of Charities insisted that the chief cause of pauperism and public dependency was nothing less than "inherited organic imperfection, vitiated constitution, or *poor stock*," and the New York Association for Improving the Condition of the Poor concluded that "the excess of poverty and crime, also, among the Irish, as compared with the natives of other countries, is a curious fact, worthy of the study of the political economist and the ethnologist." The United States Bureau of the Census gave its imprimatur to all such talk in its report upon the American population in 1860. Besides devoting special discussion to the Teutonic and Celtic components of the populace, the Census routinely subdivided the nation's white inhabitants into "native," "foreign," and "Irish" for purposes of classification and analysis.[39] In 1820 the Irish had only been one of several European immigrant groups regarded suspiciously because of their tutelage under authoritarian political and religious regimes. By 1860, Anglo-Americans had not only separated the Irish out from other immigrants and given them special status as an alien "race" but had also come to treat Irish character as the cause rather than the consequence of their particular Old World condition.

That the evolution of Paddy was more than elite invention is evident from inspection of some of the more homely repositories of verbal culture. The changing stereotype of the Irish in the mid-century United States and all of its implications was captured by the stage Irishman of American popular theater and his cousin in the pages of contemporary prose fiction. Emphasizing the dramaturgical *function* of stock character types in English and American popular theater, students of melodrama customarily point out the timeless features of the stage Irishman.[40] Early in this century, drama scholar Maurice Bourgeois wrote that in all English language melodrama:

The stage Irishman habitually bears the general name of Pat, Paddy, or Teague. He has an atrocious Irish brogue, perpetual jokes, blunders, and bulls in speaking, and never fails to utter, by way of Hibernian season- ing, some wild screech or oath of Gaelic origin at every third word. . . . His hair is of a fiery red: he is rosy-cheeked, massive, and whiskey- loving. His face is one of simian bestiality with an expression of diaboli- cal archness written all over it. He wears a tall felt hat (billicock or wideawake), with a cutty-clay pipe stuck in front, an open shirt collar, a three-caped coat, knee breeches, worsted stockings, and cockaded brogue shoes. In his right hand he brandishes a stout blackthorn or sprig of shillelagh and threatens to belabor therewith the daring person who will tread on the tail of his coat. For his main characteristics (if there is any such thing as psychology in the stage Irishman) are his swagger, his boisterousness and his pugnacity. He is always ready with a chal- lenge, always anxious to back a quarrel, and peerless for cracking skulls at Donnybrook Fair.[41]

Only as we move from the context and costume of the stage Irish- man to the content do the features of a genuine ethnic stereotype emerge, a stereotype in words on stage that paralleled the stereotype in words used in ordinary conversation outside the theater door. As the verbal image of the Irish in newspapers, magazines, school- books, and other repositories of common culture changed, the char- acter of the Irishmen portrayed on American stages (as well as in the novel and short story) also changed. The late antebellum stage Irishman was demonstrably a creation of nature.[42] After the mid- 1840s, a new representation of the "typical" Irish blunder achieved currency in American popular theater. The chief characters of the melodramatic farce *The Irish Tiger* addressed the origin of the blunder directly. Mr. Marrowfat took the traditional view: his servants' blunders were mere accidents and ordinary mistakes. But the argument advanced by his daughter, and proved by example in the course of the play, denied that the blunder was only misfortune and treated it as the inevitable consequence of Irish feeble-minded- ness. Whatever Irishman her father should hire to serve him, the perceptive Julia contended, "Wasn't there *always* sure to be some blunder or other?" By story's end, Julia's characterization of the Irish as "wild beasts" seemed an established fact. The Irish blunder, a humorous relic of a peasant past in the 1820s or 1830s, seemed a serious natural flaw a quarter of a century later. There had always been a tendency in antebellum Irish character drama to treat the blundering Irishman as equally humorous and dangerous. When the blunder was inadvertent and the blunderer deemed educable, the danger seemed bad enough. But when the blunder was innate, the blunderer was to be avoided at all costs. Barney Williams' unlucky Pat, principal of *Irish Assurance and Yankee Modesty*, who as herder lost the cows, as jockey killed the horse, as fisherman sunk the boat, as gardener destroyed the crop, and as footman nearly murdered his mistress, must have produced some nervous smiles among audiences populated with employers of Irish help.[43]

A short story published by the *Southern Literary Messenger* in 1841 described an Irish character in conventional early antebellum fashion: "He was a low, chunky, hardy-looking person, of middle age, with sandy hair, and thin red whiskers. His head, to all appearances, had not felt the edge of a razor for a month, and his long, matted locks overhung the back of a red flannel warmus." This unremarkable portrait was only made a little more distinctive by a subsequent reference to Murty O'Hanley's "ponderous red nose."[44] A scant fifteen years later, Thomas Butler Gunn offered a very different kind of description of the Irish in fiction. In *The Physiology of New York Boarding Houses*, Gunn suggestively portrayed urban immigrants as:

Paddies in the caped and high-waisted frieze coats, the brimless cabreens, the knee breeches, woolen stockings, and rusty brogues of immemorial tradition. Paddies with the 'hanging bone' gait, the forelock (to be pulled in token of subjection), the low brow denoting the serf of fifty descents, the shillalegh and inevitable blunder.[45]

Physical appearance was treated as if it were actually indicative of interior character. In his novel of the Philadelphia riots in 1844, *The Nazarene*, George Lippard made that connection even more explicit. Of one Irish Philadelphian, Lippard wrote, "The dark eyes sunken beneath the compressed brows, the forehead with its short stiff hair . . . [gave him] a look of savage ferocity."[46] For Lippard, the conformation of the Irish skull revealed the disposition of the Irish mind. By no means was this universally characteristic of the treatment of the Irish in late antebellum fiction, but the increasingly frequent connection of human form and function was reflective of ongoing developments in American "conversation."

During the 1850s, especially, American architects of Irish parts in melodrama relied heavily upon physical description to illuminate character and to distinguish ethnic populations from one another.

John Brougham, renowned American dramatic humorist of Anglo-Irish background, created Irish characters calculated to attract some audience sympathy but at the same time to show that, innately, the Celt was qualitatively different from the Saxon. Informed by his wife that an Irishman "sick and in distress" sought succor at his door, Tom, the virtuous and good-natured Anglo-American hero of *Temptation, or The Irish Emigrant,* replied, "What, a Paddy? Don't mention it." Tom doubted that Irishmen really suffered from the same afflictions that affected Americans of British ancestry. Paddy could not be regarded as fully human for, as Brougham's protagonist made clear, "He's only an Irishman." James Pilgrim, another American melodramatist contemporary with Brougham, treated the Irish as sub-Caucasian in more than one farce. In *Katty O'Sheal* they were "colored people" unsuitable for marriage to authentic whites. But it was left to another popular comedy to portray the Irish as more akin to black than white. Among the most uproarious scenes of *The Irishman in London* was that in which Murtoch Delaney fell hopelessly in love with his perfect match, the humanoid "grinning Cuba." The African and the Irishman were made for one another.[47]

Probably few Anglo-Americans were prepared to follow as far as *The Irishman in London* led, but the way in which physical descriptions of Irish stage characters were intertwined with evaluations of Irish economic, political, social, and moral characteristics in dramatic dialogue would have made sense to them. James Pilgrim always costumed his stage Irishmen in red hair; in *The Wild Irish Girl* he used scarce-veiled double entendre to associate exterior form with interior character: "Red hair is the most pliant in the world and, I confess, requires considerable fixing."[48] This conformed nicely with the representation of Paddy in ordinary conversation as tractable and in need of much "fixing" indeed. In the late antebellum period, in melodrama as in language, the defect of inefficiency was more likely to be characterized as innate than as conditional. The Irish servants portrayed in Pilgrim's farces bore inherent "laziness" and "excessive awkwardness." Pilgrim represented inability to perform a task efficiently as endemic to Irish nature. It was the product of an "infection of idleness" passed from one generation of Irishmen to the next.[49] Idleness was physical and ethnic rather than cultural and personal. So, for example, was violence. In the early years of the nineteenth century, the "fighting Irishman" who regarded combat as a frolic—as in George Colman's *The Jealous Wife* or James Kirke Paulding's *The Bucktails*—could be viewed with some humor. But after Philadelphia, in the popular imagination at least, had been made a battleground, the Irishman's stereotyped love of a contest took on a more sinister appearance.[50]

As language increasingly associated the moral and the physical, so did literature. There was not much, after all, to laugh about in Thomas Butler Gunn's fictive descriptions of the denizens of New York's Irish slums. Even the women seemed made for a fight: "Paddyesses, whose arms were only less thick than their waists or speech." No wonder Gunn concluded that Irish condition and behavior were "predestinate." John Brougham even managed to make Paddy's most praised features seem hazardous: "Plenty of courage, but no brains; useful but dangerous."[51] How much did readers really laugh at the Irish joke in an 1859 number of *Harper's Monthly* which implied that Paddy, was, after all, a "wild beast"?

"We have in our village," says a correspondent, "two fine specimens from the 'Emerald Isle,' and without both intelligent, quick-witted, and on hand. One of them, Patrick Clark by name, is a brewer, and the other, a merchant, is named Dennis B. Smith. Patrick, the other day, got up a fine conundrum, and off he set with it to enlighten Dennis. Meeting him, he said, 'Dennis, why am I like a wild beast?' intending to have him give it up; and then the answer should be, 'Because I'm always a 'brewing' (a bruin). But as quick as a flash, Dennis replies, 'Because you are a Paddy.' This used Patrick up, of course. 'And only to think of it,' he said, in his disgust, 'he a brother Irishman, and call me a Paddy.' "[52]

The emergence in the late antebellum period of a stage Irish stereotype which identified and evaluated ethnic character by allusions to conduct and appearance was important because the "comic" stage Irishman was a stand-in for the much more seriously regarded Irish immigrant. The laughter of Anglo-American audiences scarcely disguised the anxiety about ethnicity and nationality that the fully evolved stage Irishman betrayed. A stereotyped Irishman in novel and melodrama who "looked" different from Anglo-Americans and Englishmen and was by nature predisposed to particular patterns of behavior reflected apprehension that a uniform national character could not, after all, be secured by either the effects of simple acclimation or the beneficial influences of well-crafted human institutions: homes, or churches, or schools. Innately inharmonious immigrants would not be candidates for nationalization but invaders—invaders producing unassimilable offspring. "What with their own increase an' the constant immigritting fro' all parts o' Ireland," harangued rollicking John McClosky of Lucius Sargent's "Irish Heart," "there's no dout, in the minds o'sinsible calkillaturs, but we may possiss the hull country one dee. . . . There's no country't wad be more agraable to staal."[53]

"Of the great influence of race in the production of national character," opined a correspondent for the *American Whig Review* in September 1851, "no reasonable enquirer can now doubt." Reasonable doubts surfaced in the popular press just often enough to show that the connection of "race" with national character was sufficiently widespread to inspire backlash. Development of a distinctive national character through accretion of common experience—the early antebellum expectation—was bound to be slow, too slow for many like the pseudonymous "Pennsylvania" of the *Southern Literary Messenger*, who thought it absurd that the American people did not yet manifest "some particular trait common to all, and at the same time, differing from all other nations."[54] The arrival of more and more transatlantic newcomers, especially the Irish in the mid-1840s, replete with their own lifestyles and traditions, would compound diversity of experience and further slow the homogenizing forces of American life. Sustained heterogeneity might present Anglo-Americans with the unappetizing prospect of having to acknowledge the "failure" of prized institutions—political, educational, and religious—to mold personal (and national) character in ways anticipated. Worse, over the course of the antebellum period, Anglo-American society itself—immigrants aside—grew more rather than less diverse, making the whole idea of common experience a mockery. Industrialization, urbanization, and geographical expansion all made the experiences of Anglo-Americans increasingly *dissimilar* as the nineteenth century progressed. To occupational, social class, and residential diversity was joined sectional particularity, the growing perception of which was perhaps even greater than the actuality. The complexity—and thus heterogeneity—of American life was much more widely recognized than its symptoms, elite anxieties over assertive individualism and the breakdown of traditional social deference on which historians have lavished much attention. All this must be set against the fact that few contemporaries could envision a truly pluralistic society of many lifestyles, "characters," and experiences. This was certainly proven over and over again in the ongoing debate over slavery. While the contestants often differed on the degree of racial hazard posed by freed blacks, they customarily agreed—save the most ideologically pure abolitionists—that the respective temperaments of black and white would not conveniently allow them to live together in harmony. Even those most disposed to see the African temper as a gift instead of a curse could only imagine that it must in time infect the Caucasian (for the better, they thought) and not merely coexist alongside it. So too, it was not considered possible for Irish or other European immigrants to retain a distinctive character in America. If they were not Americanized then there was no alternative but that Anglo-Americans would be partly Europeanized by the contact.

The growing tendency to connect national character with "race" in the late antebellum period emerged from such considerations. To make American national character come of nature instead of nurture was to give a distinctive American national character instantaneous creation. American character was ethnic character, *Anglo-American* character. Republican institutions, by this reasoning, had not "failed" after all. Rather, they had been given an impossible task: to nurture a character that could only be had by birth. National character was, furthermore, impervious to the heterogeneity of Anglo-American experience; occupation, class, and section would avail nothing against innate character borne in the blood. In fact, some of this diversity itself could be blamed upon ethnic variety. Theodore Parker, for instance, wondered whether the Anglo-Saxon temperament of the Northern states had not produced a different American subculture than the "Norman" temperament of the South. Historian William R. Taylor has written at length about the popularity of this point of view concerning the differences between "Cavalier" and "Yankee."[55]

Kindred ideas had been floating about in American common culture for decades. As early as 1829 the author of an article published in the *American Quarterly Review* had propounded a "doctrine of temperaments," which held that "races are distinguished into nations, and nations have their characteristics, which are transmitted from one generation to another." And just a few years later the *New England Magazine* carried a piece which grandiloquently proclaimed that to discover the true causes of national character, it would be necessary to "ascend the stream of time to its source in the creation, and watch men divide off into tribes."[56] But these were unusual comments for the early antebellum period, largely restricted to elite culture and quite unsupported by styles of language through which Anglo-Americans continued to refer to themselves and others in terms of plastic character. They were not common because they had not been necessary. As Pierre Van den Berghe, a leading student of racism, has noted, human beings, however elevated their opinion of themselves and however low their opinion of others, usually base their pride upon cultural institutions and values—upon their own creations. It takes some extraordinary incentive to incline them to treat their superiority as the creation of God or nature. The view implicit in early antebellum language and culture was that of school text author Salma Hale, whose *History of the United States* instructed American youth that the "germ" of a distinctive national character was buried in republican culture and institutions and merely needed time to grow.[57] Only when the growth began to seem too slow or to have stopped altogether did alternative treatments of national character become more popular.

Ideas about the innateness and permanence of national character, flouted so publicly at mid-century, in the early antebellum period chiefly circulated among intellectuals and can especially be traced to modernist challenges to the literal truth of the biblical story of human creation. Similar views—often of similar motivation—wafted continuously across the Atlantic from Europe, though also known only to the extraordinarily well-read. But, undoubtedly, the sheer increase of European immigration itself, especially after the mid-1840s, attended by material competition between the native and the foreign-born and sometimes actual interethnic violence, was bound to magnify Anglo-Americans' sense of distinctiveness, even when they continued to believe that the basis of that distinctiveness was moral and intellectual character only. When captured in verbal stereotypes, any alleged ethnic particularity took an enlarged appearance. Even under the assumptions of the early antebellum period there was bound to be some anxiety about identifying *who* the Irish were. How, after all, might they be republicanized unless they were known? Inevitably, such concern would direct attention toward immigrant conduct and appearance—toward what I have called "extrinsic" character. The Irish would increasingly be "seen" as set apart by visible conduct and appearance. This development coincided with the national self-satisfaction that accompanied the working out of the United States' "Manifest Destiny" through geographical expansion. Expansion, and the displacement of Indians and Mexicans that it entailed, was made more palatable if it seemed demanded by nature. Roy Harvey Pearce has shown very clearly how alleged Indian "savagism" was rendered progressively more innate in the popular imagination of white Americans as the latter sought to cast expansion as the inevitable march of progress. By the same token, conflict with Mexico during the 1840s led to a decided inclination to maximize the physical distinctions between Anglo-Americans and their adversaries, who were described by one contemporary as "in no way deserving to be called white."[58] National pride had its correlate in personal pride. Emerson put his finger on this exactly: "Men gladly hear of the power of blood or race. Everybody likes to know that his advantages cannot be attributed to air, soil, sea, or to local wealth, as mines and quarries, nor to laws and traditions nor to fortune, but to superior brain, as it makes the praise more personal to him."[59] Anglo-Americans' sense of self certainly changed in advance of their sense of others. They began to treat themselves as inherently and permanently distinctive before they began to think that way of anyone else.

The ruminations of Marsh or Storrs, the thunderings of New York's *Daily Times* about the prospect of "race war," or the textbook discussions of Celts and Teutons, all such talk was sure to accelerate the ongoing drift of ordinary language. If the Irish were innately different from Anglo-Americans and impervious to improvement, it was imperative that they be seen for who they were, else their baleful influences might not be properly resisted. As long as American nationality was taken to be a product of character, descriptions of intelligence and morality were sufficient to depict the alien Irish. But if Irish character was not environmental but biological in origin, then descriptions of immigrant character were not nearly so useful. What was required were reliable indicators of "race." With a kind of hysteria, the editors of the *New York Times* wrote that the danger from "hostile races" was compounded by the fact that "the descendants of the half-brutal, ignorant Irish peasant . . . are scarcely to be distinguished from our intelligent native population."[60]

In the late antebellum period, ethnicity was no longer treated as a matter of "character," culture, and environment but of blood, and nationality was no longer understood as attainable by any who met certain standards of intelligence and morality. Nationality was neither to be had by nurture nor by choice. This, of course, made ethnicity a primary source of identity for many Anglo-Americans, a means by which they proclaimed themselves as Americans and disqualified others from sharing their nationality.

In defining themselves ethnically, good republicans by no means intended to identify themselves completely with Englishmen, Germans, or others who shared "Saxon" or "Teutonic" blood. They were insistent upon the distinctive aspect of the Anglo-*American*. As one contemporary put it, it was only in the United States, freed of the impediments of monarchy, aristocracy, poverty, and the other encrustations of antiquity, that the Saxon temperament might fully flower.[61] This, I suppose, was testimony to the endurance—at least in truncated form—of early antebellum environmentalism, as well as a practical necessity if ethnicity was to be of any value in giving definition to American national character. Still, Anglo-Americans were willing to acknowledge a special relationship with those they accepted as ethnic kin. Germans, for example, compared to the Irish, as noted earlier, received remarkably gentle treatment in the language of American common culture. Although Germans, too, were frequently Roman Catholic, had been raised under monarchical institutions, could sometimes be tarred with the brush of political radicalism, and spoke a foreign tongue besides, German immigrants to the United States were not scourged by words like the Irish. Despite—or perhaps even because of—the growing Anglo-American habit to define themselves ethnically, the German stereotype held up well even against the Anglo-American self-image.[62]

The verbal image of the Irish changed as the purposes it served changed. As the language used to treat the Irish in incidental conversation became dominated by "extrinsic" descriptives, it institutionalized a certain way of "seeing" both Anglo-Americans and Irishmen. It institutionalized a kind of ethnic prejudice. Putative membership in the ethnic group designated "Irish" disqualified an individual from being acknowledged as an authentic "American." This stereotype made no distinctions between immigrants and native-born Americans of Irish descent. In fact, under the terms of the stereotype, the latter were denationalized, virtually rendered un-American by definition.

Is this evidence of the emergence of an Anglo-American "racism" strong enough to produce an ethnically stratified society in which ethnic group membership was a major criterion for assigning individuals to social positions and thus to social and material rewards? Undoubtedly the sense of ethnic difference implicit in the late antebellum verbal stereotype of the Irish conforms to conventional definitions of "racism" in important respects. Van den Berghe calls racism "any set of beliefs that organic, genetically transmitted differences (whether real or imagined) between human groups are intrinsically associated with the presence or absence of certain socially relevant abilities or characteristics, hence that such differences are a legitimate basis of invidious distinctions between groups socially defined as 'races.' "[63] By mid-century language had built into American folk culture a sense that "Americans" and "Irish" were innately and permanently—physically—different from one another and that intelligence, morality, religious inclination, political affiliation, social conduct, and economic behavior were all derivatives of "race." Anglo-Americans unquestionably got into the habit of nationalizing themselves and denationalizing the American Irish by the routine use of a verbal stereotype which made the Irish seem "racially" distinct. Doubtless this ranks as "invidious." There is at least one historian who argues that denationalizing any group of people is the most invidious distinction of all, for it interferes with untrammeled participation in the political community, which is the basis of all civil rights. But "Celticism" did not automatically exclude many from employment, prevent economic and social mobility, or restrict access to facilities of public entertainment or accommodation.

Nor could "race" be used effectively to "place" the Irish, because it foundered on the rock of reality, the reality that the physical differences between Anglo-Americans and Irishmen were too few to make physical appearance a reliable basis for identification and "invidious" distinction. For the Irish, "passing" into Anglo-American society was too easy to make a specifically ethnic prejudice very effective. "The foreigners in Massachusetts," a student of European immigration wrote in 1856, "are chiefly of Celtic origin. In twenty years from the present time, one-half of the young men and women in the State will be of direct Celtic ancestry, and there is no doubt that they will also brag and boast of their Pilgrim fathers, their revolutionary ancestry, and especially of the Anglo-Saxon blood in their Celtic veins." A contemporaneous commentator on the street life of New York City made exactly the same point by telling the story of one Tommy Ryan, an ambitious newspaper dealer. "He is a good looking lad," G. G. Foster explained, "and we will lay a handsome wager that all of his sons will be Whigs."[64] These were the statements of empiricists who knew what they saw. In the twentieth century, Harvard anthropologist Earnest A. Hooton would prove them good observers (as if they needed to be verified). Hooton evaluated the physical characteristics of 10,000 male inhabitants of Ireland of all regions, classes, religions, and ethnic ancestries. He took thirty-three metric measurements (height, weight, girth, etc.) and sixty-four morphological ones (eye color, shape of nose). Published in 1955, his analysis concluded that the physical differences between the so-called native Irish, Scots-Irish, and Anglo-Irish were inconsistent and generally inconsequential. In fact, some characteristics which appeared in both English and Anglo-American stereotypes of the Irish in the nineteenth century turned out to be more common among individuals with "Saxon" backgrounds. Obviously, not only had the distinctions between Celts and Saxons been overstated but there had been such extensive intermarriage between ethnic stocks that visual inspection would be a wholly unreliable way of identifying ethnicity.[65] The inability of ethnic stereotypes to provide accurate assessments of group membership in Ireland in the 1930s was approximated in the United States in the 1850s.

In the mid-nineteenth century, language and popular ideology notwithstanding, white American society could not be effectively stratified by ethnicity. To have done so Anglo-Americans would have had to make unacceptable changes in the rules of American life. To keep all those with Irish blood from the polls, for instance, would have required such infringements upon the rights of all white Americans as to be offensive to republicanism itself. To restrict, wholesale, the economic opportunities of those tainted by Irish blood would have necessitated enforcement mechanisms beyond the imagination of almost everyone in the individualistic cultural environment of the mid-nineteenth century. The racial stratification of American society, on the other hand, worked because it required no special policing. Skin color made race relatively easy to identify, and white Americans—with the exception of only a few ideologues—were willing to live with the "passing" of some persons of mixed blood. Racism was a matter of law as well as of custom, but racial discrimination could be practiced by individuals without a great deal of intrusion by the state. The morphological similarity of the Irish to those who fancied themselves pure Anglo-Americans (to say nothing of "racial" intermixture) ensured that Anglo-Americans would rarely be able to use ethnicity to structure society in a way that would guarantee their cultural, political, and economic dominance.

Nevertheless, the institutionalization of a racial perception of the Irish in language had many defensive applications for individual Anglo-Americans. For all those who suffered the real or imagined barbs of the Europeans that the United States possessed no distinctive national character, the respective images of Irishman and authentic American offered relief. For beleaguered Anglo-American wage-earners, facing both the ongoing dislocations of industrialization and the perceived threat of immigrant competitors, the largely derisive stereotype of the Irish provided both comfort and grounds for demanding preferential employment. The "'No Irish Need Apply" notices that sometimes appeared in the windows of American businesses testified that this was not an entirely unreasonable expectation. For evangelical Protestants, the "racial" word portrait of the Irish which connected faith with blood seemed no threat to home missions but rather a spur to the Christian education of Anglo-American youth and to pious vigilance in the face of the antichrist. And for Americans of conservative temper discomfited by change itself, especially by developments in social structure and political practice, it gave point to their plaints for social discipline and community supervision of individual conduct.

Furthermore, the ubiquity of a "racial" stereotype of the Irish in American common culture ensured that objective sources of interethnic hostility could not have been sealed off from subjective ones. In the late antebellum years, to identify an individual or a group as "Irish" was to mobilize a word image which portrayed its subjects as un-American, Catholic, violent in temper, politically tractable, and ideologically rigid. Conversely, to identify anyone as Roman Catholic was virtually, in the absence of obvious countervailing evidence (like a German name), to label them Irish. For the same reason, almost any episode of urban street violence was likely to be attributed to the instigation of the Irish, and if any Anglo-American workman charged that his job was threatened by Irish immigrants, he was invoking a stereotype which also implied that his competitors were politically, religiously, and even physiologically alien. It is not simply, as David Brion Davis has argued, that in antebellum America subjective anxieties about national unity and national character "magnified and gave added meaning to concrete conflicts with minority groups."[66] In the case of the Irish, at least, language made the two absolutely inseparable.

But most important of all, the late antebellum stereotype of the Irish was an autonomous source of interethnic prejudice quite independent of material or ideological conflict. Because the verbal image of the Irish was so pejorative, because it connected its targets with so many unfavorable characteristics and made these seem permanent and innate, and—most of all—because this image was on almost everyone's lips, it was a source of hostility to the American Irish which might operate apart from any other. Stereotypes themselves are stimuli to "preadjustive behavior." They suggest to their users what to expect of stereotype targets and incline them to respond in an appropriate way. They are more, then, than simply a source of prejudgment but have the capacity to influence behavior itself.[67] The nature and extent of the verbal image of the Irish, ultimately, accounts for the special hostility encountered by the Irish, compared to other white ethnic minorities, in late antebellum America. The Irish faced denunciation simply for being Irish, denunciation even by those who never "saw" them except in words.

CHAPTER FOUR

Science and the Celt

"Nationality, treated philosophically, would, indeed, be a dry subject; because in order to find the origin, and explain the causes of the differences of character which exist among nations, and out of which springs patriotism, we must not only ascend the stream of time to its source in the creation, and watch men dividing off into tribes; but we must plunge into the depths of the human heart, and enter upon that wide sea of speculation where metaphysicians are lost in the mists of their own creation."

"Thoughts on National Character," *The New England Magazine* (April 1834)

AS MANY HISTORIANS would probably be quick to point out, in and of itself, the description of the Irish as a distinctive race did not *necessarily* mean much. "Race," after all, was a particularly vague term in the mid-nineteenth century and had been applied off and on to the Irish for a long time, both in England and in America.

In traditional usage, race had rarely indicated more than cultural distinction. Scholars routinely acknowledge the growing ubiquity of Anglo-Saxonist rhetoric during the last decade or two before the Civil War without suspecting that the frequency of talk about "race" reflected altered popular dispositions toward ethnic and national character.[1] John Higham argues that antebellum Anglo-Saxonism grew out of "political and literary speculation" and was more a way for elites to identify the United States with a glorious cultural heritage than for the public to make meaningful distinctions between ethnic groups or to define nationality. More serious interest in "ethnology"—the nineteenth century "science" of human differences—is customarily taken to have been characteristic of only a few intellectuals, though we know that ethnological theory was a favorite resort of white supremicists and was introduced into the national debate over slavery during the 1840s and 1850s.[2]

Undoubtedly, modern credulity is strained to accept the idea that many antebellum Americans could have viewed the Irish as anything like a separate race, distinguished by readily discernible physical characteristics linked (as the nineteenth century view of race would have it) with inheritable patterns of character and behavior. Given the obvious physical similarities between Irish-Americans and Anglo-Americans, it is difficult to see how such a perception could have stood unless propped up by some elaborate theoretical foundation. Given the arcane complexity of contemporary ethnology, it is difficult to see how such theory as did exist could circulate among more than a few devotees.

In the United States at mid-century, the application of the term "race" to the Irish was made highly meaningful by the prevailing patterns of conversation about the Irish which encouraged the consumers of language to "see" ethnic characteristics that were physical and natural rather than cultural and environmental. But, just as important, late antebellum Americans took the full draught of nineteenth century ethnologic theory, which imposed a particular interpretation upon the alleged physical dissimilarities of Anglo-American and Celt. They did so by imbibing the main points of the faddish pseudo-sciences of phrenology and physiognomy. These "sciences" legitimized the application of "race" to white ethnic groups and helped make it commonplace to connect particular physical characteristics with specific behavior/condition/character matrices. Not only did this have short-term implications for the perception of the American Irish but it also affected negatively the enduring understanding of American nationality.

The story of eighteenth and nineteenth century European ethnology, of its spread to North America, and its adoption by the theorists of white supremacy has been told in recent years by William Stanton, George M. Fredrickson, Thomas F. Gossett, and Reginald Horsman.[3] But while the conventional treatment credits Georges Louis Leclerc Buffon with introducing the term "race" to the modern European vocabulary as a way of typifying the variety of human form, it was German anatomist Johann Friedrich Blumenbach who initially confounded the adjectives "national" and "racial," making it possible for subsequent students of ethnology to apply their theories on the meaning of physical differences to discussions of European national characters. Another German, Johann Gottfried von Herder, argued explicitly that it was not only skin color groups that carried forward by inheritance characteristics resistant to the effects of environment but also "nations" or "Volk." "For every nation is one people," Herder wrote at the close of the eighteenth century, "having its own national form."[4] In Britain, ethnologic theory became the ammunition for a secularist assault upon the biblical account of unitary human creation. English surgeon Dr. Charles White was among the first to claim that "races" were so thoroughly and enduringly different that each must have originated from a different Adamic pair. This polygenetic argument first brought ethnologic theory and rhetoric to the attention of American clerics and educators. In the early nineteenth century, the Reverend Samuel Stanhope Smith of Princeton led a chorus of reaffirmation for scriptural tradition and the practical necessity of treating mankind as one species subject to one moral law. If races or "nations" differed materially, Smith wrote in his celebrated *Essay on the Causes of the Variety of Complexion and Figure in the Human Species* (first published in 1810), it was entirely because of the action of climate and other environmental conditions.[5]

Through this means—the debate between polygenesists and monogenesists—the rhetoric of ethnology entered the media of American common culture. Significantly it was a rhetoric already quite imprecise on the distinctions between nation and race. One after another, the serial publications of the church-related press in the United States jumped into the controversy. The *North American Review*, in an 1822 number, felt strongly compelled to point out "the great influence of government and peculiar form of society in opposition to . . . formation" in the constitution of human differences. Educators offered the same defense of traditional environmentalism, as witnessed by one influential early antebellum geography text, which instructed young scholars: "We should not be surprised . . . to find great varieties in the millions of the great family of man, exposed to such varieties of climate, manners, and modes of living."[6]

Still, the subject of human differences, and especially national differences, was irresistibly interesting to antebellum Americans and even a commitment to biblical authority was unlikely to prevent Americans from following developments in ethnologic science, especially when these purported to explain the character of nations. Granted the monogenetic origin of mankind, the editors of the *American Quarterly Review* offered in 1832, "It is, nevertheless, certain that there is a real and profound diversity between nations existing at this day . . . [and] it is yet interesting to consider whence arise the specific diversities among, and the peculiar characteristics of, nations." Given their passion on the subject of national character, it is no wonder that among many Americans curiosity won out over orthodoxy. More and more often after the mid-1830s, throughout the various popular media, discussions of national character turned into discussions of physical character, inheritance, and "race." "We can find instances on record of people changing their religion, their government, and their language," a contributor to the *New England Magazine* wrote among some "Thoughts on National Character," "being transplanted to another climate, and still preserving for ages their characteristic marks of distinction in spite of the continual action of causes sufficient to efface anything but innate propensities and distinctions."[7] By the 1840s, these assumptions were in the schoolbooks, too, and Peter Parley (Samuel Griswold Goodrich) could write: "There is, doubtless, such a thing as inherent character in nations, which belongs to the race, and may be traced back as far as we can investigate their records." What did Goodrich mean by "race"? He was not very explicit, but he suspected that even the inhabitants of the various *counties* of England differed in "complexion, thought, feeling, and character, which are evidently traceable to original differences in the tribes from which they are descended." The thrust of all such discussions—à la Herder—was that nations were not only political but also biological units and that the interior and exterior characters of nations alike were attributable to descent. Even the homely local historian of Chambersburg, Pennsylvania, felt that his readers would not think him overbold in predicting the town's future from its past.

After all, George Chambers wrote, "character is said to be transmissible, and that the character of descendants may be determined by what was that of their ancestors."[8]

The initial attraction of ethnologic rhetoric outside intellectual circles was probably its usefulness in silencing critics, foreign and domestic, who carped that the United States had no discernible national character and no predictable future. Continental ethnology proclaimed that all nations possessed a particular genius that they took from the "blood" of their inhabitants. There could, under these circumstances, be no such thing as a nation without a national character.[9] Doubtless it was an appreciation of the fact that ethnologic "science" might provide Americans with a way of objectively establishing their self-identity that brought the work of French natural philosopher Count Arthur de Gobineau to the attention of well-read republicans. At mid-century Gobineau's ethnological research seemed particularly applicable to the United States. In fact, Gobineau said so himself. For Anglo-Americans nervous about their nation's prospects, the central premise of Gobineau's first treatise to be published in the United States was eye-catching: "every assemblage of men, together with the culture it produces, is doomed to perish." "Degeneration," the source of national decline, issued from "continuous adulterations having gradually affected the quality . . . of blood." Adulteration did not just promote physical decay but also "loss of personal identity" and direction. Worse, it made a people unsuited to the cultural institutions, particularly laws and government, created by their purer-blooded ancestors. The results were anomie, discontent, revolution, or self-destructive passivity in the face of more homogeneous and dynamic national rivals. Powerful, civilized nations were those nearest to decline, Gobineau argued. When strong, states reach out to take other nations and people under their influence or even incorporate them directly. When civilized, they relax traditional taboos against marriages of mixed "blood." Rome, the chief historical example of these processes, had fallen as a result. The United States and Russia, the monoliths of the future, Gobineau predicted, were likely to follow the same course.[10]

While Gobineau called "race" mixture the chief threat to the United States, he left no doubt that he meant more than the amalgamation of white, red, and black. For Gobineau as for Herder, "race" and "nation" were interchangeable, and it was the "crowds which are thronging over the frontier" of the United States—throngs of European immigrants—not just the progeny of black slaves and remnants of the North American indigenes who posed a danger to American blood.[11] This was also the message of Gobineau's contemporary Dr. Robert Knox of the Edinburgh College of Surgeons, who in 1850 analyzed ethnic mixture in the United States in a book he called *The Races of Man*. As the title of this disquisition suggested, Knox assumed that European immigration was leading not to a blending of nationalities and cultures but to a union of "races," subdivisions of mankind bearing permanent, inheritable physical distinctions. According to Knox, the United States constituted the only great trial of European "race" mixture in modern times. In America, Anglo-Saxon, Celt, and Teuton mingled in promiscuous confusion. Based upon all the prior experience of man, Knox concluded, the experiment was bound to fail. Knox saw failure stamped upon the very faces of the white American populace at mid-century. "Symptoms of premature decay" in dental conformation, skin color, and muscle tone proved the biological inefficacy of "race" mixture. Furthermore, Knox argued, the confidence of the United States' founding generation that human propensities could be channeled along socially beneficial lines by the careful construction of an artificial political system had proven unwarranted. "Democracy, or socialism, or bands of peripatetic demagogues, or evil spirits, may have had something to do with the history of nations," Knox wrote, but the effect of political ideology, system, or leadership was slight compared to the impact of "race" upon government. The Celtic race, for instance, "never could be made to comprehend the meaning of the word liberty." How, then, could the distinctively Anglo-Saxon concept of representative government ever be made workable among an American populace growing increasingly Celtic?[12]

According to Knox, not only the United States' political future, but its economic future as well depended wholly upon the racial composition of the American people. Again, in Celtic blood were the seeds of blight. For the Irish had "no self-confidence, no innate courage, to meet the forest and the desert . . . and are the worst of agriculturists." Of course, some optimists liked to think that Protestantizing Roman Catholic Irish-Americans would improve the stock. "Nonsense," Knox responded; "the great broad principles of the morality of man have nothing to do with any religion. The races of men still remain distinct." The Irish, after all, were Catholics because it suited their nature as Protestantism suited the Saxon. To think that purely superficial conversion could alter the heart and mind, much less the actual behavior, of the Irish immigrant was foolishness. Ultimately, the preservation of the American experiment in democracy depended upon effective segregation of the "races" in the New World and removal of the inferior elements.[13]

American intellectuals became quite conversant with ethnologic rhetoric during the late antebellum period and some became contributors to the "science" itself. Theodore Parker engaged in a lengthy correspondence on the subject with Swiss geologist Edward Desor, and beginning in the late 1840s his essays of social criticism, like "The Political Destination of America," took on a decidedly ethnologic flavor. "Some nations, it seems," Parker wrote in 1848, "perish through defect of . . . national character. . . . Only when the blood of the nation is changed by additions from another stock is the idiosyncrasy altered."[14] Emerson seems to have picked up the ethnologic vocabulary in Britain, returning home in the mid-1850s to write his own theories of national character into *English Traits*:

> We anticipate in the doctrine of race something like that law of physiology that whatever bone, muscle, or essential organ is found in one healthy individual, the same part or organ may be found in or near the same place in its congener, and we look to find in the son every mental and moral property that existed in the ancestor.[15]

The diffusion of ethnologic theory among elites was superimposed upon an emergent romantic inclination to make particular moral and intellectual attributes the trusts of particular peoples. As early as 1838 Maine Transcendentalist Frederick Henry Hedge was enthusing that "when we trace the progress of human culture in time past, we find that there has always been some one tribe of people, to whom this culture was especially committed. . . . At present, the Anglo-Saxon race bears this charge."[16] Ethnology gave all such talk the imprimatur of science, suggesting that it was empirically verifiable.

We know very well the use antebellum white supremacists made of continental ethnology. Josiah Nott and Samuel Cartwright turned it to the defense of racial slavery. Louis Agassiz and J. Aitken Meigs, though not particularly committed to the peculiar institution, nonetheless employed ethnologic theory to prove the dangers of race mixture and the necessity of black subordination in some form.[17] But even in the United States, ethnology never became completely abstracted from the interest of its originators in analyzing the distinctions between the "races" or "nations" of western and central Europe. Even Nott divided the "Caucasian Group" of mankind into constituent "races" and "nations," including the "Anglo-American nation," the characteristics of which—physical and moral—he treated as innate and inheritable.[18]

Ethnologic theory might be thought to have no following outside circles of intellectuals and perhaps slaveholders. How could it spread among those who had no immediate exposure to Gobineau or Knox? Yet the editors of a metropolitan newspaper, commenting upon an interethnic riot in the mid-1850s, employed the ethnologic idiom: "We must remember that every nation and every form of government, which has embraced within itself the elements of mingled and hostile races, has been very weak, or has fallen."[19] They seemed to assume that a mass readership would understand what they were talking about. Much of the American public in the late antebellum period had indeed been taught to think ethnologically by the popular phrenological pseudo-sciences—to take character as a correlate of physique and national character as a product of blood—to a far greater extent than historians usually appreciate. John Davies, a leading modern student of phrenology, points out that "although it is remembered today only as a method of reading character from the contour of the skull, its true foundation was the theory that anatomical and physiological characteristics have a direct influence upon mental behavior." Historians have ordinarily treated phrenology as a faddish parlor game or, at best, an amateurish psychology,[20] but in the mid-nineteenth century, American and European scholars, including Gobineau himself, thought it held one of the keys to understanding and classifying the "nations" and "races" of man. A contributor to *Graham's American Magazine*, writing for a profoundly nontechnical audience, explained with notable economy the cardinal assumption of phrenology: "There is ever a corresponding relation between the organization of the brain, and the faculties of the mind. The mind of the Indian and the Hottentot is inferior to the mind of the European, and the organization of the brain is less perfect."[21]

The beauty of phrenology was that almost anyone could be an adequate practitioner of the discipline with little formal training, could divine the configuration of the brain and thus analyze human character by simply taking note of the topography of the skull. As the *New England Magazine* put it in 1834, "it is a mere work of observation to determine the character of any man's mind, his weak and prevailing propensities, his excellencies and defects." All one needed to do was purchase an inexpensive guidebook to the cranium, like Orson and Lorenzo Fowler's popular *Self-Instructor in Phrenology and Physiology*, or follow the prescriptions of frequent articles published in well-known magazines. In 1835, for instance, the *Western Monthly Magazine* of Cincinnati serialized a complete course on phrenology, including all the necessary head charts, directions for making observations, and descriptions of the temperaments and faculties identified by the contours of the skull.[22]

Though phrenology achieved its widest following in the United States, it originated in Germany, was brought to England in 1814 by Johann Spurzheim, and was popularized there by George Combe. By the early 1830s, Spurzheim's lectures had attracted considerable attention in the United States, but the floodtide of phrenology in America awaited the triumphal transatlantic tour of Combe in 1838–40. About the same time, the Fowler brothers of New York, capitalizing upon popular interest, set about the work of making phrenology accessible to those who could not become exposed to its mysteries through the lyceum or lecture circuit. Their popular books and serialized articles took phrenology on a geographically westward and socially downward course in the 1840s and 1850s.[23]

The enormous appeal of phrenology and the public's acceptance of it as a legitimate expositor of national as well as personal character is attested to by the fact that the treatment of ethnologic issues in the antebellum periodical press between the late 1820s and the early 1840s was nearly always couched in the language of the pseudoscience. In America, phrenology was not simply a parlor sport but a serious tool in the search for the republican national character. Unblessed by a long history and unwilling to adopt

English character in its entirety as their own, Americans saw in phrenology a way to determine the national character by objective measurement. By analyzing native American heads and foreign, the republican citizenry could establish once and for all the catalogue of national traits. Even the finest national differences could be identified. Orson Fowler asserted in a book he called *Hereditary Descent* that "though the primitive stock is English, the American head differs materially from the English."[24] This was sure to attract popular approval.

Initially, phrenology was effective in seducing skeptical Americans into accepting the biological determinism of the European ethnologists. The quick capitulation of religious journals to the attractions of the pseudoscience illustrates this very clearly. In early 1834, the *Christian Examiner,* a conventional organ of middle class Protestantism, praised the newly popular discipline as a "powerful support of the cause of morality and religion." As long as phrenology seemed a way to illuminate personal strengths and weaknesses to which Christians could tailor an education, pious editors would echo this assertion. Before the thirties were out, however, the church-connected journals were crying, "Phrenology *is* materialism." The publicists found that phrenology did not require its practitioners to adhere to the orthodox position that human beings were fundamentally alike and differentiated only by character and personality variables that were fully alterable. Instead, as the Fowler brothers openly acknowledged, phrenology was put to work to establish the innate and inherited differences between human types. So outraged were Christian editors that many continued to excoriate phrenology until the outbreak of the Civil War, long after the peak of the fad had passed.[25]

By 1840, phrenology had also fallen out of fashion with the secular intellectuals of the Northeast who had originally welcomed it enthusiastically. The cosmopolitan elites who had initially been Combe's leading devotees discovered fairly early that rigorous adherence to phrenological theory compromised cherished attempts to civilize and domesticate the urban masses through a combination of education and philanthropy. The critique of phrenology that emerged among the intellectuals, ultimately, was a good deal like the religious one. The beginning of the end of their enthrallment with the science was registered by the publication of articles like

Russell Jarvis's "On the Humbug of Phrenology" in *Burton's Gentleman's Magazine* in August 1840:

> The world has hitherto believed that talents or faculties were natural endowments, and moral character the result of education; and hence that while no training would make amends for natural stupidity, and while talents would occasionally break through all obstacles, human beings would be virtuous or vicious, honest or knavish, brutal or amicable, according to instruction. . . . According to phrenology, human character is entirely the result of bumps.[26]

Jarvis facetiously concluded that phrenologists would replace education by fitting steel caps to the heads of American children to ensure the development of the proper cranial proportions. Sophisticated Americans also noticed that some phrenologists had adopted the disconcerting habit of working backwards from the observed behavior of an individual to the cranial characteristics they "discovered" by skull measurement. Despite the repudiation of phrenology in the urban Northeast, it continued a grand and glorious career in the hinterlands of the West and South before the critiques of the coastal journals were finally replicated by Western publicists in the 1840s and 1850s.[27]

The downfall of phrenology took place not because most people dismissed its underlying principles as foolish but because more and more Americans regarded it as too imprecise and hence unscientific. Russell Jarvis notwithstanding, most did not disbelieve that character was related to physical constitution or, like constitution, was associated with inheritance. In fact, those sentiments were popular among the well-educated and ill-informed alike. Phrenology had been quite effective in making basic elements of ethnologic dogma commonplace in antebellum folk culture. Though phrenology was discredited, the association of character and physique was not, and by no means would phrenology be the last effort to objectify character analysis. Significantly, the next refinement in applied ethnology was undertaken by an American. Samuel George Morton, whose monumental *Crania Americana* was published in Philadelphia in 1839, is chiefly recognized by historians as the generator of data for the white racist theories of Louis Agassiz and Josiah Nott. But his influence was probably more extensive. It was Morton who asserted that the assessment of character, especially of racial and national character, could be made an *exact* science. It is no accident that the first widespread recognition of Morton's work in the American press occurred about the same time that phrenology took its last gasp in the major east coast journals. There is some evidence that Morton's studies brought the "unscientific" method of character analysis by feeling the contours of the skull into disrepute. In return, Morton's approach to ethnology inspired something of a fad in itself. Just as phrenology dominated the popular literature of ethnology up to 1840, so Morton's "craniology" provided a theme during the next two decades.[28]

In the first pages of *Crania Americana,* Morton acknowledged his indebtedness to both phrenology and European ethnology. "From the remote ages," he wrote, "the inhabitants of every extended locality have been marked by certain physical and moral peculiarities, common among themselves and serving to distinguish them from all other people." In reviewing Morton's work, the *American Journal of Science* reiterated the author's "*first* proposition, that the size of the brain, other conditions being equal, is in direct relation to the power of mental manifestation." Morton combined these principles with a method of measuring the internal dimension of skulls to establish the cranial characteristics of what he took to be the generic subdivisions of mankind. Based upon his measurements, Morton concluded that there were no fewer than twenty-two distinct human families, seven within the Caucasian race alone. Starting with the same premises as the phrenologists, Morton demonstrated that character could be determined with more precision than by caressing bumps.[29]

Laymen as well as students of ethnology made all of the necessary deductions from Morton's research. Robert J. Breckinridge's *Baltimore Literary and Religious Magazine* lost no time in concluding that "it is not climate alone, nor soil, nor the food, nor the manner of living, which causes such differences in mankind, but that there must be some cause in man himself, a cause which will incline him to form certain habits."[30] Ethnologists generally realized the support that Morton lent to their attempts to prove the immutability of human types. Charles Pickering argued that however equal men stood before the Creator, it was apparent that in both physique and habits they were quite unequal on earth. As early as 1849 Josiah Nott was led to make the much bolder assertion that mankind was actually composed of different "species" which manifested distinctive characteristics that were wholly "independent of climate or other physical influences," hence the products of "separate origins."[31]

Historians usually emphasize the effect Nott's theories had upon the rationalization of Southern proslavery thought during the 1850s. But his work clearly intended to show that the various Caucasian "races" were produced by distinctive acts of creation as well. Between such categories of persons, Nott saw "moral" and physical differences as significant as those between black and white. According to the ethnologist, "nothing short of a *miracle* could have evolved all the multifarious Caucasian forms out of one primitive stock. . . . If then the teachings of science be true, there must have been many centers of creation, even for Caucasian races, instead of one center for *all* the types of humanity." He was particularly impressed by the endurance of the distinguishing features of the Celtic and Teutonic "species" despite centuries of proximate residence. Nott's formulations were largely extensions and elaborations of Morton's work, but Nott refused to be bound by cranial measurements in reaching conclusions about human differences. In distinguishing one human type from another, he wrote, it was legitimate to analyze the "form and capacity of the skull, the contour of the face, many parts of the skeleton, the peculiar development of muscles, the hair, and skin."[32]

Nott and his supporters gained remarkably widespread recognition for their studies of the enduring differences among Caucasians in the popular nontechnical press. But just as the principles of Blumenbach and Herder were popularized among American laymen in the early antebellum period through phrenology, so Morton's and Nott's were simplified and disseminated by the pseudoscience of "physiognomy," the divination of character from facial configuration. Josiah Nott only cloaked with the garb of science a popular pastime in antebellum America. For decades, Americans had been informally evaluating national character through superficial analysis of personal appearance. In 1855, a contributor to *Harper's* asserted:

We have no need to go abroad to study ethnology. A walk through the streets of any great city will show us specimens of every human variety known. Not per se, of course, but transmitted (diluted too) through the Anglo-Saxon medium—special characteristics necessarily not left very sharply defined. . . . We meet faces that are scarcely human—positively brutalized out of all trace of intelligence.[33]

People naturally remark upon those who do not quite resemble them. But in the mid-antebellum period, Americans were able to point to a substantial body of "scientific" literature that gave validity to their visual impressions of ethnic characteristics. It had been Blumenbach's fundamental assumption that appearance and mental capacity were related. He wrote confidently in the late eighteenth century of the generational persistence of "national face" and "racial face." Even Samuel Stanhope Smith agreed that such a thing as "national countenance" existed and noted that facial features are an excellent "index of our feelings."[34] In some respects, physiognomy actually antedated phrenology.

The same people who found phrenology and craniology excessively materialistic and unscriptural were rather attracted to physiognomy. While it was difficult, given the limitations of contemporary science, to attribute cranial dimensions, either internal or external, to environmental causes, it was relatively easy to explain differences in face, musculature, or stature by natural processes. Reverend Thomas Price, an English physiognomist, took pains to show how differences in appearance among the peoples of Great Britain were due to the effects of climate and habit. Varying eye colors, for instance, were related to the sources of household fuel people relied upon in different regions. Coal burners acquired dark, sooty eyes; peat burners clear, blue ones. At one time, a Swede, Pieter Camper, had attempted to establish physiognomy as an exact science. Like the craniologists, he turned to precise measurements. Camper decided that what gave the human countenance individuality was facial angle, the divergence from the vertical of a line drawn from chin to forehead. Camper concluded that though individual facial angles varied somewhat, national groups possessed clearly distinguishable average rates of incline. In 1847, the English painter Sir Charles Bell proposed that different national faces could be accurately reproduced by artists simply by varying the facial angle.[35]

In the United States, despite the hopes of Smith and other Christian traditionalists that it might become a corrective to materialistic heresies, physiognomy quickly became an adjunct of popular phrenology. Orson Fowler, the chief American popularizer of phrenology, devoted increasing attention to the companion field in the 1840s and 1850s. He could hardly have avoided doing so. Fowler's phrenology was ethno-psychology for the layman, and he constantly sought ways to simplify it for mass consumption. First, he disposed of the head calipers and other phrenological instruments. Ultimately, physiognomy permitted him to eliminate head charts altogether. For if facial appearance and cranial bumps both revealed character with equal veracity, why not choose the former, more expeditious technique? Phrenology required a cooperative subject, a considerable allotment of time, and the conquest of Victorian discomfiture with physical contact in public. But physiognomy was a much more practical discipline. It required no special apparatus, gave instantaneous results, involved no embarrassing physical touching, and could be applied in the course of everyday affairs to inform human interaction. It was, all in all, a typically American solution to the problem of how to evaluate human character, being both immediately useful and thoroughly democratic. In 1852, James W. Redfield, M.D., author of *Comparative Physiognomy*, summarized the advantages of physiognomical analysis. The principal assumption of the procedure, he noted, was that "character is indicated by the *features* of the face as well as in the expressions." He continued:

Generally, the brain and face are harmonious, but . . . always the former is subservient to the latter. The devining of character by the skull is subordinate to the practical, everyday reading to which the face is appropriated. Physiognomy is available on all occasions . . . but Phrenology can be employed only professionally.[36]

For all its advantages over phrenology, physiognomy also had its limitations. It seemed, especially, to restrict artificially the quantity of evidence usable for character evaluation. Orson Fowler insisted that the basic idea of physiognomy was that there existed an immediate connection of "the *mental* and the *moral*" with the physical. If that was indeed the case, why should character analysts be restricted exclusively to evaluation of the formulation of the head and face? Fowler apparently addressed the question himself, for in *Hereditary Descent* he took a step beyond most physiognomists and concluded that "a close similarity exists between the *form of the body* or the *looks* of a person, and the tone and character of the *mind*." Fowler called character analysis which relied upon human looks—from head to toe—"physiology."[37]

Throughout the early antebellum period, many scholars and laymen alike contested the ability of "sciences" like phrenology and craniology to make substantial contributions to the understanding of national, or ethnic, differences. As a parlor sport, phrenology had been employed to illuminate the special propensities of individuals. Christian environmentalists, naturally, found little danger in such restricted use. They were, for the most part, perfectly willing to see phrenology and even physiognomy employed to elaborate personality differences which no one could possibly believe were caused by separate human origins or transmitted by inheritance.[38] Even a few academic ethnologists believed that it was impossible to rely upon the phrenological sciences to make precise ethnic distinctions. Thomas Price, for instance, thought that physiognomy was an alternative way of distinguishing the major skin color groups but did not believe that it could define smaller subdivisions of mankind.[39]

Despite the cogent reservations of some about the applicability of phrenology to ethnologic study, both American and European ethnologists increasingly relied upon this or one of its allied pseudosciences to identify national as well as racial and personal attributes. After its dismissal by a number of early enthusiasts as imprecise, phrenology was defended by Arthur de Gobineau as inexact only when applied to individual differences but entirely useful in making group distinctions.[40] Craniology was an attempt to measure human differences with more precision but was intended from the beginning to be a biological rather than a psychological science. "Physiology" drew its principles from both. It was simple, empirical, accessible to the layman like phrenology, and it was as patently applicable to the study of ethnic differences as craniology. Orson Fowler attempted to make it appealing to as many Americans as possible by describing what "physiology" could reveal: "Though the fundamentals of our race are the same in all parts of the earth, different races and nations evince lesser differences in propensity and intellect . . . and there are differences in the *tone* and *character* of different races."[41] By mid-century, Americans had taken the phrenologists' cardinal assumption that intellect was the brain and broadened it to affirm that character, including intellect, was the body.

"Physiology" was another authentically American contribution to the science of ethnology. It represented the triumph of domestic practice over imported theory. To be sure, Americans continued to be attracted to phrenology, craniology, physiognomy, and the undiluted principles of European ethnology throughout the antebellum period. The most simple-minded discussions of ethnic differences carried on by popular mid-century journals attest to that. "The Influence of Place on Race," published in *Graham's* in 1852, or "Are All Men Descended from Adam?" carried in *Putnam's* three years later, are as accurate paraphrasings of Gobineau in English as one is likely to find.[42] But "physiology" did not require the prestige of foreign authorship nor any simplification to win acceptance in the United States. Without any explicit scientific endorsement, Americans had been practicing physiology for a long time. During the 1840s and 1850s it became the accepted means by which native citizens divined the character of the European immigrants settling among them.

Physiological principles appeared in the most unlikely places in antebellum printed matter. Sometimes the applications of this "science" were ludicrous. An advertisement for "Ward's Vegetable Hair Oil" in the Charleston, South Carolina, *Mercury* asserted that "each genuine bottle is wrapped in a thirty page treatise on the hair, including a disquisition on the national differences of the hair." In the mid-1830s the *New England Magazine* devoted a sizable article to a discussion of "National Postures" in which the meaning of the characteristic stance and attitude of members of the United States' constituent ethnic groups was examined. The piece concluded with the allegation that "every bodily posture is in itself inert, the instrument of the mind; it, therefore, can assume no position, but under the direction of the soul." A few years later, Emerson showed the extent to which physiological or physiognomical ideas could triumph over the critical faculties of even liberally educated Americans. With dead seriousness, Emerson insisted that all one needed to do was look at Irishmen, "deteriorated in size and shape, the nose sunk, the gum exposed," to know that they operated with "diminished brain."[43] Serialized travelogues in late antebellum magazines were notorious for applying physiological premises to ethnological description. A contributor to an 1855 number of *Harper's* described a European this way: "His aspect at once betrayed him to be a Russian. The round head, flattened cheek, light hair and eyes, and low nose with the tip flattened so as to expose the nostril, were unmistakably Muskovite." The author deduced from these physical characteristics that "Russians are defective in inventive faculty and creative power." Other articles in contemporary magazines urged readers to examine passing faces on the street in order to test their own ethnological sensitivity.[44] Of course, popular works such as those authored by Orson and Lorenzo Fowler not only explained to the masses what identifying marks to look for and how to interpret them but placed the stamp of science upon such homely observations as well.

The suspicion is certainly not misplaced that few Anglo-Americans could ever have heard of Herder, Blumenbach, or Arthur de Gobineau. To be sure, "ethnology" itself was sometimes an object of discussion in the antebellum press, and the more pretentious American political and literary magazines were sure to review the latest works of the ethnologic school. But few outside the ranks of scholars and educated elites could have been conversant in this "science." Nonetheless, by the 1850s, Anglo-American common culture showed signs that it had absorbed the elemental ethnologic principles. These included the ideas that humanity was divided into discrete races and into distinctive varieties or families within races (including, within the Caucasian race, Celtic, Anglo-Saxon, and according to some authorities, even Anglo-American), that particular attitudes and behaviors were connected with particular physiological characteristics, and that the only enduring nations were those that grew out of the "instinctive germinal force" of a homogeneous human family. The correlate of them all was that personal character and ethnicity alike—and thus nationality—were externally visible.[45] Such was the legacy of phrenology, physiognomy, and physiology. Each suggested that mentality, morality, and behavior were revealed in physical form. Originally, they were only intended to expose personal character, but even without special prompting the public that consumed these pseudosciences probably would have begun to rely upon them to reveal national character in time. As it was, they were explicitly encouraged by the popularizers of these techniques to do so. The pervasiveness of the phrenological vocabulary in the late antebellum period guaranteed that an ethnologic interpretation of human differences would become almost reflexive among Anglo-Americans.

The popularity of the phrenological pseudo-sciences showed up unmistakably in the late antebellum verbal image of the Irish. A thoroughly "extrinsic" stereotype, it treated its subjects as physically distinctive. But it also implied that behavior and condition—even belief—were associated with physical form. Unlike the early antebellum word portrait, it did not dwell much upon the alleged intellectual and moral character of the Irish but understood these to be logical corollaries to physique. As already suggested, the transformation of an intrinsic stereotype into an extrinsic one was influenced by circumstances having little to do with *systematic* thought, pseudoscientific or otherwise. After all, Anglo-Americans had taken themselves to be a distinctive people, as a result of their republican environment if nothing else, from the outset of the antebellum period. When it became apparent that the republican environment did not affect all persons the same way, it was easy to take national character as innate rather than as conditional. Under these circumstances, the growing influx of European immigrants after the mid-1840s was likely to place a premium upon physical and behavioral descriptions capable of separating citizen from alien. Popular phrenology and its sister studies gave such descriptions "scientific" legitimacy. The phrenological pseudosciences "proved" that the simultaneous display of particular physical characteristics and particular character/behavior matrices was far from coincidental. The physical actually governed the mental, moral, and behavioral, and all of these properties were inevitably linked. Moreover, the really important physical differences among human beings were invariably "national." According to phrenology, physiognomy, and physiology, then, the identification of nationality was elementary. It required no more than a layman's informed observation to divine both an individual's nation and character. Significantly, in the parlance of popular ethnology, nationality was called "race."[46]

No wonder, then, that in the "conversation" of mid-nineteenth century America, the Irish were the subjects of "extrinsic" description and also of a descriptive vocabulary that drew attention to *particular* physical characteristics treated as significant by phrenological pseudosciences. In the mid-1850s, a contributor to *Harper's Monthly* described two "bogtrotters":

> They were a couple of the short, frieze-coated, knee-breeches and gray-stocking fellows who are as plentiful on Irish soil as potatoes. From beneath their narrow-brimmed, old, weather-beaten hats streamed hair as unkempt as their horses' manes. The Celtic physiognomy was distinctly marked—the small and somewhat upturned nose, the black tint of the skin; the eyes now looking gray, now black; the freckled cheek, and sandy hair. Beard and whiskers covered half the face, and the short, square-shouldered bodies were bent forward with eager impatience.[47]

Notwithstanding the mild misapplication of the term "physiognomy" (the author of this word portrait by no means restricted his observations to the face), the undoubted implications were that the Irish possessed characteristic physical features and that these were revelatory of interior character. And the physical attributes mentioned here were typical of those connected with the Irish in the language of antebellum common culture. Dark eyes, florid complexion, red hair, robust figure, and simianized face (prominent cheekbones, upturned nose, and projecting teeth) were emphases of verbal portraiture. Two of every three references to the physical character of the Irish in the literature sampled for this study drew attention to just such traits. Although typical of physical descriptives applied to the Irish throughout the antebellum period, they became much more commanding elements of the stereotype after the mid-1840s.[48]

Not only did many of the words applied to the Irish in antebellum conversation seem to come directly from the phrenologist's or physiologist's handbook but so did the interpretations placed upon these physical descriptions. The Irish were stereotypically small but robust. According to the Fowlers' *New Illustrated Self-Instructor in Phrenology and Physiology* (1859), the last word in popular character analysis, a short, full figure indicated a person "inactive," "slothful," and "lazy." Coarse, red hair—standard in the Irish stereotype—suggested emotions that were "excitable," "sociable," and "gushing." A ruddy complexion revealed "hearty animal passions" and considerable "selfishness," while dark eyes bespoke "ardor" and "sensuality." The Fowlers offered some predictable advice to people of such physical, moral, and emotional character.

They should, the phrenologists counseled, "never turn dentists or clerks, but seek some outdoor employment, and would be better contented with rough, hard work than a light or sedentary occupation . . . for they require a great amount of air and exercise." Surely the actual salience of the American Irish in "outdoor," manual occupations during the late antebellum period was no coincidence. The Fowlers—and probably all of their pseudoscientific brethren—reflexively worked backward from the popular verbal image of the Irish (containing both objective and subjective components) to their character analyses of persons displaying allegedly Celtic physiognomy or physique. Thus the reading of what was already considered a peculiarly Celtic characteristic, a protrusive eyebrow ridge, was crafted by James Redfield's *Outline of a New System of Physiognomy* out of Paddy's familiar parts.[49] By no means did pseudoscience create the extrinsic Irish stereotype of the late antebellum years. But it doubtless helped establish the *particular* vocabulary of ethnic description in American "conversation" and gave it the endorsement of "science."

Portrayed by words as innately and permanently distinct in ways that the rhetoric of popular ethnology labeled "racial," the American Irish could be alternatively viewed as a discordant or complementary element in the republican populace. During the late 1840s and the 1850s there was much discussion in newspapers and magazines of the natural antipathy between the "races" that would never permit them to live in harmony. In late 1844 editorials in both the *New York Times* and *Putnam's Monthly* gloomily predicted that the "races" in America would inevitably gravitate to rival political parties and that republican politics was destined to take on the quality of a blood feud. A decade later the *National Era* joined the *Times* in labeling interethnic election riots at Louisville a "conflict of the races."[50]

There was another way of looking at the "racial" diversity of white America. According to the Rev. William Lord, author of *A Tract for the Times: National Hospitality*:

The progress of civilization keeps pace with the mixture of races. It is no small advantage to a people to combine two or three distinct types of national character, when they can unite harmoniously and peaceably. A people of which all its individual members are referrable to a single tribe is, among nations, what a celibate is among individuals. Its life is unproductive and monotonous.[51]

Lord's "tribes" were the tribes of popular ethnology, Saxon and Celt included. The late antebellum periodical press was as full of the advocates of "race mixture" as of the pessimistic forecasters of racial incompatibility and "race war." Contributors to the *Christian Examiner* and the *North American Review*, J. D. B. DeBow of the journal that bore his name, and the editors of the *American Whig Review* were among many who took the ethnologic premise that the "races" of Europe were innately different in exterior form and interior character and used it to turn European immigration to the United States into a virtue. "It is a principle laid down by every physiologist," wrote one of these optimists, "and proved by abundant observation, that man, like other animals, is improved and brought to its highest perfection by an intermingling of the blood and qualities of various races."[52]

Such sentiments virtually mirrored those of contemporaneous antislavery "romantic racialists." Romantic racialism, George M. Fredrickson explains, was "a doctrine which acknowledged permanent racial differences but rejected the notion of a clearly defined racial hierarchy." Its chief adherents—Harriet Beecher Stowe, Lydia Maria Child, Oliver Wendell Holmes, Sr., come to mind—usually argued that Americans of African descent had something precious and unique to contribute to republican culture.[53] Stowe, for one, thought that the black race would moderate the icy, materialistic Anglo-Saxon temperament if it was permitted a fuller participation in American life. "The negro race is confessedly more simple, docile, childlike and affectionate than other races," Stowe wrote in *A Key to Uncle Tom's Cabin.* Child's *National Antislavery Standard* agreed that, compared to the Saxon, the African was "docile, humble, grateful and commonly forgiving." Both insisted that the republic required an infusion of such character. But this temper might also come from another source. Since by mid-century it had become conventional to treat the Irish as a distinctive "race" too, it is no surprise that romantic racialists often announced that immigrants from the Emerald Isle might make a distinctive contribution to the national character as well. Margaret Fuller Ossoli disliked what she took to be the "ignorance" and "pliancy" of the Irish but found these outweighed by the Celts' natural domesticity, generosity, gratitude, and good nature. Of this class, she concluded, "we must regard them as most valuable elements in the new race."[54]

Fuller and Child and others demonstrated that it was possible to take the Irish in America as a distinctive "race" without automatically disqualifying them from inclusion in the national family. But they did nothing to question the underlying ethnologic premise that the Irish were a people inherently different from Anglo-Americans. If anything, they reinforced it. And, considering the ethnocentrism of most of their Anglo-American contemporaries, Stowe and Child would stand out as unusual for their charitable assessment of the Irish. For others, any hint that there were innate differences between Anglo-Americans and Irish-Americans was likely to lead to dismissal of the Irish as unsuited for American nationality. At least a few contemporaries perceived the drift of popular sentiment—and worried about it. A contributor to an 1854 number of *Harper's* addressed it in an article appropriately titled "Are We One or Many?":

Of course, we think ourselves at the top of the scale. . . . Who that knows anything of man . . . can doubt that the widening distinction would go on, until one despotic tribe would come to regard itself as the only real homo, and in the maintenance of such a chain treat all the rest as the legitimate instruments of its pleasure or its profit? The Negro, the Papuan, the Hottentot, the Laplander—these surely are not men, but how long before the Anglo-Saxon pride would assume a similar attitude toward the Celt, and the idealizing Teuton dream himself into a generic superiority to the Slav?[55]

Of course the Irish were no "race" in the modern sense of the word, nor did "race" govern character as nineteenth century ethnology would have it. But antebellum Anglo-Americans, seduced by the phrenological pseudosciences, would have it so, and the illusion was quite as powerful as the reality would have been. That the traditional environmental interpretation of ethnicity and national character was falling into disuse by mid-century, the verbal image of the Irish is testament. Popular ethnology lent to the decline of environmentalism the imprimatur of "science." It helped legitimize the increasingly "extrinsic" quality of ethnic portraiture in language, providing affirmation that character could be read in appearance and condition. By making the description of the Irish as a "race" habitual, the phrenological pseudosciences were sure to magnify Anglo-Americans' perception of difference from those they would (or could) identify as Irish. And the racial label would make it hard for Anglo-Americans to exempt individual Irish-Americans from the consensual stereotype, even when they seemed not to display the predicted character. Doubtless, under the right circumstances, such an extreme sense of alienation could influence interethnic conduct. It was at least a convenient rationale for the more horrible cases of urban violence that the newspapers sometimes called "race war." And the allegation that particular behavior *always* issued from particular physique was calculated to encourage Anglo-Americans to take verbal stereotypes as predictive, inciting inflammatory rhetoric or aggressive posturing. Contemporaries were often aware of the implications of a "racial" perception of the Irish. An unsigned editorial, attributed to Roman Catholic Archbishop John Hughes, appearing in the *New York Tribune* the autumn following the Philadelphia riots denounced political rhetoric aimed at the Irish "which implied that they were not identified in interest and feeling with the American people, but existed as a distinct race."[56] At the same time, popular ethnology would minimize the distance between Anglo- and German-Americans; they were, after all, called members of the same "race." Perhaps this helps account for some of the benignity of the verbal image of Germans. They would be victims of a conventional cultural ethnocentrism, but that was all.

The most enduring influence of popular ethnology, however, was upon Anglo-Americans' *self*-image, upon what was taken to be the image of American nationality. The phrenological pseudosciences provided an explicit rationale for connecting nationality, ethnicity, and "blood" simplistic enough to be absorbed at all levels of folk culture. They suggested that the really important qualifications for American nationality could not be taught. Religious and political identity, in particular, were rendered contingent upon ethnic identity. Applied to Anglo- and Irish-Americans, this idea could not hold up for long. In fact, the perception of the Irish as a separate race would not endure, in part because a verbal stereotype which directed attention to physique would in time bring to its holders' attention how superficial the physical distinctions really were. Nonetheless, it could still leave in its wake the conviction that at the heart of American nationality stood the qualification of race. Even while it flourished during the years around mid-century, however, a "racial" perception of the Irish would not appeal to every Anglo-American. It was least attractive of all, perhaps, to the "nativists," whom we have come to identify as the immigrants' chief detractors.

CHAPTER FIVE

Paddy and the Know-Nothings

"The question of identity as a people . . . will bear looking at. No identity! We deny it, physiologically. Who ever saw an American, reared on his native soil and under his country's institutions, that could not be recognized at a glance, and distinguished, in nine cases out of ten, from the men of any other Caucasian nation on earth? There is something in the physiognomy and structure of an American, even in the first descent from a European parentage, that is peculiar and characteristic, and generally recognizable in an instant."

"Who Are We?" *The Republic* (August 1851)

CHANGES IN THE character of Paddy—the Irish stereotype—over time suggest that perceptual conditions favoring a sense of Anglo-American ethnic peoplehood were in place by the middle of the nineteenth century. In the case of many Anglo-Americans, any such disposition toward ethnicity must have been more reflexive than calculated. But there was enough explicit, if homely, ethnological discussion in popular media to suggest that the recasting of republican nationality was not strictly subconscious for everyone. Historian Jehoshua Arieli has written that there was actually an organized campaign in the late antebellum period to define "a new type of nationalism" for Americans, a nationalism based upon "common descent" which would help the United States resist sectional division. This was, Arieli said, the nativist or "Know-Nothing" movement.[1] The role of these noisy and visible critics of European immigration in the propagation of an increasingly hard and unforgiving stereotype of the Irish is certainly worth examining. So, conversely, is the ability of the nativists to capitalize upon interethnic imagery. That Arieli was unaware of the patterns in American "conversation" which indicated that a disposition hospitable to the concept of Anglo-American ineradicable peoplehood was widespread only makes the relationship of popular thought to the proselytizing of the nativist movement more intriguing.

When nativist publicists or rhetoricians took up the subject of the Irish during the 1820s and 1830s (which, significantly, they were not as prone to do as to discuss "immigrants" or "Catholics," in general), they put to work descriptive adjectives already circulating in the conversation of their fellow citizens. They described—and usually denounced—Irish "character," particularly intellectual and moral character. The Irish, in nativist parlance as in more popular patterns of language, were stereotypically illiterate and uneducated, degraded and depraved. The words themselves suggested that nativist ideologues shared the prevailing popular wisdom that character came from experience and environment and that the Irish in both respects had been rendered ill-suited for American nationality. Nativists, of course, talked more directly about immigrants' politics and religion than most of their contemporaries did, but in doing so they still used words which hinted at their adherence to an environmentalist interpretation of both ethnicity and nationality, words like "priest-ridden" or "oppressed."

The real surprise is that when the fashions of Anglo-American conversation moved off in new directions in the mid-1840s and the 1850s, the treatment of the Irish in nativist rhetoric stayed behind. Ordinary "conversation" picked up a tendency to describe the Irish by, first, conduct and condition and, subsequently, physical appearance. It implied that the marks of ethnicity—and the qualifications for American nationality—were habitual and probably innate. Temporarily, in the mid to late 1840s, Paddy bore the influence of some notorious, and what the public took to be especially stressful, developments in interethnic relations—particularly the Philadelphia riots. But nativists retained the old Paddy: a portrait of the Irish which highlighted interior character and connected character to nurture, not nature.

"The Irishman has nothing national about him except his rags." In 1855, when American "conversation" was becoming surfeited with descriptions of Celtic physiognomy, physiology, and putatively "habitual" conduct, Frederick Saunders, author of the nativist tract *The Progress and Prospects of America,* was still emphasizing the environmental origin of ethnic and national character.[2] By no means did he stand out from contemporaries in the nativist societies, who preferred to all others words like "impudent," "ignorant," "depraved," and "quarrelsome"—critiques of character—for describing the Irish. One Barney McGinniskin, a nativist magazine reported, was unsuitable for employment as a policeman because he was a representative "paddy-whack," "from the bogs of Ireland," which was to say that he was not only a Roman Catholic but also "ignorant, incompetent, swaggering, riotous." What made the Irish so? According to anti-Catholic publicist Nicholas Murray, it was entirely owing to "their low culture, their squalid poverty . . . all the results of the despotism of their priests." That is also how the self-appointed historian of the American party, John Hancock Lee, accounted for the conduct of the Irish "rioters" at Philadelphia in 1844. Avoiding elaborate hypotheses about Celtic "habit" and "nature," Lee found the unexampled violence sufficiently explained by the fact that the combatants were "paupers, beggars, half-naked starvelings."[3]

The real problem with the Irish, Lee wrote in *The American Party in Politics,* was that they were "raw," unaccustomed to Americans ways and as yet without a substantial share in the American experience.[4] Nativist ideologues like Lee were not usually sanguine that the immigrants could be seasoned easily. *The American Protestant* for January 1848 conceded that the Irish were "naturally shrewd and intelligent" but "inaccessible" to education "by reason of their early associations." Appropriately, this journal of the American Protestant Society, an organization devoted to proselytizing amongst Catholics, cautiously predicted that "the Irish heart, though cased in prejudice as in armor, can be reached, and the way is the power of love." Such late antebellum verbiage clearly sustained nativists' unmatched preference for ethnic adjectives prefixed "un-".

Earlier, to Samuel F. B. Morse, the Irish had been "*un*approach-able," to Lyman Beecher "*un*educated," "*un*acquainted with our in-stitutions," and "*un*accustomed to self-government."[5] It was not, in nativist parlance, what the Irish *had*—physically or culturally—that set them apart, but what they allegedly lacked.

The divergence between the Paddy of conventional conversation and the Paddy of nativist discourse reveals both the nature of orga-nized nativism and the relationship between nativist and popular thought in the immediate pre-Civil War decades. Confirmed is the description that nativists gave to themselves—reduced to a word, "conservative," by Grand Sachem Simeon Baldwin of the Order of United Americans in a letter to the American party's 1856 presi-dential candidate, Millard Fillmore.[6] Historians who indicate that nativists sought to *lead* a late antebellum redefinition of American nationality are confounded.[7] For, in fact, any movement to recast "nation" as "people," as traditional as the latter may have been as a basis for nationhood in the Old World, was far from conservative in the New. It would have been a radical departure from traditional American republican thought. But, for the most part, those we can call nativists did not even try. Their rhetoric shows that they stood by an identification of nation with ideology and citizenship with an appropriately nurtured character. Such a construction of nationality was fully compatible with exclusivity and bigotry, with the reserva-tion of full citizenship rights and protections to a privileged class. But it does render organized nativism apparently irrelevant both to Anglo-Americans' changing perception of immigrant minorities and later popular fashions of thought about the nature of American na-tionality. The verbal image of the Irish was no cipher for nativist interests; the stereotype gave fraternal and political nativism only limited encouragement—the stereotype may even, in the long run, have helped along nativism's demise.

In 1854, on the eve of the autumn elections, Phelim Lynch, edi-tor of New York's *Irish-American,* sized up the opposition. To a readership of "fellow countrymen and friends," Lynch reported:

You have at present opposed to you a bitter, inimical, and powerful secret society called the Know-Nothings; opposed to you, to us Irishmen particularly, on the grounds that we are impudent and voracious cor-morants of petty places under government; that we are ignorant, turbulent, and brutal; that we are controlled by our clergy; that we are willing subjects of a foreign prince, the Pope; that we are only lip-republicans; that we are not worthy of the franchise; that by the largeness of our vote and the clannishness of our habits we rule or aspire to rule in America; that we are drunkards and criminals; that we fill the workhouses and prisons; that we heap up taxes on industrious and sober and thrifty citizens. . . . And I can tell you that outside the secret organization of the Know-Nothings, outside and beyond its influence and power, an anti-Irish and anti-Catholic sentiment prevails.[8]

Lynch was trying to capture what he took to be the popular stereotype of the American Irish. And while this study of the Irish in antebellum conversation might not confirm his view in every particular, it lends support to his contention that a standardized image of the Irish—distinct from images of immigrants, naturalized voters, or even Roman Catholics—circulated widely in antebellum society. Lynch, however, was talking about more than just a stereotype. He was also talking about a "sentiment" and, moreover, about behavior.

The popular sentiment that concerned Lynch was, particularly, anti-Irish. An interethnic attitude may be more or less a conscious assent that a stereotyped perception is true.[9] The late antebellum stereotype of the Irish suggested that Irish character and conduct were functions of physical conformation and that the latter was a product of ethnicity or, in the parlance of the time, "race." If not all were devout Roman Catholics, all Irish possessed the psychological character that might make them susceptible to papish error. If not all were active criminals, all bore the seeds of violence and turbulence. If not all were misled voters, all had the intellectual and emotional characteristics that could all too easily put them under the sway of demagogues. No wonder that Lynch called the sentiment that was nourished by such a stereotype anti-*Irish* rather than anti-Catholic or anti-immigrant. Hostility toward the Irish in late antebellum America was something more than the manifestation of a nationalism antagonistic to anything "un-American." There was indeed a specifically anti-Irish sentiment—differentiable from anti-Catholicism, anti-foreignism, or anti-monarchicalism—which grew from what may have been a half-conscious but surely was a widely shared sense that American republicanism could only be sustained by a people who possessed a particular innate ethnic character.

But editor Lynch was also talking about behavior, a kind of behavior we would have to call discrimination and—to the extent that it was directed especially at the Irish, as Lynch alleged—specifically ethnic discrimination. Lynch seemed sure that the Irish were susceptible to special treatment and abuse for no more reason than that they were Irish. Undoubtedly the prevailing image of the Irish in the language and lore of late antebellum Anglo-Americans encouraged individual citizens to commit ethnic slights, and Lynch's editorial hints at this. But Lynch was primarily concerned with systematic discrimination, with efforts to regulate the naturalization, franchise, and political privileges of the Irish in America, with attempts to institutionalize ethnic prejudice. Lynch was convinced that anti-Irish sentiment was widespread among Anglo-Americans. He identified the most aggressive proponents of such discrimination as "Know-Nothings."

The organized nativist movement—culminating in the American or "Know-Nothing" political party of the 1850s—appeared to threaten the most extreme discrimination. For it was the nativistic organizations that spearheaded efforts to institutionalize invidious distinctions between "natives" and "foreigners" in law. Of this network of religious, fraternal, and political bodies that began to play an important role in American life during the early 1830s, the first were chiefly religious. The Second Great Awakening left behind it many evangelical Protestants who believed that the future of the nation depended entirely upon the personal salvation of its citizens and who often seemed convinced that the chief impediment to this goal was the Roman Catholic Church. From 1831, with the founding of the New York Protestant Association, to 1849, the year in which the American and Foreign Christian Union emerged from the combination of the three principal nationwide institutions of Protestant evangelism, anti-Catholicism remained at the center of nativism. Anti-Catholic rhetoric circulated through the local auxiliaries of evangelical agencies and an extensive evangelical press. Since Catholicism was labeled a foreign device and European immigrants seemed to be the principal source of American Catholicism's increase, anti-Catholicism and institutional anti-foreignism were closely identified throughout the antebellum period.

Nativistic social and fraternal organizations first emerged in numbers during the mid-1840s and flourished for a dozen years. Replete with carefully guarded codes and handshakes, mysterious ranks, and pompously titled offices, the secret societies came to seem to many then and since the essence of antebellum nativism. All exhibited an exaggerated patriotism, a self-conscious Unionism, and a quasi-military camaraderie; theoretically membership was restricted to approved "true Americans." New York City's Order of United Americans and Philadelphia's United Sons of America, both established at the end of 1844, were among the first nativist fraternities, but by far the most successful was the Order of the Star-Spangled Banner, founded in 1849, reorganized in 1852, and dubbed "Know-Nothing" by the press in 1853. The secret societies conventionally combined the appeal of a social club and a self-improvement association with the traditional rhetoric of patriotism and anti-Catholicism, but their chief importance rested in their ability to mobilize large numbers of adherents for political action, and their real growth accompanied the emergence of a nativistic political movement in the 1850s. In 1854 the Order of the Star-Spangled Banner prepared a national charter; by 1855 the Order of United Americans counted chapters in no fewer than sixteen states.

The organization of nativists for political purposes took place relatively late. A New York Native American Democratic Association active in municipal politics in the mid-1830s and a "national" Native American party chartered in 1845 were relatively short-lived experiments in political protest, temporary coalitions of aggrieved interests that betrayed little desire to create endurant third parties. More durable nativistic organizations emerged in the early 1850s when the secret societies began to dabble in political contest. The Order of United Americans staked out a public position in the New York state school law referendum of 1850 while the Order of the Star-Spangled Banner provided a disciplined cadre for a New York City American party in 1853. The statewide "American" organizations that appeared in Massachusetts and New York in 1854 had quite ambitious goals: to revise state requirements for voting and officeholding to the exclusion of certain categories of immigrants and Catholics and even to alter federal standards for naturalization. These, too, were the objectives of the national American party, which nominated Millard Fillmore for President in 1856. Fillmore promoted "Americanism" as a Unionist device to combine voters of all sections and mute the divisive issue of slavery, and for this reason nativism was attractive to many in the Southern and border states.

Religious, fraternal, or political, the institutional forms of ante-bellum nativism were interconnected. Much of the leadership of the fraternal Order of United Americans was simultaneously active in the American and Foreign Christian Union. In turn, the principal figures in the Order of the Star-Spangled Banner came out of the Order of United Americans with the express purpose of creating a political arm for the secret societies, which ultimately became the American party. Not surprisingly, this rendered the objectives of the various nativistic organizations quite harmonious. Active participants consistently agitated for a Protestant atmosphere in the public schools, for exclusion of Roman Catholics from public office, for more stringent enforcement of the naturalization laws, and for enactment of a fourteen- to twenty-one year probationary residence requirement for naturalized citizenship.[10]

Just what place did the Irish stereotype and the ethnic prejudice it encouraged have in the nativist—or, in Lynch's words, "Know-Nothing"—movement? The nativistic organizations subsisted within a particular cultural environment, and their successes and failures in attracting popular support doubtless bore some relation to developments in that climate. The question just raised, however, is not an easy one to answer, not least because, as John Higham once observed, "Nativism has been hard for historians to define."[11] This is particularly true of the antebellum version of American nativistic activity. Historians disagree over not just the sources of broadly nativistic sentiment in American culture but even the bases of institutional organized nativism. The antebellum nativist "movement" has been variously attributed to the intrusion of evangelical perfectionism upon politics, to militant ethnocentrism, to impatience with multi-constituency mass political parties, and to desire to submerge sectional hostilities in a patriotic cause. Alternatively, it is treated as a conservative reaction to disordering modernizing forces, as a product of material competition between groups, or as a manifestation of "ideological tensions" in a pluralist, competitive, individualistic society.[12] Any thorough understanding of nativism is complicated by the fact that the nativist secret societies were also, in nearly all cases, fraternal and beneficiary. They attracted some men for no other reason than that they offered, especially in the cities, the secure status of brotherhood in a competitive and increasingly impersonal environment, as well as practical economic protection through the system of mutual assessment insurance.[13]

Historians' disparate understandings of the sentiments behind the nativist phenomenon in the mid-nineteenth century actually echo contemporary uncertainty about what "Know-Nothingism" was. Southern Democrats denounced political nativism as antislavery "conscience" Whiggery in disguise. Northern Free Soilers called it conscienceless "cotton" Whiggery, fully acquiescent to the aggressions of the slave power. Some old Whigs sympathetically endorsed it as true Unionism, but others insisted that it was nothing but a locofoco Democratic conspiracy.[14] To more than a few it was a much-needed movement for authentic naturalization law reform. Many, on the other hand, attributed it to the self-serving opportunism of professional politicians who would drop the nativist banner as quickly as they had taken it up.[15]

There is no question that prejudice—categorical judgment and generalized hostility—was elemental to organized nativism. Nativists took no care to confine their animus to identifiable criminals, drunkards, paupers, or illicit voters; they denounced much broader classes of persons: "Catholics" or "immigrants" or "radicals." Obviously, antebellum nativism was riven with religious prejudice, and it also manifested a rather indiscriminate political prejudice, victimizing any and all who by the wildest stretch of imagination could be regarded as emissaries of European monarchicalism or, paradoxically, as dangerously liberal disturbers of Old World order and tranquility. There was, besides, an unmistakable xenophobia or reflexive anti-foreignism in nativistic enthusiasm.[16]

But was there also ethnic prejudice at the heart of the nativist movement in antebellum America? Did the Irish attract special nativist hostility on account of being Irish? On the whole, historians have found little enthusiasm among out-and-out nativists for antebellum ethnological theory and its characterization of white "races" and are inclined to make much of this. "The Know-Nothing movement of the 1850s, the principal prewar manifestation of anti-immigrant feeling," one writes, "placed very little reliance on a quasi-racial contrast between Celts and Anglo-Saxons, despite the fact that the Irish were its principal targets. . . . Its central theme was anti-Catholicism." Nativism was only derivatively anti-Irish. "Even the Know-Nothings . . . depended far more on the evils of Popery than they did on racism in pressing their cause," adds another student.[17] The first thrust of such comments seems to be that genuine ethnic prejudice lacked a convincing rationale before the Civil War, that only almost pathologically xenophobic temperaments could have been persuaded that Irish "Celts" were disqualified by nature from American nationality and the rights it conferred. Mid-century Anglo-Saxonism, John Higham maintains, was little more than a "romantic cult," chiefly attractive to literati as a way to explain the historical sources of American national greatness but without the "intellectual and emotional pungency essential to a serious, nativistic appeal." "Race" would not become the basis for distinction between white ethnic groups until science and pseudoscience had refined the concept further and spread it to a larger audience, an audience more anxiety-ridden than the antebellum population. The second thrust of historiographic convention, implied in the first, is that if ethnic, or "ethno-racial," prejudice *was* to be found anywhere before the Civil War, it was *only* to be found among the most enthusiastic nativist votaries. If the most dedicated participants in the nativist organizations cannot be found to have made much of distinctions between Celts and Saxons or Anglo-Americans then, presumptively, such distinctions could not have carried much weight among the Anglo-American citizenry at large.[18]

Actually, these conclusions partly reflect contemporary assessments of nativistic prejudices before the Civil War. A few observers called the emergence of Know-Nothing political agitation nothing less than the beginning of a "war of ancestries," or alleged that nativistic animus was based upon "the ground of race." During the 1850s, New York's Roman Catholic Bishop John Hughes denounced the American party for its special hostility to "Irishism." As early as the 1830s William Lloyd Garrison diagnosed malice toward the Irish as something more than ethnocentrism, actually a product of the "detestable spirit of caste" that debased American racial minorities.[19] But those who reported that the nativist movement rested upon a foundation of specifically ethnic prejudice were a minority, even among those who found the nativist organizations distasteful. James Hall of the *Western Monthly Magazine* thought that the uproar over European immigration was the result of unseemly "fanaticism," but an exclusively anti-Catholic fanaticism. Cincinnati's *Daily Gazette* called it "the War on the Catholics." In the mid-1840s, the *New York Herald* traced the rise of nativistic politics in the metropolis entirely to "hostility to Catholicity."[20] Others took the nativists to be not so much anti-Irish or anti-Catholic as anti-*foreign*. During the 1850s this was the consensual interpretation. The Know-Nothings were hostile to foreign immigration, foreign-born voters, the Germans, Irish, Swiss, and even the English.[21]

The connection of nativist enthusiasm with religious—or, more broadly, ethnocultural—prejudice corresponds well enough with the early antebellum image of the Irish in American "conversation." During the 1820s and 1830s everyday language perpetuated a stereotype which traced all ethnic conduct to character and character itself to nurture. To nativists, religion and custom were among character's chief nurturants, and all who bore the taint of "foreign" doctrine or habit could expect to find their "character" placed under suspicion. The anti-Catholic strain of evangelical Protestantism doubtless drew sustenance from the verbal image of the Irish that prevailed before the mid-1840s. If the American Irish lacked sound character, then indict their religion. But the apparent thinness of specifically ethnic prejudice in organized nativism contrasts sharply with our discovery through content analysis that, in the late antebellum period at least, ordinary American "conversation" sustained a stereotype of the Irish that connected character, conduct, and belief with nature and used physical appearance as a yardstick of nationality. By propagating an ethnoracial definition of national character, the phrenological pseudosciences, as we have seen, popularized and legitimized ethnic prejudice. It is interesting that nativist ideologues did not make much effort to tap this sentiment.

If both modern historians and contemporary observers are right in doubting the strength of ethnic prejudice among nativist enthusiasts, even during the late 1840s and the 1850s, then the nativist organizations must have had powerful reasons for clinging to an anti-Catholic, anti-immigrant ideology at some variance with popular prejudices, which increasingly treated religion and culture as symptomatic of blood. Furthermore, under these circumstances, thoroughgoing nativists can scarcely be understood to have exceeded their contemporaries outside the movement in zeal to refine the distinctions between natives and aliens. If anything, they lagged behind, consistent with the conservatism they always claimed as their hallmark.

If activists in the nativist movement were really resistant to the construction placed upon "nation" and "race" in ordinary conversation during the late antebellum period, it ought to surface in the word image of the Irish preserved in authentic nativist discourse. So should any alternative understandings of ethnicity and nationality. How did nativist rhetoric depict the Irish—by intrinsic descriptives (references to moral, intellectual, and relational character) or extrinsic (behavior, appearance, condition, and affiliation)? Did the nativist image of the Irish change much over time; did changes correspond with apparent developments in the nature or context of interethnic relations? In the gap between the nativist image of the Irish and the contemporaneous stereotyped Paddy circulating in nonnativist conversation lurks suggestive evidence concerning the ideological attractiveness of nativism to antebellum Anglo-Americans.

There is, of course, much nativist rhetoric to go on. One standard bibliography of mid-nineteenth century nativist literature runs to nearly 600 items, not only monographs, tracts, and even novels, which flowed from the anti-Catholic evangelistic agencies, nativist secret societies, and "American" political organizations, but also many periodicals, each containing separate issues and articles devoted to nativist concerns.[22] Such materials are the source of not so much a nativist "conversation" but of what ought to be called a "rhetoric." For this was a self-consciously polemic literature intended to persuade. The fulminations of anti-Catholic clerics, the mummeries of Order of United Americans "Sachems," and the diatribes of Know-Nothing politicians were quite calculated. There was nothing incidental about most references to Catholics, immigrants, foreigners, or Irishmen in this literature. For that reason, it is significant that specific references to the Irish in nativist rhetoric were not more common. Less than half of the overtly nativist documents sampled for this study yielded any "unit-perceptions" of the Irish at all.[23] And together, these contained a modest 240 descriptive references. The Irish were not the principal objects of nativist discourse.

An obvious pattern displayed by references to the Irish surfaced in the literature under review. In nativist materials published between 1820 and 1844, for example, two-thirds can be assigned to just four of the fifteen categories of ethnic description we used to assess the treatment of the Irish in ordinary Anglo-American "conversation." Nativist verbiage particularly drew attention to alleged deficiencies of intellect and morality, accused the Irish of aggressiveness and violence, and tagged them with religious and political labels. This word image was not so different from the descriptive pattern that characterized nonnativist sources in the early antebellum period. It was, first of all, an image that nearly balanced intrinsic and extrinsic descriptive terminology. "Character" was central to the nativist understanding of ethnicity.[24] Predictably, nativist imagery was more critical of Irish character than the contemporaneous societal stereotype. Among the documents examined there was not a single indisputably favorable treatment of Irish moral, intellectual, or social "relational" character. Nativist imagery also meets our expectations by giving pronounced attention to Irish religious and political affiliation and by emphasizing the violence of the Irish temper, even before this became a major issue in ordinary American conversation.[25]

The early antebellum nativist image of the Irish was not quite the stereotype preserved in ordinary conversation, but it was remarkably close. It gave more attention to the depiction of Irish unruliness and political/religious attitudes or affiliations and less attention to economic attributes and positive intrinsic character traits, but all in all it resembled the early antebellum societal stereotype in its emphasis on character. It was, in this sense, also much like the contemporaneous image of the Irish displayed by English descriptive literature.

Anti-Catholic publicist Robert J. Breckinridge's description of America-bound emigrants at Cork in 1836 captured several principal themes of early antebellum nativist rhetoric when it touched specifically on the Irish. First of all, Breckinridge told the readers of his own *Baltimore Literary and Religious Magazine*, the emigrants were victims: "victims of the most abject ignorance and debasing superstition." They were besides, albeit "strong, hale, young and vigorous," "filthy, miserable, and squalid" in appearance. Ignorant, illiterate, credulous, and superstitious; servile, debased, degraded—these were the favorite descriptives for the Irish in nativist literature. The emphasis upon flawed character and its consequences was pronounced, as it was upon sources of character in environment. The Irish in this material were not so much "papish" as they were "priest-ridden," not so much "nationalistic" as "oppressed," "pliant" as "corrupt." The implications of the words were much like those in currency outside the nativist movement: that character came of environment and experience. Even that which the early nativist word portrait of the Irish seemed to emphasize more than the conventional stereotype—like physical description—had this quality. "Starving" and "ragged" or Breckinridge's "squalid" were the preferred adjectives.[26]

After the early 1840s, when the portrait of the Irish in the "conversation" of American common culture changed rapidly and decisively, in nativist rhetoric it did not. The nativist image became nearly an inverse of the societal one. While the descriptives employed in most repositories of ordinary language to characterize the Irish were more often "extrinsic" during the late 1840s and early 1850s, they were *increasingly* "intrinsic" in identifiably nativist material. Allegations about Irish hostility and violence increased sharply in conventional conversation after 1844 and fell off in nativist rhetoric.[27] This kind of inversion was also the case with physical descriptives: markedly up in nonnativist literature, substantially down in nativistic. The mid-antebellum nativist image of the Irish is, perhaps, best described as "traditional," for it remained an ethnic portrait that was chiefly a picture of character, not of behavior or appearance. Nativists clung to an ethnic portrait that was apparently part of Anglo-Americans' cultural inheritance from the colonial past, one sustained during the first decades of the nineteenth century but absent from ordinary conversation later.

The inverse relationship between the nativist and nonnativist stereotypes held up until the end of the antebellum period. While intrinsic descriptives characterized fewer than half of all unit-perceptions of the Irish in nativist literature published before 1845 but 60 percent after 1852, the proportion of intrinsic characterizations in ordinary conversation fell from 53 percent to 39 percent over the same period.[28] To be sure, nativist rhetoric displayed some of the heightened concern with physical description evident in language generally during the late antebellum years, but the principal emphasis of nativist verbal portraiture remained upon moral, intellectual, and relational character. And even physical descriptions focused, like Breckinridge's in the 1830s, upon tidiness and attire rather than physique. The inversion phenomenon was also apparent in the re-emphasis of Irish turbulence and violence in nativist sources at a time when this was no longer a highlight of nonnativist conversation.

The verbal image of the Irish in nativistic rhetoric was a distinctive word portrait betraying a distinctive understanding of the nature of ethnicity and, presumably, nationality—an intrinsic stereotype sustained, even reinforced, over time. Even extrinsic descriptives in nativist literature, as we have seen, were more likely to portray condition than conduct. Thus, while nonnativist sources gave substantial attention to the alleged economic aptitudes and behavior of the Irish, nativist materials emphasized economic status. And, of course, nativist rhetoric more often identified its targets with a religious faith or political principle. Compared to the stereotype in conventional sources of language, the nativist image appears quite resistant to objective developments in interethnic relations. It responded neither to the increased notoriety of interethnic violence in the mid-1840s nor to the growing popularity of deterministic theories of national character.

If an authentic stereotype is actually a verbal construct which is not so much *about* a group of people as the reflection of a relationship *between* groups, the treatment of the Irish in antebellum nativist rhetoric does not really qualify. It was thoroughly *a priori*. Perhaps more than anything else, it suggested the rigidity of nativist dogma.

Heavily laden with ideological baggage, the nativist image of the Irish endured over time and characterized the rhetoric produced by affiliates of evangelical, fraternal, and political nativism alike. It boldly displays the persistence of a self-conscious traditionalism among active nativists. Neither developments in interethnic relations nor newly popularized ethnologic theory could weaken nativist insistence that the really important determinant of national character was personal character and that personal character was made, not inherited.

"The Order of United Americans," reported its new journal, *The Republic,* in January 1851, "will not slumber until the American People are reunited, renationalized." Nativist enthusiasts of the evangelical, fraternal, or political stamp always insisted that their principal goal was preservation or, significantly, *creation* of a distinctive American nationality. John Higham displayed an acute appreciation for this when he wrote that the distinguishing feature of American nativism seems to be that nativists have always "stood for a certain kind of nationalism." To put this another way, the nativist harbors a particular understanding of American nationality, of what constitutes a "true American."[29] During the 1840s, the rhetoric of the Order of United Americans typified that of nativistic organizations generally in displaying anxious concern for what it termed "national character."[30] Mid-century nativists extracted their certain kind of nationalism from a highly selective (and interpretive) reading of the republic's founding fathers. Though it was Washington on the dangers of foreign influence to republican institutions that nativists professedly admired, it was Jefferson the federalist and, paradoxically, Hamilton the centralist who offered the most quotable advice on national character. Jefferson had written that effective civil government "must be conducted by common consent" growing out of popular subscription to common "principles," and Hamilton not only handily observed that "the safety of a republic depends essentially on the habits of a common national sentiment; on a uniformity of principles and habits," but also, more to the point, recommended that "to render the people of this country as homogeneous as possible, must lead as much as any other circumstance to the permanency of their union and prosperity."[31] Obviously ignored were founding father James Madison's injunctions on the safety of diverse interests and sentiments in a republic. Above all, mid-nineteenth century nativist nationalism demanded uniformity—uniform nationality—among the republican populace. Since sovereignty in a republic was invested in the citizens and government in the citizens' elected representatives, both had to be rendered as uniformly "American" as possible. And while there was room in the extensive territories of the United States for resident noncitizens, even these could not be permitted to be so un-American as to interfere with the stewardship conferred upon the voter. To paraphrase Hamilton, the most reliable population was a homogeneous one. The need to police the national character rationalized the very existence of organizations like the Order of United Americans. The Order, along with its confederates, not only labored to establish homogeneity as a principle but also proffered itself as a reliable judge of American nationality with continuing work to do. The Order, together with the other "American" organizations, would separate the sheep from the goats, or at least call to account the public officials whose responsibility this might be. But whence came the "true American"?

Antebellum nativists made "character" the touchstone of nationality. "Virtue" and "intelligence" were without question the most overworked words in the nativist vocabulary (along, perhaps, with their congeners "morality" and "wisdom"). "The American Republic, above all others, demands from every citizen . . . intelligence and virtue," declared a publicist for one of the leading nativist fraternities. "The morality of the nation constitutes its highest glory; when that is gone, its worth is departed," echoed an anti-Catholic periodical. Predictably, the second plank of the American party national platform of 1855 announced that the party's goal would be "the cultivation and development of a sentiment of profoundly intense American feeling . . . and of emulation of the virtue, wisdom, and patriotism that framed our constitution."[32]

The source of good character, of virtue and intelligence for avowed nativists, was unquestionably environment and systematic nurture. To some extent, nativists were prepared to credit the natural environment for contributing to the formation of the American character. The seventh volume of George Bancroft's *History of the United States*, published during the 1850s, attracted favorable comment from the nativist press for the way in which the historian linked the "general impulse" for revolution and liberty among late eighteenth century Americans with the physical influences of the North American continent itself.[33] If natural environment had been regarded as the only source of American nationality then it might have made nationality synonymous with native birth alone, but nativists always placed more emphasis upon environmental circumstances produced by human artifice than by nature. "A man imbibes the love of country at his mother's breast," explained a Know-Nothing orator in the District of Columbia. "He learns his lessons of virtue and patriotism when dandled upon his father's knee."[34] In two decades of maturation in an American home, in an American church, and in an American school, a youth acquired the "social interests," the "social ties," and the "character for freedom" that qualified him to become a full participant in community affairs at

adulthood. Sometimes this nationalist rhetoric combined the effects
of man and nature. In 1851 a nativist magazine approvingly republished a schoolgirl's patriotic address: "Ours is a land supremely
dear to her children over which hover influences constantly forming
her people's character for freedom and for God; a land rich in bless-
ings; the fair home of Liberty!" No wonder that a few years later a
Know-Nothing congressman would argue that an American-born
teenager intuitively understood republican principles that only came
to the foreign-born adult after thorough re-education. Common experience, sustained neighborly relationships, and the ether of liberty
in the New World atmosphere produced the authentic American.[35]

The way in which nativists balanced the consequences of birth
with the effects of artifice in the creation of a true American demonstrates how thorough their environmentalism really was. Chauncey Goodrich's 1850 revision of Noah Webster's *American Dictionary of the English Language* defined "naturalization" as the legal
act of conferring citizenship *or* the process of habituating an individual to a new environment. Nativists characteristically adopted
the second meaning as their own. William Campbell, keynote
speaker at Order of United Americans Washington's Birthday cele-
brations in New York City in 1852, made plain the conventional
nativist position on the acquisition of American character. "Experience is the teacher of individuals," he instructed the faithful. Experience alone conferred "that practical knowledge that fits men to
be partakers in the government of a great country."[36] An expression
of nativist orthodoxy which appeared in the *American Whig Review* during 1849 identified four contributants to nationality or, as
the author put it, "elements which tend to union," that could only
be assimilated through experience: language, civilization, interest,
and political character.[37]

Language was a necessary but not a sufficient indicator of nationality. Common tongue was critical to common experience, but
alone it could not distinguish genuine Americans from other En-
glish-speakers who were the bogus article. "Civilization," in nativist parlance, meant something more than the cultural inheritance
that Americans shared with the rest of the English-speaking world;
it specifically referred to the prevailing customs, institutions, and
even popular art forms of the republic itself. Thus one nativist magazinist repeatedly filled the pages of his journal with pleas for the

encouragement of "purely national" drama, poetry, painting, and literature which would reflect the history, values, and lifestyle of the American people.[38]

Samuel F. B. Morse, notable nativist politician and publicist as well as artist and inventor, once explained what nativists meant by the "unity of interest" that forges nationality. "The foreigner," Morse wrote in an 1835 anti-Catholic tract, "when he arrives on these shores, finds a great insulated community, a large family, separated from all others; independent, each individual of which is bound to the general mass, and the general mass to each individual in certain settled relations."[39] Implicit in this appealing domestic metaphor was the idea that unity of interest emerged without effort from the interdependence among people participating in a sustained social relationship.

"Unity of government," that is, political unity, also carried special meaning in this context. The contributor to the *Whig Review* made it clear that it involved something more than simple subscription to a frame of government and a body of civil statutes. To committed nativists, it meant that nationality was displayed by the incorporation into personal character of the spirit and values that energized those instruments of rule.[40] "Republicanism," warned nativist Congressman William Cost Johnson of Maryland, "is a grand machine of government, but woe betide us if we bring the wrong power to bear on the wheels that it sets in motion. The springs of government, touched and controlled by ignorance and vice, the worst form of bad ambition, produce nothing but confusion worse confounded." Mid-nineteenth century nativists professed to take seriously the admonitions of the founding fathers that the success of a government of the people required a universal display of intelligence, virtue, and civic-mindedness by the people. Thomas Whitney of the Order of United Americans construed that to mean that under "American republicanism," guided by nativist principles, the people "shall govern to the extent of their intellectual and moral capacity."[41]

"Can the tenants of the poor houses of Europe who land on our shores with faculties so formed by nature, or so fashioned by education . . . become the conservative element of our free institutions, whose very basis demands intelligence, patriotism, and virtue in the voter?"[42] This was the classic question of nativist rhetoric. As their treatment in nativist literature suggested, the Irish largely ran afoul of the movement's ideologues because they allegedly lacked an American character. They were deficient in American experience and drew their character from another, less felicitous environment. "There is nothing in an Irishman's nature that renders him bloody-minded and atrocious beyond the people of other lands. . . . the disease is of a moral character," one anti-Catholic pamphleteer pointed out. "Utterly divested by ignorance and crime of the moral and intellectual requisites for political self-government" is how a Know-Nothing politician characterized the danger in Irish and, for that matter, all European immigrants.[43]

Nativists usually regarded European arrivals, the Irish included, as likely to display character values that would disqualify them for Americanization—values produced by ill-education, oppressive poverty, and false religion. "The Europeans are studiously kept ignorant and servile, and are deformed with the vices which accompany such ignorance," Frederick Saunders wrote in his anti-immigrant tract, *The Progress and Prospects of America* (1855). Twenty years earlier, Samuel Morse had described the way in which European tyranny "blotted out . . . reason, and conscience, and thought," turning human beings into "mere human machines."[44] A contemporaneous anti-Catholic publication also portrayed the immigrants as conscienceless machinery but attributed this condition less to the neglect of education than to impoverishment and harassment. "In all ages," offered Protestant evangelist Lyman Beecher, "religion, of some kind, has been the former of man's character." The most benighted immigrants were, of course, the "progeny of Popery." Roman Catholicism, another cleric counseled true Americans, left much of Europe's populace "six centuries behind all other people in knowledge, and morals, and religion."[45] Whatever their particular emphasis, nativists' consensus was that character came of condition.

In any case, none of these circumstances applied exclusively to the Irish. Nativists believed them characteristic of Europeans generally. Even the English—though they were relatively free of "papish" influences, and though they (at least the better classes of them) were beneficiaries of education—were still subject to the oppressions of monarchy, enlightened though it might be, and consequently lacked the character that was common among authentic

Americans accustomed to self-government. Well after strident criticism of England's rule over Ireland had fallen out of popular fashion, nativists kept up rapid-fire denunciation of English mismanagement and its deleterious effect upon Irish character. If more and more of the Anglo-American public found Irish condition inevitable, nativists loudly protested that *they* did not. "Seven-tenths of our population deride the idea that Ireland was ever else than an oppressed and down-trodden country," protested an 1856 American party campaign tract. "Ireland always degraded—Ireland the evangelist of all Europe . . . No!" The reduction of the Irish to their present misery and malignity was a modern accumulation of priestly oppression and the burdens imposed by "blunt, curled-nose England."[46] This was a far cry from either contemporaneous Anglo-Saxonist rhetoric circulating among intellectuals, which lauded mother England, or the tendencies of Paddy in popular conversation, which implied that Irish character and condition were unchanged and unchangeable.

Most nativists were so committed to the proposition that environment conditioned character that when it came to explaining the Europeans' flaws they were willing to concede that "the same might be equally true of Americans in reversed circumstances." Americans drew no immunity to moral or intellectual misguidance by blood. Nativist ideologues often took pains to absolve immigrants from personal responsibility for their alleged lapses, calling them "victims." The moral and intellectual deficiencies of both German and Irish immigrants, one pamphleteer explained in the mid-1850s, were entirely understandable, "if we keep in view the education of these men, the peculiar influences which were active in nurturing their character, and unavoidable predilections which the form of government under which they grew up produced in their minds."[47] American party publicist Saunders went so far as to suggest that among the white population of the United States there were really only "two classes of persons, the European and the American." The former were strictly to be distinguished by the fact that they had been "kept ignorant and servile . . . and . . . deformed with the vices which accompany servile ignorance."[48]

But even birth upon American soil was no absolute guarantee that a bad environment could be avoided. Nativists openly worried about the character of American-born youth who spent their formative years in the ethnic neighborhoods of large cities where they would be exposed not to the atmosphere and experiences of the New World but to a transplanted slice of the Old.[49] "The interminable hordes of immigrants who seek our large cities," one wrote, "constantly frequent the same localities which renders them exclusive; so that an American entering certain neighborhoods, would fancy himself in Germany or Ireland. The denizens have little communication with the outside world—have their own papers, clubs, and gatherings—and are practically a distinct people."[50] An object of general concern in public discourse during the early antebellum period, anxiety over the retardants to acculturation passed increasingly into the hands of spokesmen for the nativistic organizations which continued to link character and culture and took it to be their responsibility to supervise the nurturing process that made citizens. Likely it was the need to sustain some important role for themselves which lent an optimistic note to even their most bitter denunciations of immigrants. For the "poor, ignorant, half-clad Irish Papist who comes to these shores" after the priests had "steeped them in the grossest superstition," anti-Catholic author Nicholas Murray held out scant hope of recovery, though hope was not entirely gone. But American-born Catholics under the best circumstances were conditioned by the happy influences of their nativity to recognize the degradation of their coreligionists and, in fact, profit from witnessing what would happen to those too long under the priestly "yoke."[51]

By tracing character to nurture and environment, the nativist organizations implied that character could be reformed—but not easily. "Man is a creature of habit and custom, wherever, and under whatever auspices his lot is cast," preached *The Republic*'s founder and editor, Thomas R. Whitney. "Opinions, morals, usages are all the fruits of training and education, and all these, by training and education, become, not impressions merely, but absolute convictions, or what is sometimes called second nature. To root out these convictions, to annul this second nature, is not the work of a day or of a few years." Character and conduct, in other words, became habitual. Even if immigrants could be broken of their bad habits, they started out ignorant of American customs, institutions, and, especially, polity.[52] Compounding the difficulty of reform were the circumstances of immigration itself. "A man, coming from the twilight of bondage into the broad meridian of freedom," Whitney offered, "is dazzled with the unaccustomed glory that surrounds him. He is lost." Such profound bewilderment would, presumably, make adaptation to American ways slow and difficult. An unsettled mind and heart were ill-suited for learning. Too, many immigrants' background had prejudiced them against American habits and principles. An ingrained Roman Catholic jealousy of Protestants, a publication of the American Protestant Society submitted, made at least some of the Irish virtually "inaccessible" to education. It was for these reasons, nativists alleged, that candidates for naturalized citizenship required an extended probationary period and that unreconstructed Roman Catholics could never be safely entrusted with important public offices.[53]

These reservations notwithstanding, nativists usually were adamant that immigrant character—manifestly including Irish character—*could* be reformed. "Domestication" was a favorite term to describe the process by which immigrants might acquire an American character. An artificial adolescence of twenty-one years, the period of maturation for American-born youth, would usually suffice to instill American habits in well-disposed immigrants, though time alone was not enough. Thorough domestication meant consciously surrendering un-American habits and purposefully taking up the customs of the republican community.[54] Catholics, especially, had to work at re-educating themselves. "Laugh priestcraft to scorn," one Protestant cleric counseled immigrants. Organizations like the Order of United Americans offered education and tested acculturation. "Chapter rooms, when viewed aright," *The Republic* advised the brethren, "are schools of patriotism." The tutelage provided was expected to reach far beyond chapter hall; the proper nativist cell would be a "school of oratory and debate" preparing true Americans to evangelize both natives and immigrants in Americanism. It would examine the effects of education and acculturation as well. Thus a Know-Nothing orator differentiated between the un-American Catholic who "acknowledges a foreign power superior to the authority of the United States" and patriotic Catholics "who do not acknowledge the supremacy of the Pope." Only an "American organization" was qualified to make this distinction.[55]

Leading nativists were eager to publicize the success of these agents of Americanization. Noting Roman Catholic complaints that the names of second generation Irishmen in the United States were frequently missing from parish rosters, Thomas Whitney pridefully announced to *The Republic*'s readers, "To the question asked, 'Where are they?' it might be safely answered, *all around;* but they have become native Americans, and possibly are now protesting against Papal rule in these United States."[56] Because of their confidence in the possibility of "domestication," nativist politicians often seemed quite comfortable appealing to "Americanized" ethnic minorities for political support. There was considerable cross-pollination, for example, between the Order of the Star-Spangled Banner, the Order of United Americans, and the American Protestant Association, an anti-Catholic fraternity of Orangemen. In 1854 and 1855, the nativist ticket in the New York City municipal elections garnered the combined support of all three of these organizations as well as the German Protestant community. During January 1855 the New York State Grand Council of the Know-Nothings voted to open membership in the Order to native-born Protestants of foreign parentage, and in August the Massachusetts Know-Nothing State Committee went a step further, admitting naturalized Protestants of foreign birth.[57]

Despite the complaints of a few contemporaries that nativists indulged in a virulent form of "race" prejudice as well as in religious and ethnocultural bias, many nativists professed to see more danger in ethnic segregation than in intimate association or even intermarriage among the different ethnic elements of the white community. At a time when the *New York Times* was calling interethnic violence "race war" and a popular national magazine, *Harper's,* was explaining the contrasts of "blood" between Anglo-Americans, Teutons, and Celts, a nativist pamphleteer insisted that "Many distinct nationalities flow together and must blend into one, to insure harmony and permanency to our government." Of course, immigrants "must give up their peculiarities and become American in feeling, in thought, and in devotion to our republic, before they can be considered good citizens," but this was a matter of experience and education, not inheritance.[58] Mid-century nativist literature was permeated with impassioned discussions of the weaknesses of a society divided into distinctive ethnic communities. No fears were expressed here about the possible adulteration of Anglo-American blood. Roman Catholicism and the rapid pace of immigration were indicted because they encouraged clannishness and discouraged intermarriage.[59]

The Order of United Americans' *Republic* devoted an entire string of editorials in 1852 to denouncing resurgent Celtic nationalism and the touring lecturers who were its expositors in the United States. Rhetorical Celticism, the columns charged, only served "to excite the 'animosities of race.'" It was the concept of white "races" itself that *The Republic* seemed to find objectionable. The editors were quite blunt. If there were such things, ethnically, as Celtic-Americans and Anglo-Saxon Americans then there could be no "real" Americans at all. For American character was taught and learned, not transmitted in blood. In the same series, *The Republic* criticized efforts to persuade the Irish that they were *innately* Catholic, ridiculing an article in the *American Celt* which pronounced the inseparability of "the Irish from the Catholic temperament." The decibels of complaint from the New York nativist journal peaked as the autumn elections neared when the editors castigated politicians for going after the Irish vote by advertising their own pure Celtic blood.[60]

All of this made nationality and citizenship separable issues among active nativists. No simple legal act could transform the foreigner into an authentic American. Back in the 1830s, Samuel Morse acidly called the immigrant who had sworn the oath that would make him a voter without first habituating himself to the ways and principles nativists termed "American" a "naturalized foreigner," not a "naturalized citizen." While many contemporaries could not envision the possibility of the United States becoming the domicile of permanent residents without citizenship, nativist ideologues had no apparent difficulty conceiving of appropriate intermediate statuses between citizen and alien. New York City's American Republican Party of the mid-1840s declared as one of its cardinal principles that "It is deemed just and right that those foreigners who shall come here at a future period shall be permitted in taking the oath of allegiance, etc., to hold and convey real estate, and, in short, be citizens in all respects, saving and excepting the right of voting, and for this they shall remain twenty-one years." In 1856 the Order of United Americans' Whitney urged the adoption of a system of "affiliation" in place of conventional naturalization which would "identify the respectable resident immigrant with the *social family*, but not with the *political family* of the country."[61]

So convinced were some nativists during the mid-1850s of the capacity of environment and nurture to *create* nationality that they actually endorsed the claims of free, American-born blacks to full United States citizenship. This was exceedingly risky for nativists since the American Party openly courted conservative Whigs, southern and northern alike, who were not usually of a progressive temper in matters involving race relations.[62] But freedmen did undoubtedly have those exposures and experiences that went to form the national character. The American-born Negro, one New York nativist leader asserted, understood full well that the United States was "his country" and deserving of his loyalty. "Patriotic" is the word that Thomas R. Whitney chose to describe blacks' attachment to homeland. To patriotism, blacks joined common interest with their white neighbors, an interest born of nothing more than sustained coexistence in the same land.[63] Denying such persons the title of "American" and the rights accompanying it, at least a few outspoken nativist theorists believed, threatened the very rationale for "American" organizations, whose whole responsibility it was to teach Americanism and guarantee that none but authentic Americans by experience took on the responsibilities of the franchise.

Out of considerations like these, Whitney's New York City-based Order of United Americans publicly assaulted the program of the American Colonization Society at mid-century, despite the fact that the Society was popular among the very constituency of conservative Whigs that the Order was just then trying to attract to a fledgling nativist third party.[64] The American Colonization Society alleged that blacks were in "physiologic principle" alien to American society and could never have an equal part in it. While they might have some use as controlled labor and doubtless benefited from their exposure to white civilization, blacks could not remain as free, noncitizens in a republic that made no provision for second-class participation. Therefore, free blacks must be removed to some place where they might conveniently rule themselves. The American Colonization Society offered Liberia, a newly independent African nation of ex-slaves. If the United States required a larger population, why not encourage the immigration of white Europeans who would find—because of the same "physiologic principle" mentioned above—integration into American society most "felicitous."[65] The Order of United Americans' theorists considered the colonizationist argument ludicrous. "To speak plainly, what knaves, or fools, or both, are they who will refuse the right of suffrage to the native-born, and bred, honest and intelligent man of color, while at the same time they actually force it upon the foreign-born and bred vicious, ignorant, degraded ruffian?" the Order's Alfred Ely offered warmly. Ely found it imperative to turn the discussion of nationality and its privileges away from physiology—as the colonizationists would have it—and back to nurture and environment, to make sure that "honesty" and "intelligence," "viciousness" and "ignorance"—teachable and testable characteristics—remained central to all debate over national character. Of course, freedmen would balk at colonizationist schemes. "America, the United States of North America, is the home of their birth, the land of their nativity, and they have no idea of being sent off to foreign lands," Thomas Whitney pointed out.[66]

The Order of United Americans' position on black nationality and citizenship was not quite that assumed by authentic abolitionists (whom the Order repeatedly denounced as trouble-makers). According to Whitney and the brotherhood, nationality was conferred by nurture and experience; in proportion to their acclimation to the ways of the white majority, blacks were American too. But to most abolitionists, of both races, blacks had earned the right to be called American without reference to the ways of whites. "Their fathers fought bravely to achieve our independence during the revolutionary war," William Lloyd Garrison propounded. "They spilt their blood freely during the last war [the War of 1812]; they are entitled, in fact, to every inch of our Southern and much of our western territory, having worn themselves out in its cultivation." Black activist Frederick Douglass was bolder: "We live here—have lived here—have a right to live here, and mean to live here." Compared to this, the Order's enunciations on the subject displayed a definite cultural chauvinism.[67] But the importance of the nativists' pronouncements on colonization was not their liberality nor even their questionable sincerity, much less the willingness of nativists to make black citizenship an actual cause, but rather the evidence they offered of the seriousness nativists invested in their particular definition of nationality. American nationality derived from a particular character and character came from habits and associations. Some nativist thinkers were willing to make risky statements about black rights for no other reason than to maintain the consistency and persuasiveness of this position.

This outlook also made it possible for the Order of United Americans in 1852 to welcome into its ranks (and to make something of a public to-do about it) George Copway, a Chippewa Indian who had been trained to be a Methodist missionary to his tribesmen in the Lake Superior region. *The Republic* advertised him as "a real North American," making a play on words nativists often employed to describe themselves.[68] And, in their terms especially, indeed he was. Educated and Christianized, Copway made a point during the 1850s of cultivating acquaintanceships with leading American literati: William Cullen Bryant, James Fenimore Cooper, Henry Wadsworth Longfellow, and Francis Parkman in particular. Romantic in his self-professed attachment to American soil, patriotic in his sentiments concerning the United States and its founding father George Washington (claimed as patron saint by all nativistic organizations), Copway was just the right example of the American *made,* not born (ironic as that may seem).[69]

Even Copway's particular pet project in the late 1840s and early 1850s appealed to the Order and its supporters: creation of a self-administered Indian territory east of the Missouri River that would not be a reservation in any conventional sense but a candidate state of the Union, conferring ordinary American citizenship upon its (appropriately educated) inhabitants. This scheme, advanced by Copway in books, memorials, lectures, and, in 1851, his own weekly newspaper, *Copway's American Indian,* called for removal of the Indians of Michigan, Wisconsin, Minnesota, and Iowa to a triangular region in what is now eastern South Dakota bordered by the Big Sioux River on the east, a line drawn from the headwaters of the Big Sioux to the Missouri River on the north, and the Missouri itself on the west and the south, along with the creation of a government on the pattern of other United States territorial administrations but staffed by Indians. This plan, Copway hoped, would replace the government's haphazard removal and confinement program, which he believed kept Indians as perpetual children in tutelage to no particular end, left their title to land insecure, and

New clothes, same old Paddy: cartoon, *Harper's Monthly*, November 1854

"Celtic" physiognomy: cartoon of New York cabmen from *Harper's Weekly*, October 6, 1860

Lantern-jawed, low-browed Irish threaten the public schools: cartoon from *Harper's Weekly*, October 1, 1859

Paddy as member of the animal kingdom: *Harper's Monthly*, September 1852

"Wanted—Protestant Girls": advertisement, *The New York Times,* August 24, 1852.

A half-human Irish family: cartoon, *Harper's Monthly,* March 1856

"Hans", in contrast
to Paddy, comic and
benign stereotype of
German immigrant:
cartoon, *Harper's
Monthly,* February,
1856

HANS SCHWILLANPUFF'S VALENTINE.
"Ach, mein Vaterland!"

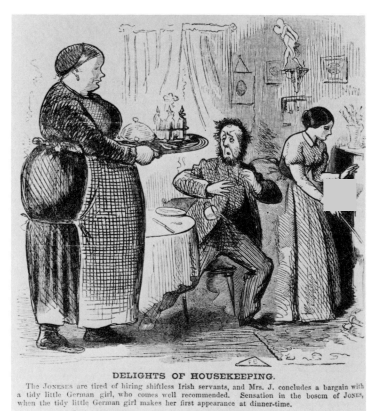

DELIGHTS OF HOUSEKEEPING.

The JONESES are tired of hiring shiftless Irish servants, and Mrs. J. concludes a bargain with
a tidy little German girl, who comes well recommended. Sensation in the bosom of JONES,
when the tidy little German girl makes her first appearance at dinner-time.

A "tidy little" German housemaid: cartoon, *Harper's Weekly,*
March 10, 1860

BRIDGET MALONY'S VALENTINE.
"Sure, Patrick is a jewel ov a boy."

Mr. Simpkins applies at an Intelligence Office for a sober, tidy, respectable servant.

The Keeper sends him one, with first-rate recommendations from her last place.

Mrs. Simpkins wonders why Bridget will always draw corks with her teeth.

The cork-drawing mystery is solved—not to Mrs. Simpkins's satisfaction.

Paddy, the "ape" behind the angel: cartoon, *Harper's Monthly*, February 1856. Bridget, vulgar, drunken, and violent: cartoon, *Harper's Monthly*, August 1855

CONTRASTED FACES.

"Look on this picture, and then on that."—SHAKSPEARE.

Fig. 747. – FLORENCE NIGHTINGALE.   Fig. 748.—BRIDGET McBRUISER.

"Contrasted Faces":
ethnic caricatures from
New Physiognomy
(New York, 1866)

AMERICAN PHRENOLOGICAL JOURNAL.

GALL

A Repository of Science, Literature, General Intelligence.

VOL. XXI., NO. 1.]   NEW YORK, JANUARY, 1855.   [$1.00 A YEAR.

"A Repository of Science, Literature, General Intelligence": masthead from
American Phrenological Journal, January 1855
Courtesy, Library of Congress

The untrained, blunt, coarse bog-trotter (fig. 423) walks heavily upon his heels in parlor, church, or kitchen, his gait being more like that of a horse on a bridge than like that of the cultivated gentleman. The slow, heavy tramp of the iron-shod "hedger and ditcher" is in keeping with the "don't-care" spirit of the lower ten thousand, be they white or black. When they dance, it may well be called a "jig," or a "break-down." The walk is a hobble, a shuffle, and a sort of "get along." The humble man has a humble walk; the dignified man, a dignified walk; the vain man, a vain walk; the hopeful man, a light, buoyant, hopeful walk; the desponding, hopeless man, a dragging, hopeless step, as though he were going to prison rather than to his duty; the executive man, an executive walk, and the lazy, slothful man, a walk corresponding with his real character.

Fig. 423.   Fig. 424.

Where there is little executiveness, propelling power, and small aspiring organs, there will be a slovenly, slouchy step, with one foot dragging lazily after the other (fig. 424). No energy, enterprise, or ambition here, and the person appears like one between "dead and alive," a sort of "froze and thawed" substance, good for nothing. He complains, grunts, whines, finds fault, and doses himself with various quack medicines—for

The "untrained, blunt, coarse bog-trotter": the Irish as represented in *New Physiognomy*

Nativist self-image with alien as serpent: icon of the Order of United American, *The Republic,* 1851

Nativist nightmare: Irish and German immigrants stealing ballot box, 1850s cartoon
Used by permission of the Astor, Lennox & Tilden Foundations Collection, New York Public Library

"Beware of foreign influence": nativist campaign broadside, 1850s
Courtesy, American Antiquarian Society

"Simian" Irishman: caricature by Thomas Nast, *Harper's Weekly*, April 6, 1867

provided little incentive for Indians to relinquish a seminomadic hunting and gathering lifestyle for the settled argiculture he regarded as prerequisite for "civilization." Copway particularly denounced the distribution of annuities for Indian land cessions, which he insisted encouraged dependence, waste, and alcoholism.[70] This fit right into the nativist understanding of character and condition. Indians were debased by their environment and their associations. But after they had been operated upon by missionaries and teachers, made part of the economic family of Americans by learning to till their land and market its bounty, and, finally, tutored in self-government in a controlled territorial situation, they would be ready to become American in the cultural and political as well as in the natural sense. They already had the attachment to American soil that would dispose them to patriotism. Copway himself seemed proof the scheme might work. By supporting it, nativists might not only give themselves new work (someone had to judge the suitability of the new citizen candidates) but also might prove their contention that *nothing* prevented the well-disposed individual from acquiring the hallmarks of American nationality.

Copway understood how appealing his plan would be to the nativist fraternal and political organizations, too. Others had proposed Indian territories and Indian citizenship, and other contemporaneous "friends of the Indian" shared Copway's optimistic environmentalist outlook on Indian character and its susceptibility to reform.[71] But Copway distinguished himself from them all by targeting the nativistic "American" organizations of the east coast as his natural political allies and lobbyists. As a missionary in the northwest in the early 1840s he had already ingratiated himself with anti-Catholic zealots in the Protestant evangelical agencies by vilifying his "papist" competitors for Indian converts. In 1849, however, after moving to New York City, Copway took direct aim at the "American" fraternities which were just beginning to dabble in politics. He published his plea for an Indian territory in the conservative *American Whig Review* and specifically asked for the support of "every *true American*." As he lectured up and down the east coast in 1849–50 he drew laughter and applause by introducing himself as a "native American" to capture the sympathy of those whose "native Americanism" had nothing to do with aboriginal bloodlines. From Washington, D.C., he wrote stirring paeans to the memory of the first President and asked, at a time when the nativist fraternities were taking donations for the completion of the Washington Monument, whether the Indians might not build their own memorial to the great father.[72] In 1850 Copway denounced the diversion of public funds for Indian education to "discordant religious elements" just when the Roman Catholic archbishop of New York was pursuing tax dollars for parochial schools. No one missed his meaning. And he took a parting shot at his birthland, British Canada, alleging that he had been denied his share of the annual Chippewa annuity for several years by Canadian authorities because "I had been *too much with the Americans,* the enemies of the British government." His rejoinder was sure to warm patriots: "I would rather never see a blanket again."[73]

When Copway felt comfortable that he was drawing the nativist societies into his corner, he sought to make use of their political clout. He called on "true Americans" to recommend his Indian territorial plan to their representatives in the Congress. He took up the cudgel of Unionism and endorsed the New York nativists' professed desire to bury the slavery extension question in the name of intersectional harmony. In 1856 he announced himself in the pages of the *New York Times* as a Fillmore man because during his presidential administration Fillmore had proven himself "kind to the Indians." At the same time he proclaimed that "the interest of the Indian identically belongs to the American Party . . . as Americans we will try to do what we can for the Indian, which is the crowning mission of the American Party in this country.[74] Copway was only exaggerating, not inventing.

George Copway never got his Indian state but he could not have been disappointed with the words and works leading nativists expended on his and his kinsmen's behalf during the 1850s. At least one nativistic congressman memorialized the President on the subject of an Indian state.[75] Another—George Briggs of New York— helped Chippewa delegates secure a presidential audience in 1852. President Fillmore himself, still a Whig in 1852, told the Congress in his last annual message that some permanent arrangement had to be made for the Indians who now effectively "were tenants at sufferance, and liable to be driven from place to place at the pleasure of the whites."[76] The 1861 inventory of Fillmore's personal library still showed Copway's *Organization of a New Indian Terri-*

tory East of the Missouri River on the shelves.[77] Other politicians and publicists of nativist persuasion contributed to Copway's short-lived newspaper. At least one proto-nativist patriotic fraternity advertised meetings in its pages. Copway responded by pandering to the prejudices of such supporters, printing a good "Paddy-whack" joke now and then.[78]

During debates on the Kansas-Nebraska and Homestead bills, nativist congressmen offered the most unflattering distinctions between Indians and immigrants. Senator John B. Thompson of Kentucky repeatedly argued that he saw no point in subjecting Indians to "bullying and browbeating, to obtain territory, and when you have obtained it . . . to turn around and say that you will give it to these foreigners and emigrants." The latter, he argued, were, in their capacity for harm to the American republic, much "worse than the Indian occupants."[79] There were, of course, some simple rhetorical points to be gained by nativist politicians in making such comparisons. How effective to denigrate the immigrant by scaling him below not only free blacks but also Indians. It is equally clear that championing real native Americans while criticizing the foreign-born fully conformed with the nativist outlook on character and nationality. Thomas Whitney, Whig/American party representative from New York City to the 34th Congress, founder and editor of *The Republic,* and past Grand Sachem of the Order of United Americans, caused much irritation among western congressmen in 1857 by repeatedly asking who were behaving more like savages along the frontier, whites or Indians. By their lawless conduct many whites proved themselves no Americans while many Indians showed themselves well advanced toward "assimilating the habits of civilization."[80] As editor of *The Republic,* Whitney had run a number of articles on the Indians attributing Indian character to environment and suggesting its capacity for development. Whitney's own poetic ode to the Indians, *The Ambuscade,* emphasized the native Americans' natural fealty to the land of their fathers.[81]

Expressions of nativist support for Indians and George Copway's efforts to connect "true Americans" of all hues may not have brought Indians much in the way of tangible benefits. But both are important in showing the seriousness with which nativists took their rhetoric about the environmental bases of character and American nationality. Some were serious enough to announce a preference for the admission of red and black men to citizenship before many whites at a time when Anglo-American racial sensitivity was, if anything, growing. Copway, *The Republic* was glad to point out, was "one of the pure aboriginal blood."[82]

This ought to tell us much about why nativists so infrequently used the language of popular ethnology to describe national character, even when it was becoming fashionable in Anglo-American folk culture during the 1850s. If nationality was largely determined by biology, then the importance of molding and testing individual character was denied altogether. Intellectual and moral character would come automatically of blood. What purpose would there be then for "American" organizations to nurture and separate? It would, of course, be wrong to say that nativists never spoke of "race" in connection with nationality. But when they did so it was usually in a special way, not quite in the fashion of their contemporaries.

For many nativist authors and lecturers, "race" was simply synonymous with cultural heritage. In nativist rhetoric, Roman Catholics were frequently described as a distinctive "race" or even as a "nationality," as were Protestants. When Thomas R. Whitney talked about the "Anglo-Saxon race," he was referring to the Anglo-American Protestant tradition, not what he took to be a biological reality. Other nativist ideologues discussed Anglo-Saxonism not as a religious heritage but as a political one.[83] Free, republican institutions were traceable to "Anglo-Saxon" origins, wrote Frederick Saunders in his lengthy *Progress and Prospects of America*. He was really describing not a physiological foundation but rather distinctive "character, custom, or opinions." Saunders decided in the end that the American nation was not Anglo-Saxon anyway—even in the cultural sense—but "Anglo-American."[84] It was Anglo-American because this people had been nurtured in a unique environment, taken on characteristic habits, and easily absorbed non-Saxon stocks. Other nativists, too, called the Anglo-Americans a "race,"[85] which only made sense if race meant something other than what it had come to express in contemporary common culture—that something being an original national character, an acquired national character. Nativists occasionally called the Irish a separate race, but a race by virtue of custom and environment, not blood, and hence scarcely disqualified from Americanization. "The famine and the landlords have actually created a *new race* in Ireland," Philadelphia nativist pamphleteer John Sanderson approvingly quoted an observer of Irish life in 1849. "I have seen on the streets of Galway, crowds of creatures more debased than the Yahoos of Swift—creatures having only a distant and hideous resemblance to human beings. Gray-haired old men, whose faces had hardened into a settled leer of mendicancy, simious and semi-human, and women filthier and more frightful than the harpies."[86] This was the nativist conception of "race" exactly. Conditions created character—personal, "racial," or "national."

During the 1830s, William Lloyd Garrison argued that it was the inevitable tendency of nationalist prejudice, if left unchecked, to draw the bounds of nationality tighter and tighter. Now it was a white skin that many took to be the primary qualification for Americanism and Americanization, Garrison tendered, but next it would be a particular religious creed and subsequently, more than likely, "veins . . . flowing with the purest English blood."[87] It has been easy for historians to take this prediction (and others like it) as an account of what actually transpired among American nativists during the 1840s and 1850s. Because nativists denounced Catholics they fit well enough into Garrison's prognosis for prejudice. And because the nativistic agencies focused their animosity upon immigrants from Germany and, especially, Ireland, it has been convenient to assume that before the Civil War "Know-Nothingism" represented the outermost extremity of nationalist boundary-setting. Allegedly, if anyone confounded nationality with ethnicity, it was the nativist. "Never explicit about the historical or racial origins of the Anglo-Saxons, much less the meaning of the term," writes Jean Baker, "Know-Nothings were nevertheless certain of three things: America's heritage was Anglo-Saxon; Anglo-Saxons were neither foreign-born Irish or Germans nor Catholics; and Anglo-Saxons were naturally superior to others."[88] This is as close as nativists got to specifically ethnic prejudice and, allegedly, nobody went further.

"Anglo-Saxon"—and, more to the point, "Anglo-American"—were terms that had taken on more established meaning by the 1840s than Baker suspects. But we could not discover this from a reading of nativist rhetoric. Nativist ideologues avoided not only the jargon of popular ethnology but also the very idea that there might be anything like an American ethnicity or "race." Instead, they clung tenaciously to the more optimistic theory of national character that had been normative in American common culture during the early antebellum decades. "Americans only shall govern America," rung out the American Party platform in 1855—Americans by "birth," Americans by "education," Americans by "training."[89]

By mid-century an ethnic construction of American nationality was firmly entrenched in the language of common culture, where it was sure to have an impact upon popular "sentiments." We may not see much of "Anglo-Saxons" before the Civil War. But we see very often indeed the identification of nationality with character and conduct and character and conduct with "blood." It was implicit in the way in which Anglo-Americans routinely talked about the Irish—and about themselves. Language disposed many to make reflexive judgments about character and nationality alike from the superficial evaluation of behavior and "looks."

Antebellum nativism, historians are quick to point out, was a movement of "the dedicated few and the casual many."[90] "Nativist," after all, is a term routinely applied to everyone from the Know-Nothing politician, anti-Catholic cleric, and "American" pamphleteer to the participant in a secret brotherhood and the one-time American Party voter. Much has been written about the social and political origins of the nativist movement in antebellum America. But there were also cultural conditions affecting the dispositions of casual and enthusiastic nativists alike. Nativism reached its political apex in the mid-1850s, just when many Americans felt—as Michael Holt puts it—"dislocated and bewildered by the rapidity of economic change," when European immigration reached its prewar peak, when the principal political parties seemed unresponsive to constituency demands, and when the Union appeared headed down the road to partition. A decade earlier, Lee Benson points out, "the conditions which would lead the native Protestant electorate to respond politically to nativist, anti-Catholic issues had not yet developed."[91] But these were not just economic conditions—or political ones.

The cultural environment of the early 1850s was at least partly responsible for making the political program advanced by nativism's dedicated few attractive to a casual many. Those conditioned by language to find "Irishism" incompatible with Americanism were sure to have sympathy with a platform that promised to suspend immigrant naturalizations and restrict the influence of Roman Catholics. Nativist theorists were not the authors of hostility to "Irishism" but were unquestionably beneficiaries of it. Nativism tapped ethnic as well as religious and cultural prejudice, even if ethnic prejudice was antithetical to the official ideology of institutional nativism. To indulge in a cliché, what one hand gave, the other took away. Reflexive anti-Irishism encouraged by the patterns in American "conversation" was capable of repelling as many from the nativist program as it attracted. If the danger posed to the republic in European immigration was really borne in "blood," discrimination against immigrants and Catholics without ethnic distinction was bound to strike many observers as draconian and utterly misguided. Actually, the only solution to the immigration "problem" consistent with authentic ethnic prejudice was restriction of immigration to selected ethnic groups. But before the Civil War few Americans were willing to delegate the powers to the state necessary to carry out such discrimination. In a society still short on labor but long on space the alternative—acquiescence in open immigration combined with outspoken cynicism about its consequences—was easier.

It is certainly worth reemphasizing that the treatment of the Irish in nativist rhetoric was not just different from the ethnic stereotype that circulated in nonnativist "conversation" but *had* to be different. To justify their very existence, the "American" organizations of the mid-nineteenth century—religious, fraternal, and political— found it imperative to cleave to a strictly environmental definition of nationality. The pattern of ethnic description in nativist rhetoric would necessarily remain "intrinsic." By contrast, as "racially" determinist theories of nationality were popularized by pseudoscience among the public at large, the treatment of the Irish and other putative aliens in ordinary conversation increasingly favored "extrinsic" representations of behavior, condition, and appearance. Nativists remained true to the perfectionist temper of the Second Great Awakening well after perfectionist optimism had slipped out of style in American common culture.

Nativism's political influence did not survive the mid-1850s, historians point out, largely because the movement neither addressed the broad range of public issues nor seemed relevant in the midst of the sectional crisis. However, nativist organizations were fractured by forces within as well as without. Although the American party committed itself to the principle of Unionism, it was repeatedly buffeted by defections in North and South. The nativists' exclusively environmentalist definition of nationality was not responsible for all of these but doubtless encouraged unresolvable ideological tensions. Many Southern nativists, committed to a principle of social organization George M. Fredrickson calls "hierarchical biracialism," would find it more and more difficult to make invidious distinctions of any kind among white men but would regard it more congenial to insist that American nationality was uniquely available to members of the Caucasian race.[92] On the other hand, environmentalist rhetoric was liable (as in the case of the Order of United Americans' leadership) to incline some Northern nativists to betray sympathy for black Americans' claim to full nationality and its rights. But, ultimately, we learn less about nativists from their treatment of the Irish in words than, by contrast, we learn about popular stereotypes and popular prejudices. The image of the Irish in nativist rhetoric did not suggest (as Garrison, perhaps, suspected) where American nationalism was headed but rather where it had been.

CHAPTER SIX

Ethnicity and Nationality in Antebellum America

"Of late we have heard much of both Saxon and Celt. But where is the Saxon—and how is one to know him? The Irish are called Celts, the English Saxons, in reference, at least, to the blood which is supposed to *predominate* in each, but . . . there is probably as much Celt in the English as in the Irish; as much Saxon in the Irish as in the English; as much of Norman in both as either of Saxon or Celt."

"The New Exodus," *The Christian Examiner* (May 1852)

ORIGINALLY COINED before 1820 to describe a printing process employing metal plates with fixed type, the term "stereotype" was being used as an adjective outside the publishing trade by the 1840s. The Civil War era edition of Noah Webster's *American Dictionary of the English Language* treated "stereotyped" as an appropriate word to describe anything "formed in a fixed or unchangeable manner; as, *stereotyped* opinions." But a decade earlier, "stereotype" had already been put to work to identify generalized, undifferentiated perceptions of other peoples. In 1853 a review of Sir Francis Head's *Tour in Ireland* for the *New York Times* charged that the author apparently "carried with him to the island the stereotyped ideas of Paddy's insouciance, blundering, and broguery."[1] Uncluttered by the social-psychological jargon of our own times, comments like these betrayed antebellum Americans' awareness of ethnic stereotypes, in general, and stereotypes of the Irish, in particular. What they probably did not suspect was the extent to which a consensual image of the Irish had become locked up in the very language of American "conversation." Nor were they likely to have had much sensitivity to the metamorphosis of the Irish stereotype over the course of the antebellum period, its responsiveness to especially dramatic developments in interethnic contact, to the influences of popular pseudoscience, or to changing definitions of nationality itself. They would most likely have been surprised—though not at all dismayed—to find that the verbal image of the Irish in American common culture was more than a simple reflection of stereotypes propagated by English verbal traditions. We may not know better than antebellum Americans that a stereotyped Paddy existed before the Civil War, but we do have a better sense of its cultural ubiquitousness and, consequently, of its ability to condition popular attitudes and even, under the right circumstances, to influence behavior.

Especially, the verbal image of the Irish in ordinary conversation shows us that ethnicity was a meaningful distinction in antebellum common culture. It meant something to label an individual "Irish" or "German," something different from tagging him as "immigrant" or as "Catholic." And this held true outside of intellectual or nativist circles where American nationalism was an object of systematic thought. It was both a cause and a symptom of this that throughout the four decades preceding the Civil War to invoke the terms "Irish" or "German" was to trigger mental images propagated by patterns in language that were not only descriptive but, because they placed the objects of conversation on a scale leading to "true" Americanism, were highly evaluative too. Ethnicity helped define the boundary between American and alien and, derivatively, offered predictive models of group behavior that might be applied in day-to-day social transactions.

Although verbal images of the Irish shaped interethnic perception and attitude throughout the whole period 1820–1860, the stereotype doubtless had the most important consequences during the last decade and a half before the Civil War. For the late antebellum Irish stereotype seemed to draw boundaries not just between native-born and foreign, Protestant and Catholic, well-educated and ill, but between Celt and Saxon (or, more to the point, Anglo-American), setting the Irish outside the pale of "true" Americanism much more thoroughly and finally than the other principal white ethnic minorities in the United States. When the editors of the *Detroit Catholic Vindicator* observed during the mid-1850s that "the native American hate is more fiercely directed against the naturalized citizens of Irish descent than of any other foreign extraction," they were probably not being hyperbolic. Language propagated an image of the Irish that distinguished them not only from Anglo-Americans but even from other "immigrants" and "Catholics." This offers considerable support for historian Edward Pessen's comment on mid-nineteenth century America that "almost everywhere the Irish made a convenient scapegoat for disgruntled groups dissatisfied with other aspects of their lives."[2] The verbal image of the Irish circulated throughout the United States was insurance of this despite local variations in the circumstances of ethnic interaction and the sources of Anglo-American "dissatisfaction."

The very ubiquitousness of a standardized Irish stereotype in antebellum "conversation" requires us to take the prescriptive function of words seriously, placing in new perspective all sides of the endurant historiographical debate over the sources of prejudice encountered by Irish-Americans in the mid-nineteenth century. It certainly demands that we approach with caution any treatments implying that Anglo-American hostility toward immigrant minorities was sufficiently mechanistic to rise and fall in direct relation to confidence-shaking political, economic, or diplomatic developments—essentially the view John Higham took of anti-immigrant sentiment in the late nineteenth century and, in the opening sequence of *Strangers in the Land: Patterns of American Nativism*, projected back into the years before the Civil War. It should make us equally wary of attributions of interethnic prejudice primarily to more or less calculated material, political, or cultural competition between groups, pretty much the approach that Oscar Handlin, sometime Higham critic, made famous in successive editions of *Boston's Immigrants*.[3] Likewise, it necessarily cautions us against relating anti-immigrant attitudes to self-serving invention designed to salve social and psychic anxieties, approximately the position adumbrated by David Brion Davis in a couple of influential journal articles and subsequently elaborated by others. Arguing that antebellum immigrant stereotypes were projective mechanisms that cast national failings upon alien "enemies" and rallied a divided Anglo-American citizenry to the defense of common traditions, Davis indicated that the stereotypes bore only the scantest relation to their targets' objective character or to developments in intergroup relationships. For this reason, Davis suggested that perceptions of immigrants and Catholics were essentially interchangeable with the popular images of ideological minorities like Mormons and Masons.[4] Our suspicion of all these interpretive emphases is provoked not because interethnic attitudes in antebellum America were unaffected by economic frustration or intergroup rivalry or even psychological projection, but rather because it is apparent that these mechanisms could only work against the backdrop of culturally normative verbal stereotypes—like Paddy. Such verbal portraiture ensured that there were underlying dispositions toward the Irish perpetuated by language through the waxing and waning of the business cycle, through periods of social and political anxiety, and even through the vagaries of ethnic interaction. In the case of the Irish, furthermore, the content characteristics of verbal imagery suggest that the principal bases for those dispositions were not—as historians have sometimes surmised—simply historical anti-Catholicism or some notions about the "wild Irish" borrowed from English precedent.[5] The Irish stereotype—in either its early or late antebellum editions—indicates that Anglo-Americans were conditioned to see the Irish as Irish, not just as Catholics, and to see them from a distinctively American perspective. This is not to say that the verbal image of the Irish was shaped *only* by prevailing popularized understandings of character, ethnicity, and nationality. But these did form the vessels that held the *particular* verbal content of the stereotype at any point in time. The vessels were filled by observation and experience, self-interest and even invention. But, even so, Americans could only talk about what they "saw" in the Irish, and ideas about nationality and ethnicity would powerfully direct their vision to at least broad areas of conduct, character, and physical appearance.

The verbal image of the Irish in antebellum America was relatively resistant to conscious manipulation by any organization or interest, but the mind-set it encouraged could give much comfort to Americans with particular interests or anxieties at particular times. It could be exploited by nativists, although less well than we might anticipate. The late antebellum variant of the Irish stereotype, especially, placed some real limits upon the ability of anti-Catholic zealots and naturalization law "reformers" to capitalize upon ethnic prejudice. Nativist remedies simply did not seem to match the problems in ethnic diversity posed by the verbal image of the Irish. Still, when it came to organizing a public meeting or raising a mob, nativists were able to tap a reservoir of discomfiture with the Irish traceable in no small part to the prevalence of a stereotype which treated them almost as an alien "race." The late antebellum stereotype probably offered more satisfaction to contemporaries who did not share nativists' enthusiasm for limiting the rights conferred by naturalization or for proscribing Roman Catholics but who did share their loudly announced anxiety about the divisive influences of sectionalism and the "demon of Party Spirit" in the mid-century republic.[6] Nativist theoreticians offered to suture the wounds in national harmony with common principles and common institutions (producing common "character"), but many other Anglo-Americans were liable to locate national salvation in "blood." For the understanding of nationality propagated in language—in ethnic stereotypes—attributed character, ideology, and institutions alike to that agency. This made it easy to hope that from Anglo-American blood the United States derived a fundamental unity that could never be completely sundered by regionalism or political partisanship.

The verbal image of the Irish must have offered some solace to those who shared a plaint (heard frequently in settings like New York's New England Society in the years around mid-century) that public opinion had become a dangerously "sovereign" agent in American political life. Public opinion brooked no restraint and was not subject to the institutional checks and balances of the Constitution. It was not only potentially tyrannical but was all too easily manipulated by parochial interests—"local feeling" George Perkins Marsh called them—armed with a printing press. But if the public mind was irresistibly directed by some predictable inner "impulse" or "law" then there was less reason to fear its will.[7] To anxious traditionalists of these views, ethnic stereotypes offered encouragement that nationality, national character, and national "impulse" resided in Anglo-American blood. "In the primal germ of nations and social bodies," Horace Bushnell told an appreciative audience in 1849, "there is a secret Form or Law present in them, of which their after-growth is scarcely more than an actualization or development."[8]

The verbal image of the Irish in its fully developed late-antebellum form was satisfying to the speculative members of American society; it was also satisfying to the active. Robert Wiebe points out that in a society characterized by considerable social and economic fluidity, it was difficult to judge the "character" or predict the objectives of individuals either by sustained experience or by connecting them with an occupation, family, or community. Instead, Wiebe writes, "What was no longer available through intimacy revealed itself through standardized tests of the external record, uniformly applicable criteria that could sort virtue and vice among people they [Americans] barely knew." Ethnic and racial stereotypes made effective "shorthand devices" that gave instant readings of character from mere inspection of behavior and appearance.[9] At a time of rapid European immigration, particularly, ethnic stereotypes were immediately applicable in day-to-day interpersonal transactions. Stereotypes—especially the Irish stereotype—also had utility for those who were not merely content to live in antebellum society but felt a compulsion to reform it. In the early antebellum period, an interpretation of personal and national character which traced virtue and intelligence to nurture was doubtless encouraging to those who wished to spread temperance or education and eliminate juvenile delinquency or crime. The perfectionist outlook which had spawned much reform set expectations that were hard to fulfill. "The unexampled growth of our country in population and wealth, and the power which, for good or for evil, is put into our hands, make it all-important that our mental and moral cultivation should keep pace with our material civilization," a New England essayist enthused. The nation was ripe for reform and its republican mission required it. When intemperance or crime did not evaporate as expected, reformers were reluctant to blame either the nation or the measures. There was some comfort to be taken in the late antebellum Irish stereotype that represented the character and condition of one rapidly accumulating portion of the population as borne in blood and resistant to much improvement.[10] But this stereotype, a pattern in the language of a whole society, was not the creation of frustrated reformers nor of any other constituency or interest group that may have incidentally benefited from it. No authentic societal stereotype is so manufactured or manipulated.

"The election of 1856 was the deathblow of the Know-Nothing Party, because it identified itself with slavery," Fr. Augustus Thébaud reminisced a quarter of a century later. "The permanent downfall of the enemies of the Church in the United States," observed the Catholic priest, "resulted from an outbreak of men's passions in another direction . . . Civil War."[11] Thebaud was certainly too optimistic about the impact of war upon American ethnic and religious prejudices. Just as his memoir was published in the early 1880s, anti-Catholicism was beginning to make loud noises in politics once again. And in just a few years' time, Republican state conventions in Ohio and Pennsylvania would add national immigration restriction to party campaign platforms. As both Paul Kleppner and Richard Jensen have demonstrated, ethnocultural animosities did not disappear from postbellum America.[12]

Thébaud was only right in the narrowest sense. Institutional nativism did not survive the Civil War—at least not in its familiar antebellum forms. A last-ditch effort to identify itself with the principle of Unionism failed to save the rump of the American party in the election of 1860. Only a handful of local chapters of a once-powerful nativist fraternity like the Order of United Americans limped through the war years and lived on as social lodges, their political influence gone.[13] But nativist enthusiasm, as we have seen, was scarcely coincident with the ethnic prejudices that—sustained by language—circulated among Anglo-Americans at large, and there is no reason to think that Know Nothingism's demise necessarily presaged a transformation in interethnic attitudes and relationships.

But, especially when it comes to assessing popular dispositions toward the Irish in America, historians often take Thébaud's side, agreeing that the Civil War weakened the most intense prewar ethnic hostilities. Their analyses are contingent upon what they take to be the principal sources of those animosities. Oscar Handlin, who traced antipathy to the Irish in antebellum Boston largely to ethnocultural rivalry, was bound to emphasize the reconciliation of Irish-American and Anglo-American cultures encouraged by war-

time patriotism and resurgent Anglophobia. Earlier, Marcus Lee
Hansen had advanced much the same argument, though in order
reversed, stressing the acculturative influences of war upon ethnic
minorities rather than the new cordiality of Anglo-Americans who
discovered that they needed immigrants' loyalty and labor in a time
of crisis. John Higham, who traced interethnic tension in antebell-
lum America to material and status rivalries exacerbated by nationalist insecurities, called the immediate post-Civil War era an "Age
of Confidence" in which relative prosperity and proven military
prowess made Anglo-Americans much more tolerant of social and
cultural diversity. Historians who emphasize the subjective nature
of anti-foreign hostility routinely notice that the outbreak of intersectional combat obviated the need to invent alien enemies in order
to build loyalty and community; there were enemies enough by the
spring of 1861.[14]

If popular dispositions toward the Irish were neither wholly
products of objective interethnic competition nor of subjective in-
traethnic anxiety but in large measure reactions to an ethnic stereotype that had become normative in antebellum "conversation," then
taking the Civil War as an important turning point in ethnic attitudes seems quite arbitrary. Certainly Father Thébaud's belief that
"the bravery and military virtues displayed on both sides; the
prominence given to the true patriotism of the Catholics" trans-
formed Anglo-Americans' regard for the Irish will not stand too
much scrutiny.[15] In the first place, it confuses dispositions toward
the Irish with dispositions toward Catholics—which the verbal image of the Irish in antebellum conversation suggests lacked identity.
In the second, it is much too sanguine about the effects of wartime
contact and camaraderie upon interethnic perceptions. Among
members of the armed forces, especially, intimacy did not always
build understanding. Unit rivalries and the cynical songs and jokes
that lightened camp life frequently intensified stereotypes rather
than diminished them. German-Americans, whose names and ac-
cents gave them special visibility, were particularly made the butt
of ethnocentric wartime humor. Anxious to maintain at least the
appearance of Anglo-American patriotism and commitment to victory, northern leaders announced that desertion from the battlefront
was "a crime of foreign rather than native birth."[16] This could only

reinforce prevailing extrinsic stereotypes which implied that behavior as well as physical appearance were functions of ethnicity.

Science and pseudoscience gave the late antebellum verbal image of the Irish intellectual legitimacy, of course. Mid-century ethnology, popularized through phrenology and its ilk, helped rationalize the connection between blood, character, behavior, and nationality. It was altogether predictable that the ethnological community would see the Civil War as an unparalleled opportunity to systematize the measurement of ethnic distinctiveness. After all, the armed forces pulled together hundreds of thousands of men from all classes and descents and delivered them into the hands of a variety of surgeons and inspectors. During 1863 and 1864, the United States Sanitary Commission tried to evaluate "the most important physical dimensions and personal characteristics" of some 16,000 northern soldiers. Most of the measurements taken would have been altogether familiar to the devotees of phrenology, physiognomy, and "physiology," for they not only included height, weight, and girth but also size and shape of the head and even facial angle. What seems especially striking about these studies, published as *Investigations in the Military and Anthropological Statistics of American Soldiers* four years after Appomattox, was the compilers' conviction that such measurements would not only clarify the external marks of ethnicity but also the internal. As was implicit in the late antebellum Irish stereotype in American conversation, physical appearance was connected with character and character was connected with "blood."[17]

If such wartime efforts to objectify ethnic differences—studies in "anthropometry," John S. Haller calls them—reinforced the conventional late antebellum understanding of the relationship between "blood" and nationality in general, they often challenged the content of the Irish stereotype, in particular. There was, as we have observed, a real fragility to the association of American nationality with a narrowly conceived "Anglo-American" ethnicity. As some of the scientific and pseudoscientific props for the verbal image of the Irish began to be knocked away, it was possible for the ethnic boundaries of the late antebellum period to be redrawn. The result would not be the rejection of the connection between nationality and blood altogether. The verbal image of the Irish had circulated too long in American conversation not to have enduring consequences for popular thought.

There is no question that Civil War "anthropometry" made much of blood but little of the culturally normative distinctions between the United States' principal white ethnic groups—locked up in verbal stereotypes—which had been standard in the late antebellum period. While the United States Sanitary Commission was taking its skull and body measurements of a few thousand men, the United States Army's Provost Marshal General's Bureau was embarked upon a much more ambitious examination of nearly half a million Union recruits. The results of this study directly challenged important elements of the late antebellum Irish stereotype. The *Statistics, Medical and Anthropological, of the Provost Marshal General's Bureau* indicated that the typical American adult male of Irish descent was neither so short, dark, and brawny nor as prone to insanity and disease as the conventional extrinsic image of the Irish would have it. The army's own measurements showed that the allegedly "tawny" or "mottled" Irish were, on balance, more fairly complected than either Anglo- or German-Americans. They were even less likely to be afflicted by skin diseases than the stereotypically clean and robust Germans. Findings like these did considerable violence to particular features of a particular ethnic stereotype. But there is, nonetheless, little doubt that the originators of the army study remained confident that interior and exterior character were traceable to the same sources and that "race" had a bearing upon nationality.[18]

It was also in the midst of the Civil War that the legitimate American scientific community first struggled with the implications of Charles Darwin's *The Origin of Species*. Despite their differences over the methods and conclusions of Darwin's research, American naturalists seemed agreed on one thing: the *Origin* drew attention to the ambiguity of all such terms as "varieties," "species," "tribes," "genera," and "races," whether they were applied to plants, to animals, or to human beings. Francis Bowen, a critic of Darwin's analysis, pointed out that it was becoming more and more clear that "the distinction between Varieties and Species is entirely vague and arbitrary," while Asa Gray, a supporter, concurred that such terms were always "subjective and ideal," applied or not applied "according to the bent of the naturalist's mind."[19] Although most of the

Anglo-American public was not aware of comments like these, they were common enough among intellectuals to draw into question some of the more extravagant late antebellum assertions about the extent of the differences between Celts and Saxons or Anglo-Americans. The extrinsic image of the Irish in words seemed well-matched with interpretations of ethnic differences that treated them as ineradicable "racial" differences, but it was likely to suffer—at least in some elite circles—when the fuzziness of terms like "race" and "tribe" was pointed out.

Obviously, all of this—Civil War anthropometry and Darwinian debate alike—led not so much to a repudiation of the association of "blood" with character and behavior as to a challenge to existing applications of that idea. As Charles Loring Brace explained in his *Races of the Old World* (1863):

> The mysterious and far-reaching property of blood—of Race, is becoming more and more recognized in modern science. That power whereby the most distant ancestor shall influence his remotest descendent, and—still more wonderful—that accumulated effect of a line of ancestors in the final progeny, so that a clear stream of inherited physical and mental peculiarities can flow unmingled through human history in every variety of external circumstances and internal influences—is something not to be lightly weighed in the philosophy of man or in the history of his actions.[20]

But Brace was not nearly so convinced as many students of "race" and nationality had been during the 1840s and 1850s that physical appearance was the best guide to descent. Throughout the world, and particularly in the United States, blood was too intermixed for physique to display the inherited propensities of individuals. Brace thought that language was a better indicator of ancestry and relationship. And similarities in language showed Brace that Celts and Saxons were not nearly of such different "blood" as had often been assumed—and as the verbal image of the Irish implied. They were close enough, anyway, to make intermixture of these ancestral types in America possible and probably desirable, as each would bring to the union characteristics born of distinctive experiences and customs. Brace implicitly questioned the form and contents of the extrinsic representation of the Irish in language, in particular; he said nothing, however, that challenged the connection of blood with temperament, morality, and habit, in general. He was insistent that blood was central to nationality, for the irresistible imperatives of blood gave each nation "its peculiar office and duty in the world's development."[21] This kind of analysis, especially its treatment of the "racial" compatibility of Celt and Anglo-American, was sufficiently widespread that by the mid-1870s there was considerable discussion among students of population about the "death" of the Anglo-American as a distinctive ethnic type. Concurrently, other terms were being coined to describe the United States' ethnic majority, terms like "Celtic-American," popularized by James Gordon Bennett of the *New York Herald*. As early as 1862, a committee of the United States House of Representatives had pronounced that the "natural" population of the nation was "the white race, whether Anglo-Saxon, Celt, or Scandinavian."[22]

But while arguments for the inclusion of Irish Celts in the core blood group of the American nation—granting them the prerequisite for full American nationality—accumulated during the Civil War era, new evidence was generated in ethnologic circles concerning the "racial" unsuitability of other peoples. The two phenomena were related. There was much approval among Americans who devoted sustained attention to such matters for the research of Swedish ethnologist Anders Retzius. Retzius's work, begun much earlier but published in America by the Smithsonian Institution on the eve of secession, had—as American ethnologist J. Aitken Meigs summarized it—"divided the races of man into two great groups according to the form of the head, or rather according to the ratio existing between the length and breadth of the skull." These two groups Retzius labeled the dolichocephaloe (long-heads) and the brachycephaloe (shortheads). The former allegedly included most of the native inhabitants of northern and western Europe, including *both* Celts and Saxons. The latter were represented by the native peoples of southern and eastern Europe, Africa, Asia, and the Americas.[23] This bifurcation of mankind was clearly related to such traditional ethnologic practices as phrenology, craniology, and the computation of facial angle. Yet because it avoided grand claims based upon the smallest alleged physiological differences, and because it employed sophisticated terminology, it seemed more "scientific" and won the endorsement of legitimate naturalists. The division of humanity into halves rather than parts, for example, proved attractive to New York University chemist and pre-Darwinian evolutionist John W.

Draper, who in *Thoughts on the Future Civil Policy of America* (1865) argued that the northern states of the Union had actually gained strength from the assimilation of immigrants from Ireland and Germany while the late rebellious southern states had been weakened by their relatively undiluted Anglo-American blood.[24] Still, northern blood remained essentially "homogeneous" because of the hereditary compatibility of Celts and Saxons. The principal differences between these tribes were of condition. Their physiological similarity was assured because both derived from the same climatic zone. The real differences between human types were between peoples of divergent climatic background, between peoples of the temperate zones and those of the tropics. No successful union of the two classes was possible, not only because of physical dissimilarity but also because of dissonant moral and intellectual capacities. The future of the United States, Draper insisted, depended upon "a common direction of thought" and the chief impediment was not the presence of persons bearing German or Irish ancestry but those exhibiting African. The crucial distinctions between peoples—at least as they affected nationality—were racial in the broadest sense, not ethnic.[25]

This too, ultimately, is where the "anthropometric" studies of Civil War soldiers seemed to lead. The Provost Marshal's *Statistics* had minimized ethnic differences; it maximized racial. And always, the exterior form of the examinees was connected with the interior character. United States Army surgeon Sanford Hunt thought that by taking "external measurements of the cranium" of black soldiers, it would be possible to ascertain not only their "comparative intellectuality" but even their "capacity to learn tactics."[26] If this did not conform to the antebellum ethnologic tradition which divided Americans into parts, not halves, it did carry on the ethnological premise, sustained in ethnic stereotypes, that there was unity between mind and body.

All of this should seem very familiar, for Civil War era science endorsed the premises of the antebellum phrenological pseudosciences and continued to make connections between physique, character, and conduct, confirming what had been rendered commonplace by the patterns in American language—that "blood" had something to do with capacity for good citizenship and thus with nationality. At the end of the Civil War, New Orleans physician

Josiah Nott could announce with the same confidence as New England Society orators before the rebellion that: "it must be remembered that man's civil history is a part of his *natural* history."[27]

Nott's remark actually appeared in a racist apologetic, which denounced General O. O. Howard and the work of the Freedmen's Bureau in the postwar South. "The Races of Men," Nott alleged, "if not distinct species, are at least *permanent varieties*" and the "instinct, reason, and intellect" of Negroes was so bound up with their physical nature that they could not function effectively in American society outside of slavery or some other custodial connection to whites.[28] Civil War science, which minimized ethnic distinctions, played right into the hands of unreconstructed racists like Nott, for it suggested that the really important social and national boundaries were not between the "races" of northwestern Europe at all but between much larger classes of human beings. It could easily be taken as a vindication of antebellum African colonizationists like southern magazinist J. B. D. DeBow, who had insisted that American nationality rested on a "physiologic principle," which was the adaptability of all white blood to "true" Americanism and the inadaptability of all black.[29]

The association of nationality with blood—but not with ethnicity—was cheerfully endorsed by the Irish themselves. In 1864 an anti-Lincoln, antiwar, Democratic campaign newspaper, the *New York (Caucasian) Day Book*, played upon the sensitivity of Irish-American voters to the stereotyped perception that they were representatives of an inferior "race" by attributing a "recent pamphlet entitled 'Miscegenation' " to the Administration. This fabrication read, in part, "there is the strongest reason for believing that the first movement towards amalgamation in this country will take place between the Irish and negroes. The fusion, whenever it takes place, will be of infinite service to the Irish. They are a more brutal race and lower in civilization than the negro. The Irish are coarse-grained, revengeful, unintellectual, with few of the finer instincts of humanity."[30] This ploy was bound to have some effect among the Irish not only because, as historians have regularly pointed out, it appealed to the racism and status anxiety common among the mid-nineteenth century urban working class, but because there seemed to be some basis for the sentiments the bogus publication expressed in the patterns of Anglo-American conversation—in the

Irish stereotype. It was during the Civil War that Americans were first able to read the book that English actress Frances Kemble had made out of the diary she kept while mistress of a Georgia plantation twenty-five years earlier. One of her observations was that the more closely Irish and black Americans were equated with one another (she personally thought the resemblance between the "low Irish" and southern slaves remarkable), the greater the hostility between the two.[31] In any event, Irish-Americans were sure to be enthusiastic about any treatment of American nationality that stressed the relevance of "race" while putting the Irish safely within an Anglo-Celtic racial majority. In California Irish-Americans would be most aggressive in claiming the privileges of "white" Americans in contradistinction to nonwhites, assuming virtual leadership of efforts to expel Chinese immigrants and in so doing earning a reputation as "Irish Know-Nothings."[32]

Given the sustained popularity of the notion that nature and nationality were closely related, it is perhaps not surprising that when, in 1868, the Congress of the United States finally passed an expatriation act which specifically affirmed the right of naturalized citizens to renounce prior allegiance, it made no provision for Americans to exercise the same privilege. Such equivocation suggested that the critique of perpetual allegiance implied in the legislation was more practical in motive than ideological. Indeed, it was precipitated by some specific incidents in foreign relations. There is little wonder that the Fourteenth and Fifteenth Amendments to the Constitution of the United States did not effecively secure the citizenship of black Americans. For fastened in common culture was the idea that whatever their legal status blacks still lacked the nature that qualified them to be "true" Americans. This made southern efforts to separate state from federal citizenship all the more morally palatable. As Frederick Douglass observed when the Supreme Court endorsed such a distinction in the *Slaughterhouse* cases of 1873, the effect was to create "two citizenships" and thus no citizenship for black Americans at all if citizenship implied a natural right to nationality and all of its privileges.[33]

During the antebellum period of American history, ethnicity was a concept bound up tightly with the popular understanding of nationality. Americans' conception of what constituted an ethnic group and their perception of what seemed to be the most important indicators of ethnicity were channeled by the connection of nationality with "character" and by changing notions about the seat of "character" itself. Popular pseudosciences like phrenology, which met Americans' demand for a way to objectify character assessment, identified the areas of behavior and appearance worth scrutinizing. These ideas became locked up in ordinary language, in ethnic stereotypes. The verbal image of the Irish especially, because of its ubiquitousness, propagated these understandings and made them normative in common culture.

But even with the help of confirmative stereotypes which prescribed perception, the late antebellum understanding of American nationality, which made it coincident with a narrowly conceived "Anglo-American" ethnicity, could not easily be sustained. The real distinctions—especially physical distinctions—between putative Saxons who could acquire American nationality and putative Celts who could not were simply too obscure (if they existed at all). Consequently, the endurance of such an understanding relied heavily upon the theoretical underpinning of popular ethnology, which postulated that character differences between ethnic groups—linked to physical form—*must* exist.

During the Civil War era some of the ethnological props to the popular understanding of nationality and ethnicity and, derivatively, to prevailing ethnic stereotypes, were permanently weakened. Ethnological "research," as noted, increasingly divided the peoples of the world and the people of the United States into halves rather than parts. Systematic discourse about this research circulated only in scientific or pseudoscientific circles. But ethnology had so long been such a favorite subject in the mass media that popularized renderings of such material soon circulated much more widely. They were, if nothing else, put into the service of racists like Nott who found a receptive audience in the postwar South. And, doubtless, by positing a "racial" kinship between Anglo-Americans and Irish-Americans, they intersected with all the wartime developments in ethnic relations that historians routinely discuss. The idea of a "Celtic-American" ethnicity, for example, certainly held appeal for Anglo-Americans anxious for assurance of Irish-American loyalty in the secession crisis. It was attractive to the Irish themselves, who recognized that their claim to "true"

Americanism was strengthened by their wartime services, military and civilian. And it conformed with the postwar mood of national self-congratulation over having survived a great crisis and having closed a breach—significantly, a breach between white men.

None of this forced Americans to jettison in its entirety the prevailing stereotype of the Irish. Paddy was too well-established in the patterns of American "conversation" for anything so revolutionary. But it did mean that, progressively, verbal portraiture became charged with a different significance. To the extent that "ethnicity" lost its synonymical relation to "race," stereotyped renderings of Irish conduct and physical appearance forfeited their capacity to reveal inherent character. Americans' gradual withdrawal of faith from phrenology and physiognomy made character analysis from observation of temple, brow, and chin suspect. Stereotyped distinctions between Irish and Anglo-Americans remained but could easily be taken as cultural rather than as "racial" distinctions. Paddy was still capable of nourishing interethnic hostility— ethnocultural hostility.

The redirection of Paddy was a long-term process; two more decades passed after the Civil War before references to the Irish as a separate "race" disappeared from ethnological discussion. As Barbara Miller Solomon points out, it was not until the late 1880s that leading exponents of an Anglo-Saxonist nationalism began to treat the Irish as honorary Saxons. But there is some reason to doubt the conclusion of L. P. Curtis, Jr., that the height of Anglo-Saxonist derision of the Irish was not reached until after the mid-1860s.[34] Notwithstanding the increasingly simianized portraits of the Irish in Thomas Nast's highly visible postwar cartoons of urban life, the verbal stereotype that could sustain such caricatures in the public imagination had long since peaked. This is not to say that in the 1870s and 1880s Paddy had shed all of its malign qualities but only that the stereotype was beginning to lose some of its bite, taking on a gentler comic quality for which it would be most remembered in the twentieth century.

The reversion of Paddy to an ethnocultural stereotype gave scant comfort to other racial and ethnic minorities. In fact, the late antebellum form of the stereotype left an unhappy legacy, for it had helped circulate very widely certain ideas about the centrality of "blood" or peoplehood to nationality. That language no longer seemed to treat the Irish as a "race" was no help to other groups still defined in that fashion, blacks and other nonwhites, and also the immigrants from the eastern and southern margins of Europe arriving in the United States at an accelerated rate toward the end of the nineteenth century.

The collapse of the late antebellum "racial" image of the Irish represented the collapse of a perception of the population of the United States as divided into many parts, some more qualified and some less qualified for American nationality. In its place grew a perception of a population divided into halves: "Anglo-Saxons" (or "Anglo" and "Celtic-Americans") and everyone else. This may only have had a marginally intensifying effect upon racist perceptions of the unsuitability of blacks for "true" Americanism; nevertheless it was liable to have a greater impact upon the perception of Asian immigrants and still more important consequences for the perception of "Mediterraneans" and "Slavs," laying the foundation for late nineteenth century "scientific" nativism. The verbal image of the Irish in antebellum America took "ethnology" out of the hands of the ethnologists and put it into common language. Patterns in language shaped popular ethnic attitudes before the Civil War and would continue to shape American thought in the years that followed.

Appendix A: Content Analysis

Practitioners of content analysis look for different things in language. They may be interested in identifying syntactical patterns (conventions in sentence structure, punctuation, and phraseology) or stylized diction (word use patterns or vocabularies) or the use or repetition of a specific word or words. In prospecting for a particular stereotype in antebellum language, I have been concerned principally with diction, especially with identifying patterns among the adjectives and predicate nominatives routinely employed in "conversation" of all sorts to characterize Irish appearance, behavior, capability, condition, and belief.

The language units treated by content analysis can be space, symbols, or themes. The relative space devoted to any topic in a message or collection of messages offers a measure of concern or attitudinal salience. This study focuses upon symbols and themes. Psychologists sometimes elicit verbal stereotypes by asking people to select from a list of adjectives those they feel best apply to particular social groups. These are "closed" tests; the respondents must work with the verbal data given them. Historians, obviously, cannot restrict the universe of data in this way. The descriptive adjectives applied to the Irish in antebellum American "conversation" constitute an "open" vocabulary of indeterminate size. I am interested in the particular words that made up this vocabulary, but especially—since the words are so many—in themes and patterns, the distribution of words among meaningful categories. The relative size of each category may provide information about both the content of the stereotype and the process of stereotyping. By this means one may determine what it was about the Irish—putatively, anyway— that drew the most (and the least) comment. Through it, one can say with some confidence, "This was the stereotype; here are the words." Moreover, it can reveal the *style* of antebellum interethnic description, especially whether language highlighted characteristics apparently conditional, dependent on circumstances, or those apparently innate, allegedly products of descent. The way is opened for comparison between the various media of "conversation" and between points in time.

The direction and degree of evaluativeness conveyed by the language applied to Irish subjects is also important. I anticipated finding considerable consistency in evaluative tone among similar communications treating the Irish during a particular time interval. Otherwise nothing like a genuine stereotype would exist. One might even look for evaluative consistency among diverse kinds of sources, in so doing gauging the representativeness of sources. Changes in the social and intellectual environments in which stereotypes subsist, furthermore, ought to produce changes in the favorability or unfavorability of language over time.

A commonplace technique for measuring the evaluative quality of text is "evaluative assertion analysis." It considers both the meaning and the grammatical context of words revelatory of underlying dispositions toward the object of conversation. This procedure involves analysis of subunits of communication—nothing as clear-cut and convenient as words but rather "assertions." A complex sentence may carry several descriptive statements or assertions, none of them in a simple declarative form. We can, however, recast such a sentence into one or more declarative statements in which the subject is described by a single adjective or a predicate nominative.[1] Evaluative assertion analysis helps us determine the effective character of language in a systematic way. It takes into account both descriptive terminology and the directness and certainty of attribution implied by verb form. By assigning numerical values to descriptive adjectives (and predicate nominatives) and verbs alike, we can compute a mean evaluative score for all assertions contained in a single source of verbal data, in a particular type of source, in all "conversation" within a certain time span, or in all text sampled.

Applied to an appropriate sample of antebellum "conversation," these content analytic techniques can help us identify and explore the treatment of the Irish in language, and can help us understand the role of words in shaping and propagating American ethnic attitudes. The power of such analysis is increased by using the same procedures to examine smaller, but in other respects comparable, samples of verbal data in which Anglo-Americans described other ethnic minorities and depicted themselves, in which contemporary Englishmen described the Irish, and in which avowed nativists treated the same targets.

"In principle," writes Morris Janowitz, "content analysis implies the standard procedures of scientific investigation: the formulation of explicit propositions, the development of categories of analysis, and the collection of standardized bits of information in order to assess the adequacy of the initial formulation."[2] The propositions for fulfilling these prescriptions in this study of "Paddy" are clear:

1. There *was* a verbal image of the Irish—a dedicated sublanguage of adjectives and predicate nominatives—in ordinary American "conversation."
2. This sublanguage was different from those applied to other white ethnic groups or to "immigrants" generically.
3. It had particular emphases which directed attention to specific areas of conduct, character, condition, affiliation, and physical appearance.
4. This word image was sustained across diverse media of antebellum public "conversation."
5. Despite its consensual and habitual nature, the image changed over time.

[1] See Ithiel de Sola Pool, "Trends in Content Analysis Today: A Summary," 194–95, and Charles E. Osgood, "The Representational Model and Revelant Research," 41, in Ithiel de Sola Pool, ed., *Trends in Content Analysis* (Urbana, Ill., 1959).
[2] Morris Janowitz, "Harold D. Lasswell's Contribution to Content Analysis," *Public Opinion Quarterly* 32 (1968), 647.

The "standardized bits of information" in this study are of three kinds; in the first instance, words: adjectives and predicate nominatives; in the second instance, "unit-perceptions," declarative statements containing a single descriptive reference to the Irish (a single adjective or predicate nominative) fashioned from ordinary (and usually more complicated) sentences; finally, documents, items which represent media of "conversation" touching upon the Irish, the bearers of both descriptive words and remanufactured sentences (unit-perceptions). These "bits" have been culled from diverse media of antebellum conversation selected to cut across region, class, and interest. (A separate appendix treats the criteria of selection.)

To test the propositions, I subjected bits of information, by classes, to two analyses. The first—and probably the most useful—is categorization of the descriptive terms applied to the Irish in the sample of conversation. The second is evaluative assertion analysis, intended to measure the affective quality of each unit-perception of the Irish and of the documents bearing them.

As mentioned in the text, social psychologist Howard Ehrlich has published a system of ethnic adjective classification, which, with a little modification to suit historical data, met my needs. The fifteen word categories in my adaptation of this system bring together terms referring to related forms of conduct, character, condition, affiliation, and appearance. By distributing descriptive references to the Irish among these categories I was able to determine the particular emphases of verbal imagery within sources, across sources, and over time. Categorizing the words led to the verbal image of the Irish. Table 1 describes the categories and offers examples of their constituents.

This study relies heavily upon the most elemental content analytic procedure, the frequency count. What can we do with the numbers generated by these tabulations? This comes close to being—but is not quite—an exercise in "qualitative" content analysis. A purely qualitative study of text is more concerned with the mere presence or absence of words or expressions than with their frequency, focusing upon the internal characteristics of communications. Often it is used to study data samples of small size, a single document perhaps or a series of communications produced by a single source.[3] This study, however, deals with a large and diverse document sample, although presence or absence of words and themes is important to it—for example, descriptions of Irish political and religious proclivities or discussions of Irish physical features and intellectual capacities. This study is also concerned with quantity/frequency—although in a somewhat restricted sense. Relatively speaking, how much *more* present was one word or class of words than other words or themes directed at the Irish in antebellum conversation? Can one rank presence? What symbols appear *most* often in a sample of text? Which appear second most often, third, last? To answer such questions is, in a sense, to perform qualitative content analysis with vectors which indicate word relationships and the direction of changes in word use patterns.

This study established the descriptive emphases of language by simple counting and percentage ranking. It makes no assumptions about "normal"

[3] For a discussion of qualitative content analysis see Alexander L. George, "Quantitative and Qualitative Approaches to Content Analysis," in de Sola Pool, *Trends in Content Analysis* (Urbana, Ill., 1959), 11.

TABLE 1: *Categories of Ethnic Description*

Characteristic	Analysis	Examples from sampled text
1. Positive Relational	"denote the target group's positive interpersonal qualities." They either "depict the target group and its members as familiar or no different than others" (Type 1) or "emphasize those characteristics which make the group members desirable and attractive interpersonal partners" (Type 2).	friendly, generous, good-hearted, kind, merry, affectionate, compassionate, eloquent, happy, hospitable, jolly, merciful, obliging, tolerable, warm
2. Positive Intellectual	"denote the intellectual abilities for realistic and creative behavior of the target group and its members."	educated, ingenious, intellectual, judicious, learned, shrewd, witty
3. Positive Moral	"depict target group values and/or member behavior as self-directed, sincere, and principled."	brave, honest, courageous, faithful, stout-hearted, valorous
4. Negative Relational	"denote the target group's negative interpersonal qualities." They either "depict the target group and its members as strange or alien as opposed to familiar and native" (Type 1) or "emphasize those characteristics which make group members undesirable and unattractive interpersonal partners" (Type 2).	boastful, curious, droll, extraordinary, familiar, impertinent, impudent, selfish, singular, sorrowful, unnatural, amusing, condescending, flattering, funny, inconsiderate, ingratiating, insolent, loquacious, meddling, mournful, odd, outlandish, preposterous, provoking, saucy, shocking, strange, troublesome, ungrateful, vexing
5. Negative Intellectual	"denote the intellectual deficits, ignorance, or naivete of the target group and its members."	blundering, brainless, crazy, ignorant, illogical, nonsensical, simple, stupid, uneducated, confused, foolish, illiterate, pliant, superstitious
6. Negative Moral	"depict target group values and/or member behavior as immoral, deceptive, or unprincipled."	cheating, devilish, thieving, villainous, contriving, depraved, dishonest, lying, mischievous, scheming, untruthful, wicked
7. Conflict/ Hostility	indicate "aggressiveness, conflict, or hostility as descriptive of relations with the target group or as interpersonal characteristics of target group members."	criminal, dangerous, ferocious, fighting, pugnacious, quarrelsome, savage, violent, bloodthirsty, bold, brutal, enraged, hot-tempered, lawless, terrifying, unrelenting, unruly, vicious.
8. Substantial	"depict the target group and its members as possessing the	ambitious, industrious, self-assured, useful

TABLE 1: (*continued*)

Characteristic	Analysis	Examples from sampled text
	qualities of industry, energy, and direction (Type 1) or of "continuity and persistence" (Type 2).	
9. Insubstantial	"depict the target group and its members as being capricious, fleeting, unreliable, and without direction."	fanciful, gaming, idle, improvident, lazy, light-hearted, childish, grinning, joking, playful, reckless, silly
10. Emotional	"depict the emotionality and emotional sensitivity of the target group."	dancing, drunken, frisky, gay, loving, roaring, boisterous, emotional, enthusiastic, excited, frolicking, imaginative, intemperate, lusty, romantic, temperamental
11. Political/ Religious	"describe the political and religious institutions, beliefs, and activities of the target group."	patriotic, Catholic, heathen, Jesuitical, liberty-loving, nationalistic
12. Economic	refer "to the economic status, economic attitudes, or economic relations of the target group with the dominant group."	poor, unsuccessful, begging, distressed, vagrant
13. Aesthetic/ Cultural	"relate to or deal with the arts and artistic appreciation or excellence in taste as generally associated with the quality of being cultured."	wild, rude, unsophisticated
14. Physical	"refer to the physical qualities of the target group and its members." They may refer to "directly visible and external physical characteristics such as color, physique, or physiognomy" or to "physical qualities which are visible only in behavior such as athletic ability" or even to "a present physical state such as clean or dirty."	big, broad-shouldered, brutish, clumsy, coarse-haired, dark-eyed, deep-chested, dirty, fair, florid, muscular, prolific, red-haired, stout, tall, wide-mouthed, awkward, bright-eyed, colored, dark, fat, four-legged, hungry, large, low-browed, masculine, oleaginous, ragged, round-faced, sickly, singular-looking, strong, thin, wild-looking
15. Group Subjective	describe general impressions of the target group rather than specific characteristics. They are normally highly evaluative.	miserable, cursed, detestable, infernal, offensive, unfortunate, unlucky, worthless, wretched.

NOTE: Table 1 draws upon Howard J. Ehrlich's "Preliminary Dictionary for the Classification of Ethnic Stereotypes," quoting selectively a number of Ehrlich's category descriptions. For Ehrlich's original formulation, see Ehrlich, *The Social* distributions of verbal data, nor does it study attitude salience that might require higher orders of statistics.[4] My principal interest here is in relative frequencies. Because there is only one independent variable in this study, objects of the appellation "Irish," there is no need to perform any sort of multiple classification analysis, which would be the case if we were trying to determine the relative impact of ethnicity—compared to the impact of age, class, occupation, or other variables—upon descriptive word choice.[5]

Among 2,255 "unit-perceptions" of the Irish, Germans, "immigrants," and Anglo-Americans in antebellum texts sampled for this study, 392 different descriptive terms recur. Table 2 shows the distribution of this "dictionary" of ethnic adjectives among the fifteen categories of the modified Ehrlich classification system.

The content characteristics of the antebellum "dictionary" are remarkably similar to those of a modern ethnic adjective dictionary compiled by Howard Ehrlich from the research literature of contemporary social psychology. Table 3 places the two dictionaries side by side. A simple "eyeball" comparison scarcely indicates identity between the two dictionaries, but it does suggest that the *kinds* of words employed for interethnic description in the mid-nineteenth century were not so very different from those used in the mid-twentieth. If there have been major evolutionary developments in the treatment of the Irish, and other ethnic groups, in American language, they must appear primarily in changing patterns of word use rather than in the raw material of conversation—words—themselves.

Even within the confines of the period 1820–1860, patterns of language used to describe the Irish in America did change. Table 4 summarizes the application of ethnic adjective classification to 1,592 unit-perceptions of the Irish taken from a sample of antebellum "conversation." It suggests the existence of a specific language of ethnic description—different from the ethnic adjective dictionary that was its raw material—that changed over time. Table 4 also satisfies the need for assurance that such a language was sustained across different media for public "conversation." If the distinctive content patterns discovered above are really no more than the composite of many subpatterns in different sorts of text, each wandering off in a different direction, it should give us pause. We might not be dealing with a reflexive societal stereotype at all, but instead, with a series of manipulated caricatures or at least differentiable subcultural stereotypes. The format and audience for different kinds of printed material had an impact upon language use; still, if the divergences are too pronounced we may justifiably wonder whether particular communicators were not adjusting their treatment of the Irish to fit their own peculiar needs. In that case, the spontaneity—the inci-

Psychology of Prejudice: A Systematic Theoretical Review and Propositional Inventory of the American Social Psychological Study of Prejudice (New York, 1973), 26–27. Used by permission.

[4] For some constraints on using higher order statistics see Sydney Siegel, *Nonparametric Statistics for the Behavioral Sciences* (New York, 1956), 3, 19, 31.

[5] For an example of multiple classification analysis in a content analytic study see Jane Range and Maris A. Vinovskis, "Images of the Elderly in Popular Magazines: A Content Analysis of *Littell's Living Age*, 1845–1882," *Social Science History* 5 (Spring 1981), 123–70.

TABLE 2: *An Antebellum "Dictionary" of Ethnic Adjectives*

Word list		Assigned value	Word list		Assigned value
	CATEGORY 1:			**CATEGORY 3** (*continued*)	
	POSITIVE RELATIONAL		8	merciful	+3
1	affectionate	+2	9	moral	+3
2	cheerful	+2	10	stout-hearted	+3
3	elastic	+2	11	truthful	+3
4	eloquent	+2	12	valorous	+3
5	frank	+2	13	worthy	+3
6	friendly	+2		**CATEGORY 4:**	
7	generous	+2		**NEGATIVE RELATIONAL**	
8	gentle	+2	1	abject	—2
9	good-dispositioned	+2	2	amusing	—1
10	good-hearted	+2	3	arrogant	—2
11	good-humored	+2	4	audacious	—2
12	good-natured	+2	5	bigoted	—2
13	good-tempered	+2	6	blustering	—2
14	grateful	+2	7	boastful	—2
15	happy	+2	8	bothersome	—2
16	hospitable	+2	9	clannish	—1
17	jolly	+2	10	condescending	—2
18	kind	+2	11	curious	—1
19	merry	+2	12	demoralized	—2
20	obliging	+2	13	detached	—1
21	peaceable	+2	14	discourteous	—2
22	respectable	+1	15	dispirited	—2
23	sincere	+2	16	distrustful	—2
24	sociable	+2	17	droll	—2
25	taciturn	+2	18	extraordinary	—1
26	tender	+2	19	facetious	—2
27	tolerable	+1	20	familiar	—2
28	warm	+2	21	fearful	—2
	CATEGORY 2:		22	flattering	—2
	POSITIVE INTELLECTUAL		23	funny	—1
1	educated	+3	24	henpecked	—2
2	ingenious	+3	25	humorous	—1
3	intellectual	+3	26	ill-tempered	—2
4	inventive	+3	27	impertinent	—2
5	judicious	+3	28	importunate	—2
6	learned	+3	29	imposturing	—2
7	shrewd	+3	30	improprietous	—2
8	witty	+3	31	impudent	—2
	CATEGORY 3:		32	inauspicious	—1
	POSITIVE MORAL		33	inconsiderate	—2
1	brave	+3	34	indiscreet	—2
2	compassionate	+3	35	ingratiating	—2
3	courageous	+3	36	insolent	—2
4	faithful	+3	37	loquacious	—2
5	honest	+3	38	loud	—2
6	loyal	+3	39	meddling	—2
7	manly	+3	40	miraculous	—1
			41	morbid	—2

TABLE 2: *An Antebellum "Dictionary" of Ethnic Adjectives (continued)*

Word list	Assigned value	Word list	Assigned value
CATEGORY 4 (*continued*)		**CATEGORY 6:**	
		NEGATIVE MORAL	
42 mournful	−2		
43 noisy	−2	1 cheating	−3
44 odd	−1	2 contriving	−3
45 outlandish	−1	3 corrupting	−3
46 prejudiced	−2	4 cowardly	−3
47 preposterous	−1	5 debauched	−3
48 provoking	−2	6 degraded	−3
49 rude	−2	7 demoralizing	−3
50 saucy	−2	8 depraved	−3
51 selfish	−2	9 devilish	−3
52 shocking	−1	10 dishonest	−3
53 singular	−1	11 evil	−3
54 sorrowful	−2	12 immoral	−3
55 strange	−2	13 indecent	−3
56 talkative	−2	14 intriguing	−3
57 troublesome	−2	15 licentious	−3
58 unassimilable	−1	16 loose	−3
59 ungrateful	−2	17 lying	−3
60 unnatural	−1	18 mischievous	−3
61 vexing	−2	19 roguish	−3
62 vitrioloic	−2	20 scheming	−3
		21 shameless	−3
CATEGORY 5:		22 thieving	−3
NEGATIVE INTELLECTUAL		23 untruthful	−3
		24 unwholesome	−3
1 blundering	−3	25 villainous	−3
2 brainless	−3	26 wicked	−3
3 confused	−3		
4 crazy	−3	**CATEGORY 7:**	
5 credulous	−3	**CONFLICT/HOSTILITY**	
6 distracted	−3		
7 dull	−3	1 bloodthirsty	−3
8 foolish	−3	2 bold	−3
9 gullible	−3	3 brutal	−3
10 idiotic	−3	4 criminal	−3
11 ignorant	−3	5 dangerous	−3
12 illiterate	−3	6 disorderly	−3
13 illogical	−3	7 enraged	−3
14 incompetent	−3	8 ferocious	−3
15 inert	−3	9 fighting	−3
16 insulated	−3	10 hot-tempered	−3
17 naive	−3	11 lawless	−3
18 nonsensical	−3	12 militaristic	−3
19 pliant	−3	13 murderous	−3
20 simple	−3	14 pugnacious	−3
21 stupid	−3	15 quarrelsome	−3
22 superstitious	−3	16 resentful	−3
23 thick-headed	−3	17 riotous	−3
24 uneducable	−3	18 savage	−3
25 uneducated	−3	19 terrifying	−3
26 unintelligible	−3	20 tumultuous	−3

TABLE 2: *An Antebellum "Dictionary" of Ethnic Adjectives (continued)*

Word list		Assigned value	Word list		Assigned value
CATEGORY 7 (*continued*)			**CATEGORY 9** (*continued*)		
21	turbulent	−3	9	idle	−2
22	unrelenting	−3	10	improvident	−2
23	unruly	−3	11	inefficient	−2
24	vengeful	−3	12	joking	−2
25	vicious	−3	13	lazy	−2
26	violent	−3	14	light-hearted	−2
27	virulent	−3	15	mercurial	−2
			16	nomadic	−2
CATEGORY 8:			17	playful	−2
SUBSTANTIAL			18	reckless	−2
1	active	+3	19	restless	−2
2	ambitious	+3	20	silly	−2
3	businesslike	+3	21	wandering	−2
4	careful	+2			
5	cautious	+2	**CATEGORY 10:**		
6	deliberate	+2	**EMOTIONAL**		
7	enduring	+2	1	amorous	−2
8	enterprising	+3	2	animated	−2
9	hard-working	+3	3	boisterous	−2
10	independent	+3	4	dancing	−2
11	industrious	+3	5	delirious	−2
12	laborious	+2	6	drunken	−2
13	orderly	+2	7	emotional	−2
14	painstaking	+2	8	enthusiastic	−2
15	patient	+2	9	excited	−2
16	persevering	+2	10	frisky	−2
17	phlegmatic	+2	11	frolicking	−2
18	poised	+2	12	gay	−2
19	practical	+2	13	imaginative	−2
20	productive	+3	14	intemperate	−2
21	provident	+2	15	lively	−2
22	prudent	+2	16	lusty	−2
23	self-assured	+3	17	roaring	−2
24	self-reliant	+3	18	rollicking	−2
25	sensible	+2	19	romantic	−2
26	sober	+2	20	sanguine	−2
27	temperate	+2	21	self-indulgent	−2
28	useful	+2	22	sentimental	−2
29	well-managing	+2	23	temperamental	−2
			24	unrestrained	−2
CATEGORY 9:			25	vivacious	−2
INSUBSTANTIAL			26	vociferous	−2
1	carefree	−2			
2	careless	−2	**CATEGORY 11:**		
3	childish	−2	**POLITICAL/RELIGIOUS**		
4	dependent	−2	1	atheistic	−3
5	fanciful	−2	2	Catholic	−3
6	gaming	−2	3	conservative	−1
7	grinning	−2	4	heathen	−3
8	happy-go-lucky	−2	5	infidel	−3

TABLE 2: *An Antebellum "Dictionary" of Ethnic Adjectives (continued)*

Word list	Assigned value	Word list	Assigned value
CATEGORY 11 (*continued*)		**CATEGORY 14:**	
		PHYSICAL	
6 irreligious	−3	1 awkward	−1
7 irreverent	−3	2 bewhiskered	0
8 Jesuitical	−3	3 big	−1
9 liberty-loving	+3	4 big-fisted	−2
10 nationalistic	−3	5 blue-eyed	+1
11 obedient	−2	6 bright-eyed	+2
12 oppressed	−1	7 broad	−1
13 partisan	−2	8 broad-faced	−2
14 patriotic	−3	9 broad-shouldered	−1
15 pious	+3	10 brutish	−3
16 politically ambitious	−2	11 bulky	−1
17 priest-ridden	−3	12 clumsy	−1
18 Protestant	+3	13 coarse-featured	−2
19 radical	−3	14 coarse-haired	−3
20 religious	+3	15 colored	−3
21 servile	−2	16 dark	−3
22 Socialistic	−3	17 dark-eyed	−1
23 traditionalist	+1	18 deep-chested	+1
CATEGORY 12:		19 dirty	−3
ECONOMIC		20 diseased	−3
1 begging	−2	21 fair	+2
2 debt-ridden	−2	22 fat	−1
3 destitute	−2	23 florid	−2
4 distressed	−2	24 four-legged	−3
5 economical	+2	25 grey-eyed	+1
6 frugal	+2	26 hairy	−1
7 indigent	−2	27 handsome	+3
8 mean	−1	28 hardy	+2
9 miserly	−1	29 healthy	+3
10 pauper	−2	30 hungry	−1
11 poor	−1	31 incurable	−3
12 successful	+2	32 infirm	−2
13 thrifty	+2	33 inodorous	−3
14 unsuccessful	−2	34 insane	−3
15 vagrant	−2	35 large	−1
CATEGORY 13:		36 large-mouthed	−2
AESTHETIC/CULTURAL		37 leprous	−3
1 artistic	+2	38 light-haired	+1
2 barbarous	−3	39 lithe	+2
3 cultured	+3	40 low-browed	−3
4 literary	+2	41 masculine	−2
5 musical	+2	42 muscular	−1
6 poetic	+2	43 obese	−1
7 refined	+3	44 oleaginous	−3
8 rude	−2	45 physically-offensive	−3
9 unsophisticated	−2	46 prolific	−1
10 wild	−3	47 ragged	−2
		48 red-haired	−2

TABLE 2: *An Antebellum "Dictionary" of Ethnic Adjectives (continued)*

Word list	Assigned value	Word list	Assigned value
CATEGORY 14 *(continued)*		CATEGORY 15:	
49 robust	—1	GROUP SUBJECTIVE	
50 round-faced	—1	1 contemptuous	—3
51 short	—1	2 cursed	—3
52 sickly	—2	3 detestable	—3
53 simian	—3	4 infernal	—3
54 singular-looking	—1	5 loathsome	—3
55 small	—1	6 miserable	—3
56 solid	—1	7 offensive	—3
57 stout	—1	8 pitiable	—1
58 strong	+1	9 suffering	—1
59 thin	+1	10 unfortunate	—1
60 towheaded	+1	11 unlucky	—1
61 ugly	—3	12 worthless	—3
62 unkempt	—2	13 wretched	—3
63 wide-mouthed	—2		
64 wild-looking	—3		

TABLE 3: *Distribution of Items in Two Adjectival Dictionaries Among Fifteen Categories of Ethnic Description*

Category	Characteristic	Percent of items in modern dictionary (123 items)	Percent of items in antebellum dictionary (392 items)
1	Positive Relational	6%	7%
2	Positive Intellectual	7	2
3	Positive Moral	5	3
4	Negative Relational	24	16
5	Negative Intellectual	7	7
6	Negative Moral	7	7
7	Conflict/Hostility	6	7
8	Substantial	8	7
9	Insubstantial	7	5
10	Emotional	3	7
11	Political/Religious	7	6
12	Economic	3	4
13	Aesthetic/Cultural	2	3
14	Physical	8	17
15	Group Subjective	0	3

NOTE: For the sources of the modern dictionary see Ehrlich, *The Social Psychology of Prejudice*, 28.

TABLE 4: *Categorization of 1,592 Unit-Perceptions of the Irish in Antebellum Conversation by Source and Time Period*

1820–1844
(Number of observations: N = 598)

Category	Classification	Periodicals	Newspapers	School texts	Public documents	Popular nonfiction	Melodrama	Popular fiction	Total
1	Positive Relational	17%	0%	13%	0%	22%	5%	5%	12%
2	Positive Intellectual	5	0	8	0	6	0	0	4
3	Positive Moral	0	0	6	0	2	6	8	3
4	Negative Relational	12	15	14	6	2	20	10	13
5	Negative Intellectual	9	12	10	12	22	11	10	11
6	Negative Moral	4	15	4	6	2	6	5	5
7	Conflict/Hostility	11	27	6	18	6	4	5	9
8	Substantial	2	0	3	0	2	0	3	2
9	Insubstantial	11	2	12	18	6	5	3	9
10	Emotional	9	7	6	12	8	14	15	9
11	Political/Religious	4	5	3	6	8	4	0	9
12	Economic	1	5	4	0	2	1	3	4
13	Aesthetic/Cultural	3	3	3	18	2	3	0	3
14	Physical	8	2	4	6	6	16	33	9
15	Group Subjective	5	8	6	0	2	5	0	5

1845–1852
(Number of observations: N = 520)

Category	Classification	Periodicals	Newspapers	School texts	Public documents	Popular nonfiction	Melodrama	Popular fiction	Total
1	Positive Relational	17%	12%	20%	8%	10%	9%	14%	13%
2	Positive Intellectual	2	4	4	0	1	0	2	2
3	Positive Moral	2	12	2	2	3	1	2	2
4	Negative Relational	8	8	7	7	1	12	2	7

Category	Classification	Periodicals	Newspapers	School texts	Public documents	Popular nonfiction	Melodrama	Popular fiction	Total
5	Negative Intellectual	5	0	5	7	7	8	6	6
6	Negative Moral	4	8	6	5	8	6	6	6
7	Conflict/Hostility	15	4	19	5	6	20	22	15
8	Substantial	0	8	1	7	4	1	0	2
9	Insubstantial	8	4	6	15	10	5	2	7
10	Emotional	6	15	13	5	7	17	12	11
11	Political/Religious	4	8	0	0	7	1	0	2
12	Economic	1	4	4	10	11	5	4	5
13	Aesthetic/Cultural	1	4	2	0	6	2	4	3
14	Physical	18	8	6	24	16	12	22	14
15	Group Subjective	7	4	4	5	4	3	2	4

1853–1860

(Number of observations: N = 474)

Category	Classification	Periodicals	Newspapers	School texts	Public documents	Popular nonfiction	Melodrama	Popular fiction	Total
1	Positive Relational	15%	4%	27%	0%	16%	6%	8%	11%
2	Positive Intellectual	3	2	3	0	1	0	2	2
3	Positive Moral	0	0	3	0	4	2	0	1
4	Negative Relational	11	10	5	6	11	11	11	9
5	Negative Intellectual	9	10	5	6	7	15	8	10
6	Negative Moral	0	6	0	6	8	4	8	4
7	Conflict/Hostility	7	27	7	12	9	4	5	9
8	Substantial	3	6	0	9	1	1	0	2
9	Insubstantial	11	2	9	9	11	10	5	9
10	Emotional	11	12	9	18	9	15	8	12
11	Political/Religious	7	6	6	0	12	2	2	5
12	Economic	0	2	7	9	1	2	0	2
13	Aesthetic/Cultural	1	6	3	3	4	7	2	4
14	Physical	22	2	13	21	0	23	47	19
15	Group Subjective	3	4	3	3	7	0	2	2

dental quality—of references to the Irish in most "conversation" would be suspect.

There is no such problem with Paddy. The word usage pattern for treatments of Irish subjects measured by the distribution of descriptive terms across content categories is remarkably similar for all seven principal types of literature sampled. The anomalies are predictable. In newspapers a disproportionate share of unit-perceptions focused upon allegedly violent or disorderly behavior (Category 7: Conflict/Hostility)—to the exclusion of some alternative descriptions. But, of course, it was in newspapers that the Irish appeared most often in the context of riot or crime. Not surprisingly, best-selling fiction over-represented the physical description of Irish characters; one would expect writers of fiction to portray in words characters not available to the reader for sustained physical inspection. Public documents also stressed the physical description of Irish subjects. Logic fails us here. But close examination of the individual sources suggests that many public reports touching upon the Irish discussed the medical and sanitary condition of immigrants and immigrant neighborhoods. In these, of course, physical descriptives were prominent. Once the anomalous cases are accounted for, we discover substantial agreement about the relative importance of different kinds of ethnic descriptives in different kinds of text. Conflict/Hostility, Emotionality, and Negative Intellectual Characteristics were among the most over-represented categories in nearly all source types. By contrast, Positive Moral (e.g., "honest," "faithful"), Aesthetic/Cultural (e.g., "rude," "unsophisticated"), Substantial (e.g., "ambitious," "industrious"), and Positive Intellectual Characteristics (e.g., "shrewd," "witty") were repeatedly among the most poorly-represented categories. These patterns are accentuated when the antebellum period is divided into three segments, 1820–1844, 1845–1852, and 1853–1860, and the word usage examined by source type for each of these in turn.

Since comparison is my purpose—between sources and across intervals of time—evaluative assertion analysis was also helpful. Conducting evaluative assertion analysis, which seeks to establish the relative favorability of a source of verbal data toward an object of description, requires recasting ordinary sentences into uniform unit-perceptions. Each unit-perception contains an adjective or predicate nominative and a verb representing the directness of attribution in the original sentence. If numerical values are given to both descriptives and verbs according to a formula that awards positive numbers ($+3$ to $+1$) to the most direct forms of attribution and most favorable descriptives but negative ones (-1 to -3) to the most conditional attributions and unflattering descriptives, the blanks can be filled in an arithmetic equation summarizing the evaluative character of any single assertion on a scale of -9 (least favorable) to $+9$ (most favorable). By averaging such scores one can obtain a mean favorability coefficient for a single document or for an entire class of documents. Again, these are relative measures. Evaluative assertion analysis offers an alternative to word classification for measuring stereotype consistency and stereotype change. Table 5 demonstrates the assignment of numerical values in an evaluative assertion analysis.

The chief hazard in evaluative assertion analysis is inconsistency in assignment of values to the components of each evaluative assertion or unit-perception. One can eliminate some of the subjectivity—and thus inconsistency—from this procedure by requiring particular value assignations for

TABLE 5: *Evaluative Assertion Analysis Computation*

Column: Contents:	1 Source	2 Attitude Object	3 Verbal Connector	4 Value of Column 3	5 Descriptive Term	6 Value of Column 5	7 Product of Cols. 4 × 6
Sample:	Mr. Buffer	"Paddy"	is	+3	brainless	−3	−9

Direction/Intensity Values

Verbal connectors are either associative (+) or disassociative (−); their intensity may be established by reference to the following formula:

+3 strong intensity: "to be," "to have," unqualified simple verbs in the present tense

+2 moderate intensity: verbs implying imminent, partial, probable, and incremental relationships; simple verbs in other tenses than the present; modal auxiliary verb forms, e.g. "used to be"

+1 weak intensity: verbs implying possible or hypothetical relationships

Descriptive terms acquire direction and intensity values according to the category of ethnic description to which they are assigned (Table 1):

1 Positive Relational	Type 1:	+1	Type 2:	+2	
2 Positive Intellectual		+3			
3 Positive Moral		+3			
4 Negative Relational	Type 1:	−1	Type 2:	−2	
5 Negative Intellectual		−3			
6 Negative Moral		−3			
7 Conflict/Hostility		−3			
8 Substantial	Type 1:	+3	Type 2:	+2	
9 Insubstantial		−2			
10 Emotional		−2			
11 Political/Religious		−3 to +3			
12 Economic		−2 to +2			
13 Aesthetic/Cultural		−3 to +3			
14 Physical		−3 to +3			
15 Group Subjective		−1 to −3			

NOTE: For an effective summary of the coding and scaling procedures of evaluative assertion analysis, the basis for Table 5, see Robert C. North, Ole R. Holsti, M. George Zaninovich, and Dina A. Zinnes, *Content Analysis: A Handbook for the Study of International Crisis* (Evanston, Ill., 1963), 92–96.

particular verb forms. How values are to be assigned to adjectives or predicate nominatives is a different matter. Here, experience with word counting and categorizing can help. To categorize descriptive terms according to Ehrlich's scheme is to say that the words in any single class are alike in some important respect, that they all point to the same area of human appearance, conduct, or capacity. Similarity is also liable to extend to evaluation. By assigning values to whole categories of words—or, in a few cases, subcategories—I could both ease and systematize the valuation of the terms to be treated by evaluative assertion analysis. As a descriptive term is assigned to an emphasis category, it takes on a numerical value. This does not make valuation completely objective or automatic; there is considerable subjectivity in assigning values to descriptive categories because it involves making a judgment about how Americans a century and a half ago regarded particular human characteristics. No one ought to be better suited to do this than historians. Still, words can change meaning, change category, and change value by their context, and any judgment about this will be a subjective one. Whether this is a serious difficulty for an exercise in content analysis can be gauged by comparing the work of two or more evaluators working independently on the same textual sample using a simple percentage agreement index. In this study of the treatment of the Irish in antebellum language, three evaluators working with a trial sample of 288 unit-perceptions managed 271 agreements and only 11 disagreements in assigning descriptive terms to categories and values. This 96 percent agreement rate gave me some confidence that the evaluative process used here is reliable and resistant to capricious judgments.[6]

In the incidental "conversation" of antebellum America, Irish subjects were much more likely to be treated by some *kinds* of words than by others. These directed attention to particular areas of human conduct, appearance, or belief and slighted alternatives. This sublanguage had a very pronounced character. It also carried with it a particular disposition toward or evaluation of its subject, a product not only of the meaning of the descriptive terms but also of their context within sentences. The mean evaluative assertion analysis score for all 1,592 unit-perceptions examined was −4.6, with a standard deviation from the mean of 3.1. The evidence is clear that most treatments of the Irish in antebellum discourse were quite censorious, although most of the "assertions" about the Irish in the material analyzed did not begin as assertions at all but referred to the Irish only in passing, in descriptive idioms used reflexively and without polemical intent.

I found not only consistency in content, in emphasis, among different kinds of sources for treatments of the Irish in antebellum "conversation" but also consistency in implied evaluation. The mean evaluative assertion analysis scores for documents in each variety of text were all decidedly negative, with standard deviation values low enough to indicate that departures into favorable evaluation were infrequent. In general, the more negative the mean evaluation for any particular source type, the smaller the standard deviation of the data—that is, the greater the agreement between individual communicators. Apparently, those communicators offering more charitable assessments of the Irish through their use of language were most likely to be deviating

[6] Richard L. Merritt employs this coding reliability test in his content analytic study *Symbols of American Community, 1735–1775* (New Haven, 1966), 200.

TABLE 6: *Evaluative Assertion Analysis for Treatments of the Irish in Seven Media of American "Conversation"*

Medium and measure	1820–1844	1845–1852	1853–1860	1820–1860
Journals:				
Mean EAA Score	−3.3	−3.0	−3.3	−3.3
Standard Deviation	3.9	4.2	4.5	4.2
Newspapers:				
Mean EAA Score	−7.8	−1.5	−6.0	−5.7
Standard Deviation	0.9	4.2	3.6	2.4
Texts:				
Mean EAA Score	−3.3	−2.4	−1.8	−3.0
Standard Deviation	2.7	1.5	4.2	2.7
Public Documents:				
Mean EAA Score	−7.8	−3.9	−6.9	−6.0
Standard Deviation	0.3	5.1	0.9	3.3
Nonfiction:				
Mean EAA Score	−2.1	−3.9	−4.8	−3.9
Standard Deviation	5.4	3.9	5.1	4.8
Melodrama:				
Mean EAA Score	−5.7	−5.7	−5.6	−5.6
Standard Deviation	2.6	1.3	2.6	2.2
Fiction:				
Mean EAA Score	−3.6	−4.8	−5.4	−4.8
Standard Deviation	2.1	1.5	3.0	2.4
Total:				
Mean EAA Score	−4.8	−3.7	−4.8	−4.6
Standard Deviation	2.1	3.9	3.1	3.1

from the cultural norms of word assignment. The critical evaluative tenor of the stereotype was more than a reflection of the vocabulary of ethnic description from which it was drawn. The mean evaluative coefficient for dictionary entries was very low, −3.3, but for treatments of the Irish in conversation, the evaluative assertion analysis score was altogether devastating, −4.6 on a scale of −9.0 to +9.0. Table 6 summarizes this information.

Applied to an appropriate sample of antebellum "conversation," these content analytic tools help identify and explain the treatment of the Irish in language, and help us understand the role of words in shaping and propagating American interethnic perception. Content analysis is only a beginning. But my surmise is that one can say little of value about "Paddy" without first discovering what "Paddy" was.

Appendix B: Sources and Sampling

Which public media captured—and thus preserved—antebellum American "conversation" and how to identify patterns in language that cut across class, taste, and region were key questions from the outset for this study of ethnic stereotypes. Sheer availability recommended certain kinds of documents; others seemed necessary to provide geographical breadth or social inclusiveness. Few bibliographies for any species of antebellum print media are complete. Genuine random sampling from the best of these is made difficult by problems of document access. Some materials have disappeared, others are elusive. Fortunately, this is not a study of stereotype salience. This study does not measure *how often* the Irish were mentioned in everyday conversation. Ultimately, the materials selected for content analysis fell into seven categories and cut a swath across the "popular," "mass," and "elite" subcultures of antebellum America. Because of noticeable differences in quantity, accessibility, and content, these sources could not be tapped by a single sampling procedure but required several, some more random and some less, but each calculated to capture with as little distortion as possible the incidental treatment of the Irish in conventional language.

MELODRAMA

Popular melodrama—disproportionately comedy, farce, and burlesque—was part of antebellum oral culture. In 1850, G. G. Foster's widely circulated guide to New York City numbered seven melodramatic stages on Manhattan alone, each catering to a different clientele. But professional melodramatic repertory companies existed not only in New York, Boston, and Philadelphia but also in Pittsburgh, Cincinnati, and New Orleans. Established stars of the English and American melodramatic stage, like Barney Williams, one of the great performers of stage Irish parts, repeatedly toured the United States, including the South and the upper Mississippi valley. The standard scripts were available to amateurs everywhere. Joseph Schick's *Early Theater in Eastern Iowa* suggests the ubiquity of this entertainment even on the antebellum frontier.[1]

For this study, a list of Irish character melodrama performed in the

[1] G. G. Foster, *New York by Gas-Light* (New York, 1850), 85–88; Joseph S. Schick, *The Early Theater in Eastern Iowa: Cultural Beginnings and the Rise of the Theater in Davenport and Eastern Iowa, 1836–63* (Chicago, 1939).

United States between 1820 and 1860 was assembled from three sources: Arthur Hobson Quinn's *A History of American Drama from the Beginning to the Civil War,* Perley Isaac Reed's *The Realistic Presentation of American Characters in Native American Plays Prior to 1870,* and Schick's *Early Theater in Eastern Iowa.* No truly comprehensive bibliographies of Irish character drama apparently exist. Even those that purport to be complete, like Hixon and Hennessee's *Nineteenth Century Drama: A Finding Guide,* an index to the Readex Corporation's microprint edition of American plays, have notable gaps. Stephen J. Brown's *Guide to Books on Ireland* also has many holes in its index to Irish character plays originating in the British Isles.[2] Because of such omissions, no sample of antebellum melodrama is entirely systematic and perfectly random. For this exercise in content analyis, the ninety-eight Irish character plays listed in Quinn, Reed, and Schick were consulted. Of these, thirty-three scripts offered 331 different "unit-perceptions" of the Irish.

NEWSPAPERS

American newspapers in the mid-nineteenth century propagated both oral and what folklorist Richard Dorson calls "mass" culture. Editors relied heavily upon the contributions of amateur correspondents; they shared anecdotes and took letters from their readers that had their origins in speech. Newspapers also disseminated calculated editorials, official announcements, and legislative debates that constituted some of the "centrally-directed signals" of antebellum society.[3] A few newspapers were becoming national in circulation and influence, for example, Washington's *National Intelligencer* and Baltimore's *Niles' Register,* which may have come as close to being a newsmagazine in the modern sense as any mid-nineteenth century periodical. But many other publications that were never read beyond local neighborhoods captured local and regional tastes.

The chief difficulty in tapping this material for treatments of the Irish is that there were so many antebellum newspapers carrying so many words. In 1834 the editor of Cincinnati's *Western Monthly Magazine* estimated that there were more than one thousand papers in press throughout the United States.[4] References to the Irish in antebellum newspapers were spread among thousands of issues. For this study, then, it was necessary to devise criteria for limiting the number of newspaper titles to be examined and the number of actual issues to be sampled. The decision was to select twelve newspaper titles that would represent the tastes of northern readers, southern readers, border state readers, and national subcribers. As much as possible, the twelve publications were drawn from different sized communities and were picked to represent a range of political affiliations. Since it was necessary to cover

[2] Arthur Hobson Quinn, *A History of American Drama from the Beginning to the Civil War* (New York, 1946); Perley Isaac Reed, *The Realistic Presentation of American Characters in Native American Plays Prior to 1870* (Columbus, 1918); Schick, *Early Theater;* Don L. Hixon and Don A. Hennessee, *Nineteenth Century American Drama: A Finding Guide* (Metuchen, N.J., 1977); Stephen J. Brown, *A Guide to Books on Ireland* (Dublin, 1912).

[3] Richard M. Dorson, *American Folklore and the Historian* (Chicago, 1971), 174–75.

[4] "The American Periodical Press," *Western Monthly Magazine,* 2 (August 1834) 394.

the whole period 1820–1860, papers with fairly long runs were favored over the much larger number of publications that came and went quickly. The dozen newspapers, with inclusive dates for the runs consulted were: *Baltimore American* (1834–54), *Charleston Mercury* (1820–60), *Chicago Democrat* (1833–45), *Chicago Tribune* (1849–60), *Cincinnati Enquirer* (1853–55), *Cincinnati Gazette* (1837–44), *New York Herald/Herald Tribune* (1835–41/1841–60), *The New York Times* (1851–60), *Niles' Register* (Baltimore, 1820–60), *Scioto Gazette* (Chillicothe, Ohio, 1820–60), *Springfield Republican* (Springfield, Mass., 1844–60), *Washington National Intelligencer* (1820–60).

In all, 248 newspaper-years are represented in this sample—still an unwieldy array of print to wade through in search of explicit references to the Irish. It seemed useful, therefore, to identify particular episodes in antebellum life that would have maximized the visibility of the Irish in this media. Twenty-nine such "episodes" recommended themselves, and each newspaper of the twelve in publication at the time was read for the entire month in which such an episode occurred. On the average, three newspaper observations could be located for each event; a total of ninety-four observations were collected. The "episodes" were chiefly riots, elections, sectarian debates, and public controversies. The likelihood was, consequently, that most treatments of the Irish in this material would be negatively charged. Still, a principal objective of the study was to compare non-nativist with overtly nativistic verbal representations of the Irish and the latter were almost always hostile. In an effort to achieve some balance, fifty-one "episode-free" monthly runs of the same newspaper titles were examined. In all, 145 newspaper-months yielded 135 unit-perceptions of the Irish for content analysis.

SCHOOLBOOKS

Schoolbooks were prime vehicles for the "official" culture of antebellum America. They represented the language and ideology that (to use Ruth Miller Elson's phrase) the "guardians of tradition" in American life thought appropriate for the socialization of republican youth. During the mid-nineteenth century, elementary and secondary school texts were primarily of two kinds: readers (or rhetorics) and geographies (or histories). There are, fortunately, a number of modern bibliographies for this material. This study turned to the catalogue of readers contained in Richard D. Mosier's *Making the American Mind* and to the index of geographies in Sr. Marie Leonore Fell's *The Foundations of Nativism in American Textbooks, 1783–1860*.[5] In each case, a 10 percent random sample was taken of the titles listed. The resulting thirty texts contained 357 unit-perceptions of the Irish.

[5] Ruth Miller Elson, *Guardians of Tradition: American Schoolbooks of the Nineteenth Century* (Lincoln, Neb., 1964); Richard D. Mosier, *Making the American Mind: Social and Moral Ideas in the McGuffey Readers* (New York, 1947), 356–72; Sr. Marie Leonore Fell, *The Foundations of Nativism in American Textbooks, 1783–1860* (Washington, 1941), 227–51.

MAGAZINES AND JOURNALS

Antebellum America possessed periodical literature for every taste. Frank Luther Mott counts more than 2500 magazine titles that went in and out of print between 1850 and 1860 alone, with perhaps 600 current at any one time. James Hall of the *Western Monthly Magazine* thought that in 1834 there were probably about fifty literary magazines, one hundred religious and philanthropic journals, twenty scientific or medical publications, fifty "entertainment" magazines, and a large number of political sheets published at such varying intervals that many were difficult to distinguish from newspapers.[6] Such a diverse periodical literature as this appealed to many different readerships. Some of the entertainment magazines, like *Ballou's Pictorial Drawing Room Companion* (Boston) or *Burton's Gentleman's Magazine* (Philadelphia), came close to representing popular or oral culture, devoting many of their columns to jokes, ballads, and anecdotes. All of the scientific and most of the literary journals, on the other hand, were alluvia of mid-nineteenth century elite culture. In between were the political, religious, and reform publications, didactic in content and institutional in origin. Like schoolbooks, they were organs of mass culture. This extensive periodical press was disproportionately centered in New England and the Middle Atlantic states, but no region entirely lacked its own publications.

As in the case with newspapers, the chief problem in sampling this material for unit-perceptions of the Irish was posed by sheer bulk. It was possible, ultimately, to focus upon runs of thirty magazines representing New England (eleven titles), the Middle Atlantic region (eleven titles), the South Atlantic area (two titles), the Mississippi Valley (three titles), and the Great Lakes (three titles), and also the principal kinds of publications: literary (fifteen titles), entertainment (four titles), political (two titles), scholarly/professional (three titles), religious/reform (six titles). These thirty publications ran for a total of 370 years during the period 1820–1860, with an average of ten titles in print during any given year. Relying heavily upon tables of contents and indexes, I was able to identify 341 unit-perceptions of the Irish. The titles consulted, by region, with run years were:

New England:

North American Review (Boston)	1820–50
Ballou's (Gleason's) Pictorial Drawing Room Companion (Boston)	1852–56
American Quarterly Register (Boston)	1827–43
New England Magazine (Boston)	1831–35
Massachusetts Quarterly Review (Boston)	1847–50
American Journal of Education (Boston)	1830–35
American Journal of Science (New Haven)	1846–60
The Liberator (Boston)	1831–60
Zion's Herald (Boston)	1823–60
Christian Examiner (Boston)	1824–60

Middle Atlantic:

Graham's American Monthly Magazine (Philadelphia)	1842–54

[6] Frank Luther Mott, *A History of American Magazines*, 2 vols. (Cambridge, Mass., 1957), 1:4, 2:555–65; "American Periodical Press," 394.

Middle Atlantic (continued):

United States Democratic Review (New York)	1837–59
American Whig Review (New York)	1845–52
New York Review (New York)	1832–42
American Quarterly Review (Philadelphia)	1827–37
Harper's Monthly (New York)	1850–60
Knickerbocker (New York)	1833–60
Putnam's Monthly (New York)	1853–57
Burton's Gentleman's Magazine (Philadelphia)	1837–40
National Antislavery Standard (New York)	1840–60
National Magazine (New York)	1851–53

South and West:

Southern Literary Messenger (Richmond)	1834–60
Southern Review (Charleston)	1828–32
Southern Quarterly Review (New Orleans)	1842–57
DeBow's Review (New Orleans)	1846–60
Western Messenger (Louisville)	1836–41
Illinois Monthly Magazine (Valdalia)	1830–32
Northwestern Christian Advocate (Chicago)	1850–51
Western Monthly Magazine (Cincinnati)	1833–36

BEST-SELLING COMMERCIAL LITERATURE: FICTION AND NONFICTION

Throughout the antebellum period, much American prose fiction took the form of short stories published in literary, entertainment, and religious journals. The American novel was still in its adolescence. At the outset of the period, the novel was chiefly a reading matter of elites, but by the end it was reaching much wider audiences—witness, for example, the extreme popularity of Harriet Beecher Stowe's *Uncle Tom's Cabin.* Even George Lippard's *Quaker City,* much less well-known today, sold more than 60,000 copies in 1844, its first year of publication.[7] Stories and sketches were also collected for publication in book form. Antebellum fiction was sometimes blatantly didactic. Novel and short story alike were pressed into the service of antislavery, temperance, and Protestant evangelism.

Frank Luther Mott has made an effort to establish the identity of the best-selling books in the mid-nineteenth century. A "best-seller," according to Mott's definition, was any work selling a number of copies equal to one percent of the United States' population as reported in the census at the beginning of the decade in which it made its appearance. "Better-sellers" circulated at half that rate.[8] Fiction titles in these categories are really too few to justify taking a percentage sample and too many to read in their entirety. Fortunately, nearly all are discussed in secondary literature and it was possible to pick out those most likely to offer usable descriptions of the Irish. In all, this sample furnished 151 unit-perceptions.

Commercial nonfiction includes everything from biographies and travel

[7] See introductory essay by Leslie A. Fiedler in George Lippard, *The Quaker City* (Philadelphia, 1846; reprint, New York, 1970), vii, ix.
[8] Frank Luther Mott, *Golden Multitudes: The Story of Best Sellers in the United States* (New York, 1947), 305–08, 317–20.

accounts to encyclopedias, philosophical essays, and evangelists' tracts. There is no way to sample this literature systematically, although Mott's *Golden Multitudes* offers a list of "best-selling" titles. Because any sample is wildly random, this material serves as a useful control. If word patterns in it are found to approximate those uncovered in materials sampled more systematically, this finding can strengthen any conclusion that a particular verbal image was consensual. This was, as it turned out, the case with the 185 unit-perceptions of the Irish drawn from "nonfictional" sources.

PUBLIC DOCUMENTS

Published legislative debates and investigative reports, as well as executive documents issuing from state and national agencies, did not circulate widely enough to *create* the antebellum republic's official culture, but they undoubtedly reflected it. This material is uncommonly well indexed and easy to survey. The *Annals of Congress* (to 1824), Gales and Seaton's *Register of Debates in Congress* (1825–37), and the *Congressional Globe* (after 1833) all offer a glimpse of the treatment of the Irish in "official" conversation. These are supplemented for the period after 1833 by United States House and Senate *Documents* and *Reports*. State materials, of course, are more voluminous and less well indexed. Legislative documents issuing from two states with large Irish-American populations, Massachusetts and New York, are, however, fairly accessible and were surveyed for this study. All of this material was the source of 92 unit-perceptions of the Irish. Government officials were much more likely to talk about "immigrants" or "aliens" than about the members of any particular ethnic group.

NATIVIST

Ray Allen Billington's *Protestant Crusade* includes a lengthy bibliography of nativist and anti-Catholic publications running to 45 periodical titles, 48 organizational reports, and 505 books and pamphlets.[9] A 10 percent random sampling of these 598 titles rendered sixty items for content analysis. Of these, nine were serial titles running for a total of eighty-six publication years. This material contained 240 unit-perceptions of the Irish. These were, of course, outnumbered by descriptions of "immigrants," "Catholics," and "foreigners" in nativist literature.

[9] Ray Allen Billington, *The Protestant Crusade, 1820–1860: A Study of the Origins of American Nativism* (New York, 1938), 445–82.

Notes

PREFACE

1. I have found particularly helpful the insights provided by Fredrick Barth in *Ethnic Groups and Boundaries: The Social Organization of Cultural Difference* (Oslo, Norway, 1969). See especially 9–10, 15–16, 32–33, 38.

2. Herbert Blumer, "Race Prejudice as a Sense of Group Position," *The Pacific Sociological Review* 1 (Spring 1958), 218, 224–25.

3. Gordon Wood, "Intellectual History and the Social Sciences," in *New Directions in American Intellectual History*, ed. John Higham and Paul K. Conkin (Baltimore, 1979), 34–35. For some additional discussion of symbols and images in intellectual/cultural history see Rhys Isaac, "Ethnographic Method in History: An Action Approach," *Historical Methods* 13 (Winter 1980), 43–61.

4. Editor James Hall of Cincinnati's *Western Monthly Magazine* estimated that there were more than two hundred periodicals other than newspapers in press during 1834. Among these, he thought, were some 100 religious and benevolent magazines, 50 literary periodicals, 20 medical and scientific journals, 50 family and entertainment magazines, and an indefinite number of "political" publications. See "The American Periodical Press," *Western Monthly Magazine*, II (August 1834), 394. Frank Luther Mott, a modern student, puts the number of such periodicals in 1850 at 685 and counts 2500 different titles in print between 1850 and 1865. Frank Luther Mott, *A History of American Magazines*, 2 vols. (Cambridge, Mass., 1957), 2:4. Mott is also responsible for compiling a bibliography of "best-selling" books for the early and mid-nineteenth century, using a sales figure of "1% of the total population of the continental United States for the decade in which the book was published" as the criterion for inclusion. See Mott, *Golden Multitudes: The Story of Best Sellers in the United States* (New York, 1947), 6, 7.

5. Lawrence Veysey, "Intellectual History and the New Social History," in *New Directions in American Intellectual History*, ed. Higham and Conkin, 20, 22.

6. Phillip J. Stone, et al., *The General Inquirer: A Computer Approach to Content Analysis* (Cambridge, Mass., 1966), 5.

7. See Morris Janowitz, "Harold D. Lasswell's Contribution to Content Analysis," *Public Opinion Quarterly* 32 (1968), 649–50; Harold Lasswell, "Why Be Quantitative?" in *Language of Politics: Studies in Quantitative*

Semantics, ed. Harold Lasswell, Nathan Leites, et al. (New York, 1949), 51.

8. Lasswell, "Why Be Quantitative?," 57; Edmund Ions, *Against Behavioralism: A Critique of Behavioral Science* (Totowa, N.J., 1977), 96.

9. Dale Sorenson, "The Language of a Cold Warrior: A Content Analysis of Harry Truman's Public Statements," *Social Science History* 3 (Winter 1979), 171–86.

10. See Melvin Small, "How We Learned to Love the Russians: American Media and the Soviet Union During World War II," *The Historian* 36 (May 1974), 455–78; Dean L. Yarwood, "Norm Observance and Legislative Integration: The U.S. Senate in 1850 and 1860," *Social Science Quarterly* 51 (1970), 57–69. An index of traditionalism among practitioners of content analysis is the endurance of Lasswellian frequency measures like the "Coefficient of Imbalance." Sorenson, for example, uses it. See Irving L. Janis and Raymond Fadner, "The Coefficient of Imbalance," in *Language of Politics,* ed. Lasswell and Leites, 157. To be sure, historians have innovated with content analysis. See, for example, Louis Galambos, *The Public Image of Big Business in America, 1880–1940: A Quantitative Study in Social Change* (Baltimore, 1975).

INTRODUCTION: PADDY AND THE REPUBLIC

1. Roy Harvey Pearce, *Savagism and Civilization: A Study of the Indian in the American Mind* (Baltimore, rev. ed., 1965), v.

2. Stuart Creighton Miller, *The Unwelcome Immigrant: The American Image of the Chinese, 1785–1882* (Berkeley, 1969); Winthrop D. Jordan, *White Over Black: American Attitudes Toward the Negro, 1550–1812* (Chapel Hill, 1968); George M. Fredrickson, *The Black Image in the White Mind: The Debate on Afro-American Character and Destiny, 1817–1914* (New York, 1971).

3. Jordan, *White Over Black,* 90.

4. *The Life and Speeches of Henry Clay,* 2 vols. (Philadelphia, 1855), 1:270. Clay's address, "On African Colonization," was delivered in the House of Representatives on January 20, 1827; "The Title of This Journal," *The Colored American,* March 4, 1837.

5. Charles B. Boynton, *Oration, Delivered on the 5th of July, 1847 . . . in Cincinnati* (Cincinnati, 1847), 10; "Catholicity Necessary to Sustain Popular Liberty," in Orestes Brownson, *Essays and Reviews, Chiefly on Theology, Politics, and Socialism* (New York, 1852), 375.

6. John Hancock Lee, *The Origin and Progress of the American Party in Politics* (Philadelphia, 1855), 243; "America for the Americans," *Putnam's Monthly* 5 (May 1855), 534.

7. See *Report of the Debates and Proceedings of the Convention for the Revision of the Constitution of . . . Ohio, 1850–51,* 2 vols. (Columbus, 1851), 2:550–61; Leon F. Litwack, *North of Slavery: The Negro in the Free States, 1790–1860* (Chicago, 1961), 54–57; Ambrose Doskow, ed., *Historic Opinions of the United States Supreme Court* (New York, 1935), 118–90.

8. Kirk H. Porter and Donald B. Johnson, eds., *National Party Platforms, 1840–1964* (Urbana, Ill., 1966), 22–23; Ray Allen Billington, *The Protes-*

tant Crusade, 1800–1860: A Study of the Origins of American Nativism (New York, 1938), 413.

9. Oscar Handlin, *The Uprooted: The Epic Story of the Great Migrations That Made the American People* (Boston, 1952), 270; Merle Curti, *The Roots of American Loyalty* (New York, 1946), 76.

10. Paul Nagel, *This Sacred Trust: American Nationality, 1798–1898* (New York, 1971), 161–62, 63–64, 139, 48–49.

11. Gilbert Osofsky, "Abolitionists, Irish Immigrants, and the Dilemmas of Romantic Nationalism," *American Historical Review* 80 (October 1975), 911–12; Kenneth M. Stampp, "The Concept of a Perpetual Union," *Journal of American History* 65 (June 1978), 28–29.

12. Abraham Lincoln to Joshua Speed, August 24, 1855, in Paul M. Angle, ed., *Abraham Lincoln's Speeches and Letters, 1832–1865* (London, 1957), 64.

13. Yehoshua Arieli, *Individualism and Nationalism in American Ideology* (Cambridge, Mass., 1964), 297.

14. For some discussion of the meagerness of nativist ethno-racial theory, see George M. Fredrickson, *The Black Image in the White Mind: The Debate on Afro-American Character and Destiny, 1817–1914* (New York, 1971), 99; Thomas F. Gossett, *Race: The History of an Idea in America* (Dallas, 1963), 97; and David Brion Davis, "Some Themes of Counter-Subversion: An Analysis of Anti-Masonic, Anti-Catholic, and Anti-Mormon Literature," *Mississippi Valley Historical Review* 47 (September 1960), 213n.

15. Joel H. Silbey, "The Surge of Republican Power: Partisan Antipathy, American Social Conflict, and the Coming of the Civil War," in *Essays on Antebellum American Politics, 1840–1860*, ed. Stephen E. Maizlish (College Station, Tex., 1982), 201–02. In fact, it is not altogether clear that all practitioners of ethnocultural political analysis are very careful in ascertaining the contemporaneous definitions of antebellum America's "tribes." They seem liable to draw their own ethnocultural boundaries and to create their own group labels. Lee Benson's "Puritans" and "Nonpuritans" are good examples. See Lee Benson, *The Concept of Jacksonian Democracy: New York as a Test Case* (Princeton, N.J., 1961), 198.

16. See, for example, Thomas Curran, "From 'Paddy' to the Presidency: The Irish in America," in *The Immigrant Experience in America*, ed. Frank J. Coppa and Thomas J. Curran (Boston, 1976), 101.

17. James H. Kettner, *The Development of American Citizenship, 1608–1870* (Chapel Hill, N.C., 1978).

18. J. R. Pole, *The Pursuit of Equality in American History* (Berkeley, Calif., 1978), 152.

19. Alexis de Tocqueville, *Democracy in America*, 2 vols., ed. Phillips Bradley (New York, 1945), 1:27.

20. Curran, "From 'Paddy' to the Presidency," 99; Adrienne Siegel, *The Image of the American City in Popular Literature, 1820–1870* (Port Washington, N.Y., 1981), 126–28.

21. See Reginald Horsman, *Race and Manifest Destiny: The Origins of American Racial Anglo-Saxonism* (Cambridge, Mass., 1981), 55–59.

22. "Emigration," *Knickerbocker* 16 (December 1840), 470; Edward Everett Hale, "Review of Schmidt and Gall on America," *North American Review* 17 (July 1823), 92.

23. See United States Bureau of the Census, *Historical Statistics of the United States: Colonial Times to 1957* (Washington, 1960), 57, and Maldwyn A. Jones, "Scotch-Irish," in *Harvard Encyclopedia of American Ethnic Groups,* ed. Stephen Thernstrom (Cambridge, Mass., 1980), 904–05. For an up-to-date accounting of the ethnic and religious heterogeneity of the early nineteenth century emigration from Ireland see David Noel Doyle, *Ireland, Irishmen, and Revolutionary America, 1760–1820* (Dublin, 1981), 202–30.

24. "Editor's Drawer," *Harper's Monthly* 11 (November 1855), 711; *National Intelligencer,* May 11, 1844; Nathaniel G. Huntington, *A System of Modern Geography for Schools* (Hartford, 1836), 162–63; Moses M. Henkle, *The Life of Henry Bidleman Bascom . . . Late Bishop of the Methodist Episcopal Church, South* (Nashville, 1857), 206.

25. Francis Bowen, "The Irish in America," *North American Review* 52 (January 1841), 193; U.S. Congress, Senate, *Congressional Globe,* 33rd Cong., 2nd sess., 389–91.

26. Lydia Maria Child, "Anti-Slavery Education," *National Anti-Slavery Standard,* June 3, 1841.

27. "The Irish Population," *The Liberator,* January 3, 1835.

28. "The Catholic Question," *Western Monthly Magazine* 3 (May 1835), 379.

29. H. Giles, "The Present Condition of Ireland," *The Christian Examiner* 45 (July 1848), 113; Horace Greeley, *Recollections of a Busy Life* (New York, 1868), 29.

30. For some discussion of both the flexibility and rigidity of societal stereotypes see Rosemary Gordon, *Stereotypy of Imagery and Belief as an Ego Defence* (Cambridge, England, 1962), 2; Robin M. Williams, Jr., *Strangers Next Door: Ethnic Relations in American Communities* (Englewood Cliffs, N.J., 1964), 19–20.

31. Samuel C. Busey, *Immigration: Its Evils and Consequences* (New York, 1856), 40.

32. Kettner, *The Development of American Citizenship,* 351; also see Frederick Douglass to Gerrit Smith, July 3, 1874, in Philip Foner, ed., *The Life and Writings of Frederick Douglass,* 4 vols. (New York, 1955), 4:306. Commenting upon the Supreme Court's *Slaughterhouse* decision, which excluded the rights and privileges of state citizenship from the protections of the Fourteenth Amendment, Douglass noted that "Two citizenships mean no citizenship. The one destroys the other. . . . The nation affirms, the State denies, and there is no progress."

33. See Michael B. Katz, *The Irony of Early School Reform: Educational Innovation in Mid-Nineteenth Century Massachusetts* (Boston, 1968), 180–81, 207–08; David J. Rothman, *The Discovery of the Asylum: Social Order and Disorder in the New Republic* (Boston, 1971), 243, 284; and John F. Kasson, *Civilizing the Machine: Technology and Republican Values in America, 1776–1900* (New York, 1976), 106.

34. Oscar Handlin, "The New History and the Ethnic Factor in American Life," *Perspectives in American History,* 1970, 18.

35. John Higham, *Strangers in the Land: Patterns of American Nativism, 1860–1925* (New York, 1970), 4.

36. Charles Hartshorne and Paul Weiss, eds., *Collected Papers of Charles Sanders Pierce,* 6 vols. (Cambridge, Mass., 1934), 5:297.

37. *Proceedings of the United States Anti-Masonic Convention, Phila-delphia, September 11, 1830* (New York, 1830), 118.

CHAPTER ONE: FINDING PADDY

1. Tyrone Power, *The Omnibus* (Philadelphia, 1833), 6; *Niles' Weekly Register,* December 27, 1834.
2. Samuel Griswold Goodrich, *Ireland and the Irish* (Boston, 1841), 50–51.
3. Theodore Parker, "Causes of the Present Condition of Ireland," *Massachusetts Quarterly Review* 11 (June 1850), 336; *New York Times,* June 6, 1854.
4. Richard M. Dorson, *American Folklore and the Historian* (Chicago, 1971), 91.
5. Ibid.
6. Ibid.; David Hollinger, "Historians and the Discourse of Intellectuals," in *New Directions in American Intellectual History,* ed. John Higham and Paul K. Conkin (Baltimore, 1979), 47.
7. Howard J. Ehrlich, *The Social Psychology of Prejudice: A Systematic Theoretical Review and Propositional Inventory of the American Social Psychological Study of Prejudice* (New York, 1973), 23–25. Ehrlich calls this dictionary a "preliminary compilation" of "ethnic group-descriptive words" and explains that he drew it from the "research literature on stereotypes."
8. The sample included 1,592 individual descriptive unit-perceptions of Irish subjects in American "conversation," 189 of German, 171 of "immigrant," as well as 240 of the Irish drawn exclusively from a sample of "nativist" material. An additional 347 unit-perceptions constituting a comparative/control sample were culled from contemporaneous British sources. (For a detailed explanation of "unit-perceptions" see Appendix A, p. 185.)
9. Ehrlich, *The Social Psychology of Prejudice,* 26–27. Ehrlich identifies the fourteen fundamental kinds of ethnic adjectives as those describing:

1. "Positive Relational Characteristics"—that is, interpersonal characteristics
2. "Positive Intellectual Characteristics"
3. "Positive Moral Characteristics"
4. "Negative Relational Characteristics"
5. "Negative Intellectual Characteristics"
6. "Negative Moral Characteristics"
7. "Conflict/Hostility"
8. "Substantial Characteristics"—denoting "industry, energy, and direction"
9. "Insubstantial Characteristics"—"capricious, fleeting, unreliable"
10. "Emotional Characteristics"
11. "Political/Religious Characteristics"
12. "Economic Characteristics"
13. "Aesthetic/Cultural Characteristics"
14. "Physical Characteristics"

In working with these in a historical context, I found it useful to supple-

TABLE 1.1: *Distribution of 1,592 "Unit-Perceptions" of the Irish Among Fifteen Categories of Ethnic Description*

Category	Classification	Percentage of usages (rounded)			
		1820–1844	1845–1852	1853–1860	1820–1860
1	Positive Relational	12%	13%	11%	12%
2	Positive Intellectual	4	2	2	3
3	Positive Moral	3	2	1	2
4	Negative Relational	13	7	9	10
5	Negative Intellectual	11	6	10	9
6	Negative Moral	5	6	4	5
7	Conflict/Hostility	9	15	9	11
8	Substantial	2	2	2	2
9	Insubstantial	9	7	9	8
10	Emotional	9	11	12	11
11	Political/Religious	4	2	5	4
12	Economic	3	5	2	3
13	Aesthetic/Cultural	3	3	4	3
14	Physical	9	14	19	14
15	Group Subjective	5	4	2	4
	Observations	N = 598	N = 520	N = 474	N = 1,592

ment them with a fifteenth category, which I have denoted "Group Subjective," to describe adjectives making strictly evaluative statements about the target group. Words like "cursed," "detestable," "unfortunate," and "worthless" would fit here. For a more thorough description of this classificatory scheme and sample words for each category, see Appendix A.

10. The 1592 unit-perceptions were distributed among the following kinds of text in the numbers indicated: magazines/journals (331), newspapers (135), texts (357), public documents (92), nonfiction (185), melodrama (341), prose fiction (151).

11. See Table 1.1.

12. In the adjective classification tables found in the Notes and Appendix, adjective categories 1 through 6 and category 15 contain "intrinsic" descriptives. Adjective categories 7 through 14 contain "extrinsic."

13. See Table 1.2.

14. Timothy Dwight, *Travels in New England and New York,* 3 vols. (n.p., 1822), 3:375.

15. See Table 1.3, p. 214.

16. See Table 1.4, p. 215.

17. Rollo Ogden, ed., *Life and Letters of E. L. Godkin,* 2 vols. (New York, 1907), 1:182.

18. Thomas Butler Gunn, *The Physiology of New York Boarding Houses* (New York, 1857), 266.

19. See Neil Harris, *The Artist in American Society: The Formative Years, 1790–1860* (New York, 1970), vii; Ronald T. Takaki, *Iron Cages: Race and Culture in Nineteenth Century America* (New York, 1979), 115–16; Marvin Harris, *The Rise of Anthropological Theory: A History of The-*

TABLE 1.2: *Distribution of 598 "Unit-Perceptions" of the Irish, 1820–1844*

Category	Classification	Periodicals	Newspapers	School texts	Public documents	Popular nonfiction	Melodrama	Popular fiction	Total
1	Positive Relational	17%	0%	13%	0%	22%	5%	5%	12%
2	Positive Intellectual	5	0	8	0	6	0	0	4
3	Positive Moral	0	0	6	0	2	6	8	3
4	Negative Relational	12	15	14	6	2	20	10	13
5	Negative Intellectual	9	12	10	12	22	11	10	11
6	Negative Moral	4	15	4	6	2	6	5	5
7	Conflict/Hostility	11	27	6	18	6	4	5	9
8	Substantial	2	0	3	0	2	0	3	2
9	Insubstantial	11	2	12	18	6	5	3	9
10	Emotional	9	7	6	12	8	14	15	9
11	Political/Religious	4	5	3	6	8	4	0	4
12	Economic	1	5	4	0	2	1	3	3
13	Aesthetic/Cultural	3	3	3	18	2	3	0	3
14	Physical	8	2	4	6	6	16	33	9
15	Group Subjective	5	8	6	0	2	5	0	5

TABLE 1.3: *Distribution of 520 "Unit-Perceptions" of the Irish, 1845–1852*

Category	Classification	Periodicals	Newspapers	School texts	Public documents	Popular nonfiction	Melodrama	Popular fiction	Total
1	Positive Relational	17%	12%	20%	8%	10%	9%	14%	13%
2	Positive Intellectual	2	4	4	0	1	0	2	2
3	Positive Moral	2	12	2	2	3	1	2	2
4	Negative Relational	8	8	7	7	1	12	2	7
5	Negative Intellectual	5	0	5	7	7	8	6	6
6	Negative Moral	4	8	6	5	8	6	6	6
7	Conflict/Hostility	15	4	19	5	6	20	22	15
8	Substantial	0	8	1	7	4	1	0	2
9	Insubstantial	8	8	6	15	10	5	2	7
10	Emotional	6	15	13	5	7	17	12	11
11	Political/Religious	4	8	0	0	7	1	0	2
12	Economic	1	4	4	10	11	5	4	5
13	Aesthetic/Cultural	1	4	2	0	6	2	4	3
14	Physical	18	8	6	24	16	12	22	14
15	Group Subjective	7	4	4	5	4	3	2	4

TABLE 1.4: *Distribution of 474 "Unit-Perceptions" of the Irish, 1853–1860*

Category	Classification	Periodicals	Newspapers	School texts	Public documents	Popular nonfiction	Melodrama	Popular fiction	Total
1	Positive Relational	15%	4%	27%	0%	16%	6%	8%	11%
2	Positive Intellectual	3	2	3	0	1	0	2	2
3	Positive Moral	0	0	3	0	4	2	0	1
4	Negative Relational	11	10	5	6	11	11	3	9
5	Negative Intellectual	9	10	5	6	7	15	11	10
6	Negative Moral	0	6	0	6	8	4	8	4
7	Conflict/Hostility	7	27	7	12	9	4	5	9
8	Substantial	3	6	0	9	1	1	0	2
9	Insubstantial	11	2	9	18	11	10	5	9
10	Emotional	11	12	9		9	15	8	12
11	Political/Religious	7	6	6	0	12	2	2	5
12	Economic	0	2	7	9	1	2	0	2
13	Aesthetic/Cultural	1	6	3	3	4	7	2	4
14	Physical	22	2	13	21	0	23	47	19
15	Group Subjective	3	4	3	3	7	0	2	2

ories of Culture (New York, 1968), passim; Curti, *The Roots of American Loyalty,* 77.

20. Billington, *Protestant Crusade,* 1; Handlin, *Boston's Immigrants,* 178; Higham, *Strangers in the Land,* 4–5; Michael F. Holt, "The Politics of Impatience: The Origins of Know Nothingism," *Journal of American History* 60 (September 1973), 322–23.

21. Davis, "Some Themes of Counter-Subversion," 208.

22. The riots in Kensington (March) and Southwark (July) grew out of a combination of ethnic, religious, occupational, and social class rivalries. In the public mind, however, these were obscured and the riots seem to have been regarded as principally ethnic and religious in origin. No doubt the notoriety of the Philadelphia disturbances was enhanced by their proximity to the widely publicized political struggle which took place in neighboring New York state between 1840 and 1842 over the State School Law which was also popularly taken to be an ethnic and sectarian controversy. See David Montgomery, "The Shuttle and the Cross: Weavers and Artisans in the Kensington Riots of 1844," *Journal of Social History* 5 (Summer 1972), 411–46; Vincent Lannie and Bernard Duthorn, "For the Honor and Glory of God: The Philadelphia Bible Riots of 1844," *History of Education Quarterly* 8 (Spring 1968), 44–106; Vincent P. Lannie, *Public Money and Parochial Education: Bishop Hughes, Governor Seward and the New York School Controversy* (Cleveland, 1968), 54–55.

23. The 360 unit-perceptions included 189 of German subjects and 171 of "immigrants."

24. Gunn, *The Physiology of New York Boarding Houses,* 257, 262.

25. See Table 1.5, below.

TABLE 1.5: *Distribution of "Unit-Perceptions" in Two Specialized Languages of Ethnic Description*

Cate-gory	Classification	1820–1844		1845–1860		1820–1860	
		Irish	Germans	Irish	Germans	Irish	Germans
1	Positive Relational	12%	16%	12%	12%	12%	15%
2	Positive Intellectual	4	9	2	5	3	8
3	Positive Moral	3	20	2	0	2	13
4	Negative Relational	13	1	8	2	10	2
5	Negative Intellectual	11	8	8	0	9	5
6	Negative Moral	5	0	5	5	5	2
7	Conflict/Hostility	9	0	12	0	11	0
8	Substantial	2	29	2	34	2	31
9	Insubstantial	9	0	8	2	8	1
10	Emotional	9	1	11	2	11	2
11	Political/Religious	4	1	3	7	4	3
12	Economic	3	3	4	17	3	8
13	Aesthetic/Cultural	3	5	3	5	3	5
14	Physical	9	7	16	7	14	7
15	Group Subjective	5	2	3	0	4	0
	Observations	N = 598	N = 84	N = 994	N = 105	N = 1,592	N = 189

26. This Anglo-American "norm-image" was extremely focused. Of the small, incidental sample of unit-perceptions examined, 37% highlighted Substantial Characteristics, 30% Physical, 13% Positive Relational, and 10% Positive Intellectual. These made up virtually the entire word portrait.

27. See Table 1.6, below.

28. Thomas Jefferson, *Notes on the State of Virginia* (New York, 1964), 82–84. This is a reprint of the 1861 edition. Jefferson wrote the work between 1781 and 1785 and made subsequent amendments over a period of years.

29. "Mobs," *New England Magazine* 7 (December 1834), 471–72.

30. Even Abraham Lincoln, generally critical of nativism on both ideological and political grounds, had uncharitable words to say about "immigrants." See Lincoln to Norman B. Judd, October 20, 1858, in Don E. Fehrenbacher, ed., *Abraham Lincoln: A Documentary Portrait Through His Speeches and Writings* (New York, 1964), 118–19.

31. Matthew Carey, *Vindicae Hibernicae; or, Ireland Vindicated* (Philadelphia, 1819), ix–x.

32. David Krause, ed., *The Dolmen Boucicault* (Dublin, 1964), 39; Edward D. Snyder, "The Wild Irish: A Study of Some English Satires," *Modern Philology* 17 (April 1920), 162. Horatio Sheafe Krans discusses the fictive folk sketch in *Irish Life in Irish Fiction* (New York, 1903), 26, 55, 58, 116. See also Snyder, "The Wild Irish," 147.

33. L. Perry Curtis, Jr., *Anglo-Saxons and Celts: A Study of Anti-Irish Prejudice in Victorian England* (Bridgeport, Conn., 1968), 64–65, 89–90.

34. See Table 1.7, p. 218.

TABLE 1.6: *Distribution of "Unit-Perceptions" in Two Specialized Languages of Ethnic Description*

		1820–1844		1845–1860		1820–1860	
Category	Classification	Irish	Immigrants	Irish	Immigrants	Irish	Immigrants
1	Positive Relational	12%	0%	12%	0%	12%	0%
2	Positive Intellectual	4	0	2	0	3	0
3	Positive Moral	3	1	2	1	2	1
4	Negative Relational	13	16	8	11	10	14
5	Negative Intellectual	11	16	8	15	9	16
6	Negative Moral	5	16	5	24	5	21
7	Conflict/Hostility	9	11	12	10	11	11
8	Substantial	2	0	2	0	2	0
9	Insubstantial	9	9	8	9	8	9
10	Emotional	9	4	11	5	11	5
11	Political/Religious	4	3	3	1	4	2
12	Economic	3	11	4	9	3	10
13	Aesthetic/Cultural	3	0	3	1	3	1
14	Physical	9	9	16	8	14	8
15	Group Subjective	5	4	3	5	4	5
	Observations	N = 598	N = 80	N = 994	N = 91	N = 1,592	N = 171

TABLE 1.7: *Distribution of "Unit-Perceptions" of the Irish in English and American Materials*

Category code	Characteristic	English materials: Percent of usages, 1800–1844	American materials: Percent of usages, 1820–1844
1	Positive Relational	17%	12%
2	Positive Intellectual	6	4
3	Positive Moral	5	3
4	Negative Relational	13	13
5	Negative Intellectual	8	11
6	Negative Moral	7	5
7	Conflict/Hostility	6	9
8	Substantial	2	2
9	Insubstantial	11	9
10	Emotional	8	9
11	Political/Religious	1	4
12	Economic	1	3
13	Aesthetic/Cultural	3	3
14	Physical	8	9
15	Group Subjective	4	5
	Observations	N = 349	N = 598

35. As established by "evaluative assertion analysis," measuring relative descriptive favorability, or unfavorability. The evaluative assertion analysis score for thirty items containing 349 unit-perceptions was −1.8 on a scale of +9.0 (most favorable) to −9.0 (least favorable). The standard deviation from the mean was 2.9. For a discussion of evaluative assertion analysis, see Appendix A.

36. See Krans, *Irish Life in Irish Fiction*, 216–17; John Wilson Croker, *A Sketch of the State of Ireland, Past and Present* (Dublin, 1808), 26–27.

37. R. K. Webb, *Modern England: From the Eighteenth Century to the Present* (New York, 1968), 137–38, 187–90.

38. See Snyder, "The Wild Irish," 147–48.

39. Robert Bell, *A Description of the Conditions and Manner of the Peasantry of Ireland . . . Between the Years 1780 and 1790* (London, 1804), 17.

40. Richard and Maria Edgeworth, *Essay on Irish Bulls* (London, 1815), 250; John Pinkerton, *Modern Geography* (London, 1807), 232.

41. Curtis, *Anglo-Saxons and Celts*, 31, 99.

42. This has not always been anticipated in the historical literature. See, for example, Billington, *The Protestant Crusade*, 1, or a synthetic text like David M. Potter, *Division and the Stress of Reunion, 1845–1876* (Glenview, Ill., 1973), 78. The surmise in these is that antebellum Anglo-Americans responded to a stereotype of the Irish inherited more or less intact from English cultural traditions.

43. Francis Wyse, *America: Its Realities and Resources*, 3 vols. (London, 1846), 3:43.

NOTES TO PAGES 39 TO 47   219

CHAPTER TWO: "THE SIN OF THE IRISHMAN IS IGNORANCE"

1. Tocqueville, *Democracy in America*, 1:250–51.
2. Ibid.; Arieli, *Individualism and Nationalism*, 32.
3. Arieli, *Individualism and Nationalism*, 24, 12, 188, 274.
4. I-Mien Tsiang, *The Question of Expatriation in America Prior to 1907* (Baltimore, 1942), 38; Walter O. Forster, "The Immigrant and the American National Idea," in *In the Trek of the Immigrants,* ed. O. Fritiof Ander (Rock Island, Ill., 1953), 160. Forster speculates that "non-British and non-Anglo-American elements were well-entrenched and numerous enough that any new nationalism seeking to base itself on a majority ethnic or cultural group could do so only at the price of *eo ipso* acquiring some important national minorities."
5. Kettner, *The Development of American Citizenship,* 128. See also Thomas J. Archdeacon, *Becoming American: An Ethnic History* (New York, 1983), 58, and Reed Ueda, "Naturalization and Citizenship" in Thernstrom, ed., *Encyclopedia of American Ethnic Groups,* 736.
6. Arthur M. Schlesinger, Jr., "America: Experiment or Destiny?" *American Historical Review* 82 (June 1977), 507–11, 515; see also Harris, *The Artist in American Society,* 28–29, and Robert F. Berkhofer, Jr., *The White Man's Indian: Impressions of the American Indian from Columbus to the Present* (New York, 1978), 41.
7. James Kettner offers some useful discussion of this in *The Development of American Citizenship,* 235–46. See also Frank George Franklin, *The Legislative History of Naturalization in the United States* (Chicago, 1906), 33–115.
8. U.S. Congress, House, *Annals of Congress,* "Naturalization Bill," 3rd Cong., 2nd sess., 1795, 1065.
9. Goodrich, *Ireland and the Irish,* 111–17. For a contemporary critique of Goodrich's popular style see "Peter Parley," *Western Messenger* 3 (March 1837), 548, 550.
10. See Richard A. Easterlin, "Immigration: Social Characteristics" in *American Ethnic Groups,* ed. Thernstrom, 476, 479.
11. Ibid., 476; United States Bureau of the Census, *Historical Statistics, . . . to 1957,* 57; Patrick J. Blessing, "Irish," and Maldwyn A. Jones, "Scotch-Irish," in *American Ethnic Groups,* ed. Thernstrom, 529, 904–05. See also Doyle, *Ireland, Irishmen, and Revolutionary America,* 208–13.
12. Clifford S. Griffin details the "interlocking directorates" of organizations like the American Tract Society, the American Bible Society, the American and Foreign Christian Union, and the nativistic Order of the Star-Spangled Banner. See C. S. Griffin, *Their Brothers' Keepers: Moral Stewardship in the United States, 1800–1860* (New Brunswick, N.J., 1960), 216, 178; Billington, *The Protestant Crusade,* and Louis D. Scisco, *Political Nativism in New York State* (New York, 1901), though dated, still contains the most descriptive material on anti-Catholic organizations and publications.
13. Louis Scisco's *Political Nativism in New York State,* despite its age, remains a standard reference on the history of the principal nativist secret societies.
14. Jesse Olney, *A Practical System of Geography* (n.p., 1828), 161.

15. Goodrich, *Ireland and the Irish,* 66, 72; Bowen, "The Irish in America," 205.

16. Michel Chevalier, *Society, Manners, and Politics in the United States* (Boston, 1839), 123; "Pennsylvania" (pseud.), "The Right of Suffrage to Subsequent Immigrants," *Southern Literary Messenger* 12 (June 1846), 367.

17. "On the Formation of National Character," *Western Monthly Magazine* 1 (August 1833), 348.

18. Jefferson, *Notes on the State of Virginia,* 83.

19. "On the Formation of National Character," 351; "Immigration of Foreigners," *Western Monthly Magazine* 5 (December 1836), 746.

20. See Gordon S. Wood, *The Creation of the American Republic, 1776–1787* (New York, 1969), 68–69.

21. William Wirt Henry, ed., *Patrick Henry: Life, Correspondence, and Speeches* (n.p., 1891), 591; Thomas Jefferson to George Ticknor, November 25, 1817, in Bernard Mayo, ed., *Jefferson Himself: The Personal Narrative of a Many-Sided American* (Charlottesville, Va., 1970), 324. "Wisdom" and "virtue" were also among the most overworked terms in the political vocabulary of John Adams. See, for example, John Adams to Mercy Warren, January 8, 1776, and April 16, 1776, in *Warren-Adams Letters, Being Chiefly a Correspondence Among John Adams and James Warren, 1743–1814,* 2 vols. (Boston, 1917–25), 1:201–02, 227.

22. William Hickling Prescott, "Bancroft's United States," in *The Papers of William Hickling Prescott,* ed. C. Harvey Gardiner (Urbana, Ill., 1964), 299.

23. U.S. Congress, House, "Memorial of James P. Miller and Ninety-Six Other Electors of Washington County, New York, Praying a Revision of the Laws Respecting the Naturalization of Foreigners," H. Document 154, 25th Cong., 2nd sess., 1838; Frederick Hedge, *Oration Pronounced Before the Citizens of Bangor, July 4, 1838* (Bangor, Me., 1838), 20; [Thomas Paine], *Common Sense* (Philadelphia, 1776), in *The Complete Writings of Thomas Paine,* ed. Philip S. Foner, 2 vols. (New York, 1945), 1:45.

24. *United States Anti-Masonic Convention,* 118.

25. "On the formation of National Character," 350.

26. Daniel Drake, *Discourse . . . on the West* (Cincinnati, 1834), 6; Ralph R. Gurley, *Life of Jehudi Ashmun, Late Colonial Agent in Liberia* (n.p., 1835), 107.

27. Prescott, "Bancroft's U.S.," 304–05.

28. See Franklin, *The Legislative History of Naturalization,* 117–33.

29. *Cincinnati Daily Gazette,* May 15, 1844.

30. Snyder, "The Wild Irish," 147–85, offers a useful discussion of the "wild Irish" in English literary tradition.

31. "Ireland," *North American Review* 5 (July 1840), 205; William Channing Woodbridge and E. C. Willard, *Universal Geography* (Hartford, 1833), 297; S. Augustus Mitchell, *A System of Modern Geography* (Philadelphia, 1843), 243.

32. B. D. Emerson, *The Academical Speaker: Exercises in Elocution* (Boston, 1830), 261–62.

33. "Foreign Pauperism in the United States," *New England Magazine* 7 (December 1834), 498.

34. *New York Morning Herald,* June 17, 1837.

35. *National Intelligencer,* July 6, 1844; U.S. Congress, House, "Foreign Paupers and Naturalization Laws: Report of the Select Committee," House Report 1040, 25th Cong., 2nd sess., 1838, 111.

36. Joseph C. and Owen Lovejoy, eds., *Memoir of the Rev. Elijah P. Lovejoy* (New York, 1838), 114.

37. "The Catholic Question," 388; Lovejoy, eds., *Memoir,* 104.

38. "Review of Traits and Stories of the Irish Peasantry," *Knickerbocker* 2 (September 1833), 228. For other examples of the alleged variability of Irish temperament see "All Saints Eve; or A Recollection of the Irish Peasantry," *Knickerbocker* 2 (September 1833), 188–96; "Immigration of Foreigners," 743–49; Dwight, *Travels in New England and New York,* 3:375.

39. Rev. W. C. Brownlee, *Letters in the Roman Catholic Controversy* (New York, 1834), 178; Bowen, "Irish in America," 200–01. Harvard College commencement programs in the early 1840s were full of student addresses treating the effects of environment upon character. John Chandler Nourse, one of White's classmates, discussed "The Alleged Demoralizing Influence of Large Towns," while two years later Francis Brooks would instruct his fellow graduates on the "Importance of a High Standard of Liberal Education in a Republic" and Leonard Livermore examined the effects of regionalism in the "New England Character."

40. For examples of the publicity given to civil disturbances involving (or allegedly involving) the Irish see *Niles' Weekly Register,* August 22, 1835, and June 5, 1841; "Riots in Boston and New Haven," *New York Morning Herald,* June 15, 1837.

41. "Papacy in the United States," *American Quarterly Register* 7 (August 1835), 58–60.

42. Francis Grund, *The Americans in Their Moral, Social, and Political Relations* (Boston, 1837), 79–80.

43. Frank Rahill, *The World of Melodrama* (University Park, Pa., 1967), xiv. For other discussions of the melodramatic form and its effectiveness in capturing popular concerns see James L. Smith, ed., *Victorian Melodramas: Seven English, French, and American Melodramas* (London, 1976), viii, and David Grimsted, "Melodrama as Echo of the Historically Voiceless," in *Anonymous Americans: Explorations in 19th Century Social History,* ed. Tamara K. Hareven (Englewood Cliffs, N.J., 1971), 81.

44. Editorial Introduction to George Colman, *The Jealous Wife* (New York, 1846), iv; "Amusements," *The Republic* 1 (April, 1851), 183–84.

45. See Table 2.1, p. 222.

46. Samuel Griswold Goodrich, *The Fourth Reader* (n.p., 1839), 151; Hugh Henry Brackenridge, *Modern Chivalry* (New York, 1847), 6; J. Planche, *The Irish Post* (New York, 1830), 30.

47. Edward Fitzball, *Jonathan Bradford* (Pittsburgh, 1844), 25; Power, *The Omnibus,* 6. For a more thorough discussion of the stage Irishman in antebellum melodrama see Dale T. Knobel, "A Vocabulary of Ethnic Perception: Content Analysis of the American Stage Irishman, 1820–1860," *Journal of American Studies* 15 (April, 1981), 45–71.

48. C. E. Grice, *The Battle of New Orleans* (Baltimore, 1815), 8–9.

49. John Minshull, *Rural Felicity* (New York, 1801), 61–62; James Workman, *Liberty in Louisiana* (Charleston, S.C., 1804), 35.

50. "The Catholic Question," 379; Julius Laffal, *Pathological and Normal Language* (New York, 1965), x.

TABLE 2.1: *Distribution of "Unit-Perceptions" of the Irish in Popular Melodrama and Contemporaneous "Conversation"*

Cate-gory	Classification	1820–1844		1845–1852		1853–1860	
		Melo-drama	All sources	Melo-drama	All sources	Melo-drama	All sources
1	Positive Relational	5%	12%	9%	13%	6%	11%
2	Positive Intellectual	0	4	0	2	0	2
3	Positive Moral	6	3	1	2	2	1
4	Negative Relational	20	13	12	7	11	9
5	Negative Intellectual	11	11	8	6	15	10
6	Negative Moral	6	5	6	6	4	4
7	Conflict/Hostility	4	9	20	15	4	9
8	Substantial	0	2	1	2	1	2
9	Insubstantial	5	9	5	7	10	9
10	Emotional	14	9	17	11	15	12
11	Political/Religious	4	4	1	2	2	5
12	Economic	1	3	5	5	2	2
13	Aesthetic/Cultural	3	3	2	3	7	4
14	Physical	16	9	12	14	23	19
15	Group Subjective	5	5	3	4	0	2

51. See, for example, the approaches of Handlin, *Boston's Immigrants*; Billington, *Protestant Crusade*; Higham, *Strangers in the Land*.

CHAPTER THREE: "AN IRISHMAN BY NATURE"

1. Timothy L. Smith, "Religion and Ethnicity in America," *American Historical Review* 83 (December 1978), 1155.

2. Nagel, *This Sacred Trust*, 63–64. Note, however, that Nagel does not find that the development of American ethnic "peoplehood" was complete until the late 1890s. See also Horsman, *Race and Manifest Destiny*, 134, and Robert F. Berkhofer, Jr., *The White Man's Indian: Impressions of the American Indian from Columbus to the Present* (New York, 1978), 56–57, 154–55.

3. Horsman, for example, specifically directs his attention to the American intellectual community. Horsman, *Race and Manifest Destiny*, 6.

4. For an example of mid-antebellum perceptions of "Irishism" see Francis Bowen, "The Distribution of Property—Ireland," *North American Review* 67 (July 1848), 145.

5. Cephus and Eveline Brainerd, eds., *The New England Society Orations, 1820–1885* (New York, 1901), and Clark S. Northrup, et al., eds., *Representative Phi Beta Kappa Lectures* (Boston, 1915), are useful though selective compilations of this material. Some Phi Beta Kappa lectures and all of the annual New England Society addresses were published separately. For a description of the aims and origins of the New England Society see New England Society of New York, *Annual Report—1861* (New York, 1861), 11, 15, 17.

6. Horace Bushnell, "The True Wealth or Weal of Nations," in Nor-

thrup et al., *Phi Beta Kappa Lectures*, 12–14; Robert Charles Winthrop, "Address, 1839," in Brainerd, *New England Society Orations*, 258.

7. Charles Brickett Haddock, "The Elements of National Greatness, 1841," and George B. Cheever, "The Elements of National Greatness, 1842," in Brainerd, *New England Society Orations*, 273, 290, 313–15.

8. Job Durfee, "The Influence of Scientific Discovery and Invention on Social and Political Progress," in Northrup et al., *Phi Beta Kappa Lectures*, 74–75, 64, 55.

9. George Perkins Marsh, "Address, 1844," in Brainerd, *New England Society Orations*, 414–15, 382.

10. Mark Hopkins, "Oration, 1853," and Richard Salter Storrs, "Oration, 1857," in Brainerd, *New England Society Orations*, 205, 363, 340.

11. Giles, "The Present Condition of Ireland," 113–14.

12. Ibid., 113; H. Giles, "The New Exodus," *The Christian Examiner* 52 (May 1852), 375.

13. Thomas L. Nichols, *Forty Years of American Life* (London, 1864), 71.

14. *National Intelligencer*, October 11, 1851.

15. E. J. Sears, "Ireland, Past and Present," *North American Review* 86 (January 1858), 136.

16. "Foreign Immigration Formerly and Now," *DeBow's Review* 24 (1858), 328.

17. Edward Everett Hale, *Letters on Irish Immigration* (Boston, 1852), 54–55. These essays were originally published in the *Boston Daily Advertiser* during December 1851 and January 1852.

18. Ibid., 56.

19. Edward H. Dixon, M.D., *Scenes in the Practice of a New York Surgeon* (New York, 1855), 260–61.

20. "The Foreign Vote and the Catholic Press," *United States Review* 34 (September 1854), 195–96.

21. Journalist E. L. Godkin offered a typical complaint about the manipulation of the Irish vote on the eve of the Civil War. See Ogden, ed., *Life and Letters of E. L. Godkin*, 1:182.

22. "The Irish Character," in Margaret Fuller Ossoli, *Woman in the Nineteenth Century, and Kindred Papers Relating to the Sphere, Condition, and Duties of Woman*, ed. Arthur B. Fuller (Boston, 1860), 330. Ossoli, who died a decade before the collection of these essays in a book, originally published this selection in the *New York Tribune*.

23. "Angel Gabriel," *New York Times*, June 12, 1854; "The Foreign Vote and the Catholic Press," 199; William Bentley Fowle, *The Free Speaker* (Boston, 1859), 109–12.

24. Mrs. J. Ware, "The Anglo-Saxon Race," *North American Review* 73 (July 1851), 55–56.

25. Ralph Waldo Emerson, *English Traits*, in *The Selected Writings of Ralph Waldo Emerson*, ed. Brooks Atkinson (New York, 1950), 547. *English Traits*, which first appeared in 1856, described Emerson's visit to the British Isles nine years earlier. For similar comments see "The Anglo-Saxon Race," *Ballou's* 4 (April 23, 1853), 267; William Channing Woodbridge, *A System of Modern Geography* (Hartford, 1844), 353; and Theodore Parker, *The Rights of Man in America*, ed. F. B. Sanborn (Boston, 1911), 354–55.

26. "An Irish Heart," in Lucius Manlius Sargent, *Temperance Tales* (Boston, 1848), 180; "The Catholic Question," *North Western Christian Advocate*, February 16, 1853.

27. Anthony G. Dworkin, "Prejudice, Discrimination, and Intergroup Perceptions: Exploratory Research into the Correlates of Stereotypy," (Ph.D. Dissertation, Northwestern University, 1970), 103.

28. Michael Feldberg, *The Turbulent Era: Riot and Disorder in Jacksonian America* (New York, 1980), 7. Also see Montgomery, "The Shuttle and the Cross," 433.

29. Feldberg, *The Turbulent Era*, 11, 29. Also see Elizabeth M. Geffen, "Industrial Development and Social Crisis, 1841–1854," in Russel F. Weigley, ed., *Philadelphia: A 300-Year History* (New York, 1982), 357–58.

30. Peter Parley (pseud.), *Manners and Customs of Nations* (Boston, 1845), 112.

31. "Review of Mrs. A. Nicholson's *Ireland's Welcome to the Stranger*," *Southern Quarterly Review* 13 (January 1848), 237–45; Massachusetts General Court, Senate, "Report of the Joint Special Committee of the Legislature of Massachusetts Appointed to Consider the Expediency of Altering and Amending the Laws Relating to Alien Passengers and Paupers," Senate Document #46, 1848, p. 588.

32. "Mental and Moral Pauperism," *Harper's Monthly* 16 (February 1858), 408; Theodore Parker, "Causes of the Present Condition of Ireland," *Massachusetts Quarterly Review* 11 (June 1850), 336; Charles G. Finney, *Lectures on Systematic Theology* (1846–47; reprint ed., Grand Rapids, Mich., 1951), 222.

33. Henry David Thoreau, *Walden*, in *Thoreau: Walden and Other Writings*, ed. Joseph Wood Krutch (New York, 1962), 260. Thoreau kept his diary at Walden during 1845–47 and published it in 1854.

34. Theodore Parker, "A Sermon on the Moral Condition of Boston" (1849), in *The Collected Works of Theodore Parker*, ed. Frances P. Cobbe, 14 vols. (London, 1864), 7:136.

35. Allan Nevins, ed., *The Diary of George Templeton Strong*, 2 vols. (New York, 1952), 1:318, 2:348. These were, respectively, Strong's entries for April 28, 1848, and July 7, 1857.

36. "The Brooklyn Riot," *New York Daily Times*, June 6, 1854; "An Excursion in Ireland," *Southern Literary Messenger* 16 (February 1850), 94.

37. "The Anglo-Saxons and the Americans," *American Whig Review* 14 (September 1851), 192; review of *The Rise of the Dutch Republic* by John Lothrop Motley, *Presbyterian Quarterly Review* 7 (April 1859), 583.

38. William Channing Woodbridge, *A System of Modern Geography* (Boston, 1866), 353; George Ripley and Charles A. Dana, eds., *The American Cyclopedia: A Popular Dictionary of General Knowledge*, 16 vols. (New York, 1860), 9:351–52.

39. Massachusetts Board of State Charities, *Report* (Boston, 1866), xxii–xxiii; United States Bureau of the Census, *Statistics of the United States . . . Compiled from the Original Returns and Being the Final Exhibit of the Eighth Census* (Washington, 1866), I–LVII.

40. See, for example, Frank Rahill, *The World of Melodrama* (University Park, Pa., 1967), xiv; James E. Smith, ed., *Victorian Melodramas:*

Seven English, French, and American Melodramas (London, 1976), ix, xii. Moreover, some students of theater believe that the American stage Irishman was nothing more than an English import and therefore irrelevant to American experience. See Kent G. Gallagher, *The Foreigner in American Drama: A Study in Attitudes* (The Hague, 1966), 115, 117–18. Despite their generally boundless confidence that popular theater was a vehicle of mass attitudes, American social and cultural historians have often questioned the worth of the American stage Irishman as an historical datum, too. Richard Dorson argues that mid-nineteenth century cult characters—often popularized through melodrama—like Mose the Fireboy, Sam Patch, or the stage Irishman were virtually interchangeable adaptations of stock roles usually filled in English plays by servants or peasants. David Grimsted points out that since the one-dimensional Anglo-Saxon heroes of melodramatic productions could do no wrong, foolishness and foible inevitably fell into the hands of "ethnic, racial, or regional stereotypes." According to Grimsted, what made Paddy the Irishman, Jonathan the country rube, or Cubba the black laundress the comic idol of the melodramatic stage at any given time was largely unpredictable fad. They all performed the same dramaturgical function. See Dorson, *American Folklore,* 103; David Grimsted, "Melodrama as Echo of the Historically Voiceless," in *Anonymous Americans: Explorations in Nineteenth Century Social History,* ed. Tamara K. Hareven (Englewood Cliffs, N.J., 1971), 90; and Grimsted, *Melodrama Unveiled: American Theater and Culture, 1800–1850* (Chicago, 1968), 186, 189.

41. Maurice Bourgeois, *John Millington Synge and the Irish Theater* (London, 1913), quoted in Duggan, *The Stage Irishman,* 288–89.

42. For a more thorough assessment of temporal changes in the antebellum stage Irishman see Knobel, "A Vocabulary of Ethnic Perception," 45–71.

43. John Madison Morton, *The Irish Tiger* (New York, 1856), 4; Barney Williams, *Irish Assurance and Yankee Modesty* (New York, 1848), 5.

44. George S. M'Kiernan, "Murty O'Hanley, A Tale of Olden Times on the Frontier," *Southern Literary Messenger* 7 (July 1841), 515. As students of nineteenth century literature regularly point out, the themes and style of antebellum prose fiction were virtually interchangeable with those of popular drama. One of the immediate consequences was that the "stage Irishman" lived in the short story and novel too. The content characteristics of unit-perceptions of the Irish in this sort of material were very close to those of contemporaneous melodrama. Again, over time, the proportion of unit-perceptions of Irish characters featuring "extrinsic" and physical descriptives measurably increased. For a discussion of the connection between popular drama and prose fiction see Herbert R. Brown, *The Sentimental Novel in America, 1789–1860* (Durham, N.C., 1940), 127n.

45. Gunn, *The Physiology of New York Boarding Houses,* 1:267.

46. George Lippard, *The Nazarene* (Philadelphia, 1846), 170.

47. John Brougham, *Temptation, or the Irish Emigrant* (New York, 1856), 7; James Pilgrim, *Katty O'Sheal* (St. Louis, 1854), 3; William Macready, *The Irishman in London* (New York, 1853), 15–17. The latter is an American acting edition of an English comedy.

48. James Pilgrim, *The Wild Irish Girl* (Baltimore, 1858), 27.

49. Pilgrim, *Katty O'Sheal,* 3.

50. Colman, *Jealous Wife*, 52; James Kirke Paulding, *The Bucktails* (Philadelphia, 1847), 94; Gunn, *New York Boarding Houses*, 1:267.

51. John Brougham, *The Irish Yankee* (New York, 1856), 9.

52. *Harper's Monthly* 18 (January 1859), 277.

53. Sargent, "Irish Heart," 216.

54. "The Anglo-Saxons and the Americans," 188; "The Right of Suffrage," 367.

55. Theodore Parker, "The Present Crisis in American Affairs," in *Rights of Man in America*, 446. William R. Taylor, *Cavalier and Yankee: The Old South and American National Character* (New York, 1961).

56. "Doctrine of Temperaments," *American Quarterly Review* 5 (March 1829), 122; "Thoughts on National Character," *New England Magazine* (April 1834), 35.

57. Pierre van den Berghe, *Race and Racism, A Comparative Approach* (New York, 1967), 12; Salma Hale, *History of the United States* (Cooperstown, New York, 1840), 263.

58. See Roy Harvey Pearce, *Savagism and Civilization: A Study of the Indian and the American Mind* (Baltimore, 1965); John C. Calhoun speaking in the United States Senate, January 4, 1848, on the annexation of "All Mexico" in Calhoun, *Works*, ed. Richard K. Cralle, 6 vols. (New York, 1853–57), 4:410–411.

59. Emerson, *English Traits*, 546.

60. "The Brooklyn Riot," *New York Times*, June 6, 1854.

61. G. G. Foster, *New York by Gas-Light* (New York, 1850), 102.

62. See Chapter Two for the emphases of the German stereotype. For a typical laudatory treatment of Germans in the United States see J. B. Angell, "German Emigration to America," *North American Review* 82 (January 1856), 246.

63. Van den Berghe, *Race and Racism*, 11.

64. Louis Schade, *The Immigration Into the United States from a Statistical and National-Economical Point of View* (Washington, 1856), 10; Foster, *New York by Gas-Light*, 49.

65. Earnest A. Hooten and Wesley C. Dupertuis, *The Physical Anthropology of Ireland* (Cambridge, Mass., 1955), 135–36.

66. David Brion Davis, "Some Ideological Functions of Prejudice in Ante-Bellum America," *American Quarterly* 15 (Summer 1963), 117.

67. Rosemary Gordon, *Stereotypy*, 44.

CHAPTER FOUR: SCIENCE AND THE CELT

1. Fredrickson, *Black Image*, 100–01; Gossett, *Race*, 97; and Jean H. Baker, *Ambivalent Americans: The Know-Nothing Party in Maryland* (Baltimore, 1977), 38–39.

2. Higham, *Strangers*, 11, 9.

3. See Gossett, *Race*; Fredrickson, *Black Image*; William Stanton, *The Leopard's Spots: Scientific Attitudes Toward Race in America, 1815–59* (Chicago, 1960); and Horsman, *Race and Manifest Destiny*.

4. Johann Friedrich Blumenbach, *On the Natural Variety of Mankind* (Göttingen, 1795), 264; Johann Gottfried von Herder, *Reflections on the Philosophy of the History of Mankind* (London, 1800; reprint, Chicago, 1968), 7.

5. Stanton, *Leopard's Spots*, 16–18; Samuel Stanhope Smith, *An Essay on the Causes of Variety of Complexion and Figure in the Human Species* (New Brunswick, N.J., 1810; reprint, Cambridge, Mass., 1965), 9, 23.

6. Review of *Lectures on Physiology* by William F. Lawrence, *North American Review* 17 (July 1823), 19–20; Woodbridge and Willard, *Universal Geography* (1835), 165, 216–17.

7. "Chenevix on National Character," *American Quarterly Review* 8 (September 1832), 24–25; "Thoughts on National Character," 36–37.

8. Parley (pseud.), *Manners and Customs of Nations*, 5–6; Goodrich, *Ireland and the Irish*, 46; George Chambers, *A Tribute to the Principles, Virtues, Habits, and Public Usefulness of the Irish and Scotch Early Settlers of Pennsylvania* (Chambersburg, Pa., 1856), 34.

9. Friedrich von Raumer captured the criticisms directed at American nationality: "Sometimes . . . the nationality even of white Americans is disputed; because they have no long magnificent past, no antiquity to look back to; and because a conflux of many nations, a *colluvias gentium*, excludes the possibility of a finished, independent, peculiar character." Friedrich von Raumer, *America and the American People*, trans. William W. Turner (New York, 1846), 145.

10. Arthur de Gobineau, *The Inequality of Human Races*, trans. Adrian Collins (1853; reprint, New York, 1967), 2–3, 24–25; Gobineau, *The Moral and Intellectual Diversity of Races*, Introduction by H. Hotz, Appendix by J. C. Nott (Philadelphia, 1856), 78–81.

11. Gobineau, *Moral and Intellectual Diversity*, 78–79.

12. Robert Knox, M.D., *The Races of Men: A Fragment* (Philadelphia, 1850), 57–58.

13. Knox, *Races of Men*, 216, 54–55, 98.

14. Theodore Parker, "The Political Destination of America," in *Collected Works*, ed. Cobbe, 4:80. For a good description of Parker's ethnological sensitivity see Michael Fellman, "Theodore Parker and the Abolitionist Role in the 1850's," *Journal of American History* 61 (December 1974), 666–84.

15. Emerson, *English Traits*, 546.

16. "Prospects of America," *The Western Messenger* 6 (November 1838), 33.

17. See Stanton, *Leopard's Spots*, 176, 190, and Fredrickson, *Black Image*, 132, 137.

18. Josiah C. Nott and George Glidden, *Types of Mankind* (Philadelphia, 1854), 301–17.

19. "The Brooklyn Riot," *New York Times*, June 6, 1854; "Exiles of Erin," *New York Times*, April 28, 1853.

20. See John D. Davies, *Phrenology, Fad and Science: A Nineteenth Century American Crusade* (New Haven, 1955), 3, and E. Douglas Branch, *The Sentimental Years, 1836–1860* (New York, 1934), 278–88. In his now somewhat dated overview of antebellum culture, Branch takes phrenology very lightly indeed.

21. "The Mental Character of Man," *Atkinson's Casket* (August 1837), 351–52.

22. "Phrenology," *New England Magazine* 6 (June 1834), 467; Orson S. and L. N. Fowler, *Self-Instructor in Phrenology and Physiology* (New York, 1859); "Outlines of Phrenology," *Western Monthly Magazine* 3 (April

1835), 258–60. See also "Phrenological Examinations," *Southern Literary Messenger* 1 (1834–5), 204–05; serialization of Combe's lectures in *Southern Literary Messenger* 5 (1839), 393; and "Remarks on the Science of Phrenology," *American Journal of Education* 4 (1829), 541–43.

23. Davies, *Phrenology*, 60.

24. Orson S. Fowler, *Hereditary Descent: Its Laws and Facts* (New York, 1843), 47.

25. Review of *A System of Phrenology*, by George Combe, in *Christian Examiner* 16 (May 1834), 225; Review of *Phrenology*, by Johann Spurzheim, in *Christian Examiner* 17 (November 1834), 253. While phrenology was still in favor, one magazine editor enthused that it was like "a compass for the moral philosopher." See "Thoughts on Phrenology," *Illinois Monthly Magazine* 2 (December 1831), 110.

26. Russell Jarvis, "On the Humbug of Phrenology," *Burton's Gentleman's Magazine* 7 (August 1840), 62–69.

27. In 1840 the *Western Messenger* noted the "intellectual eagerness of Cincinnatians" for George Combe's forthcoming lecture series in the city. "Monthly Record," *Western Messenger* 8 (June 1840), 94.

28. Samuel George Morton, M.D., *Crania Americana* (Philadelphia, 1839). Reviews of Morton's work began appearing almost immediately in the popular journals. See, for example, *Christian Examiner* 28 (May 1840), 248–52.

29. Morton, *Crania Americana*, 1; review of *Crania Americana*, by Samuel George Morton, in *American Journal of Science* 38 (1840), 349; Morton, *Crania Americana*, 4–5.

30. "Psychology," *Baltimore Literary and Religious Magazine* 7 (August 1841), 351.

31. Charles Pickering, *The Races of Man* (London, 1854), 3; Josiah Nott, *Two Lectures on the Connection Between the Biblical and Physical History of Man* (Mobile, Ala., 1849), 27.

32. Nott and Glidden, *Types of Mankind*, 89, 411.

33. "Passing Faces," *Harper's Monthly* 11 (June 1855), 91.

34. Blumenbach, *Natural Variety of Mankind*, 226–27, 229; Smith, *Essay*, 46–47.

35. Thomas Price, *An Essay on the Physiognomy and Physiology of the Present Inhabitants of Britain; with Reference to their Origin, as Goths and Celts* (London, 1829), 32; Sir Charles Bell, *The Anatomy and Philosophy of Expression* (London, 1847), 18–44.

36. James W. Redfield, M.D., *Comparative Physiognomy or Resemblances Between Men and Animals* (New York, 1852), 3, 10.

37. Fowler, *Hereditary Descent*, 125; Fowler, *Self-Instructor*, 121.

38. The editors of the *New England Magazine* thought that phrenology might be a useful way for individuals to learn about themselves: "We venture to say that the more enlightened the intellect is, and the stronger the moral powers, the freer is the Will, because it is unfettered by animal passions." "Phrenology Vindicated," *New England Magazine* 7 (December 1834), 441.

39. Price, *Physiognomy and Physiology*, vi–viii.

40. Gobineau, *Moral and Intellectual Diversity*, 92.

41. Fowler, *Hereditary Descent*, 33–34.

42. Ben Gaultier, "Influence of Place on Race," *Graham's* 41 (October

1852), 362–63; "Are All Men Descended From Adam?" *Putnam's Monthly* 5 (January 1855), 79–88. The latter essay was particularly blunt: "The peculiarities that mark the different races are not confined to the great families of mankind, but extend to the different tribes of each of these families; and the northern nations of Europe differ quite as permanently from the southern, as the Caucasian does from the Mongolian. . . . It is easy to distinguish an Englishman from a Frenchman, a Spaniard from a German. Now, if the varieties manifested by the two or three great families of mankind compel us to trace them to two or three different origins, why will not the differences equally ineradicable between infinitely numerous tribes, point also in each case to different origin?"

43. *Charleston* (South Carolina) *Mercury*, August 14, 1834; "National Postures," *New England Magazine* 7 (September 1834), 229–30; Emerson, *English Traits*, 547.

44. "Pictures of the Russians," *Harper's Monthly* 11 (September 1855), 434, 452. See also "A Scene from Irish Life," *Harper's Monthly* 3 (1851), 833.

45. Nott and Glidden, *Types of Mankind*, 450. Nott placed "Anglo-Americans" in the "Teutonic Family" of the "Caucasian Group."

46. Fowler, *Self-Instructor*, 51; Thomas Milner, "Distribution of the Human Race," *Graham's* 41 (September 1852), 239, 241.

47. "A Scene from Irish Life," 833.

48. See Table 1.1, page 212, for a tabulation of the growing proportion of physical descriptions among unit-perceptions of the Irish in antebellum "conversation."

49. Fowler, *Hereditary Descent*, 126; Fowler, *Self-Instructor*, 43–45, 55–56. For a good example of the responsiveness of the phrenological pseudo-sciences to popular stereotypes see James Redfield, *Outline of a New System of Physiognomy* (New York, 1850), 58.

50. "The Louisville Riots," *Washington National Era*, August 16, 1855; "The Louisville Riots—The Tragic Side of Know-Nothingism," *New York Times*, August 8, 1855; Parke Godwin, "Secret Societies—The Know-Nothings," *Putnam's Monthly* 5 (January 1855), 94–95.

51. Rev. W. H. Lord, *A Tract for the Times: National Hospitality* (Montpelier, Vt., 1855), 5, 21–44; Thomas L. Nichols, *Letters on Immigration and the Right of Naturalization* (New York, 1845), 3–4, 21–32.

52. S. Osgood, "Americans and the Men of the Old World," *Christian Examiner* 59 (July 1855), 7; "The Anglo-Saxon Race," 42; "Sources From Which Great Empires Come," *DeBow's Review* 18 (1855), 704; "The Destiny of Our Country," *American Whig Review* 5 (March 1847), 232–33.

53. Fredrickson, *Black Image*, 107. See Oliver Wendell Holmes, Sr., *The Autocrat of the Breakfast Table* (Boston, 1854), 22. Holmes expressed the "romantic racialist" faith accurately: "We are the Romans of the modern world,—the great assimilating people."

54. Harriet Beecher Stowe, *A Key to Uncle Tom's Cabin* (Boston, 1853), 25; "The African Race," *National Anti-Slavery Standard*, April 27, 1847; Lydia Maria Child, *Letters From New York* (New York, 1844–45), 244; Ossoli, "The Irish Character," 324.

55. "Are We One or Many?" *Harper's Monthly* 9 (October 1854), 690.

56. "A Catholic and an Adopted Citizen," *New York Tribune*, October

26, 1844. See also Thomas D'Arcy McGee, *A History of the Irish Settlers in North America* (Boston, 1851), 177.

CHAPTER FIVE: PADDY AND THE KNOW-NOTHINGS

1. Arieli, *Individualism and Nationalism*, 297.
2. John P. Sanderson, *Republican Landmarks* (Philadelphia, 1856), 20.
3. "Boston City Marshall Francis Tukey, An Address of an American Meeting in Boston to the State of Massachusetts," *The Republic* 2 (December 1851), 278; "The Boston *Pilot* and Marshall Tukey," *The Republic* 3 (January 1852), 40–41; Nicholas Murray, *Romanism at Home: Letters to Chief Justice Roger Taney* (New York, 1852), 191; Lee, *The Origin and Progress of the American Party*, 60.
4. Lee, *The Origin and Progress of the American Party*, 120.
5. *The American Protestant* 3 (January 1848), 10; Samuel F. B. Morse, *Foreign Conspiracy Against the Liberties of the United States* (New York, 1835), 69–70; Lyman Beecher, *A Plea for the West* (Cincinnati, 1835), 51.
6. Simeon Baldwin to Millard Fillmore, July 21, 1856. Millard Fillmore Collection, The Penfield Library, State University of New York at Oswego.
7. Arieli is not alone in suggesting that nativists were in the vanguard. Merel Curti made the same observations much earlier. See Curti, *The Roots of American Loyalty*, 77.
8. *New York Irish-American*, quoted in *New York Times*, August 30, 1854.
9. Rosemary Gordon, *Stereotypy*, 38.
10. For some discussion of these interrelationships see Griffin, *Their Brothers' Keepers*, 216, 178, and "Our Secret Societies," *New York Tribune*, May 29, 1855.
11. Higham, *Strangers*, 3.
12. For a fair sample of interpretations of antebellum nativism's sources see Billington, *Protestant Crusade*; Handlin, *Boston's Immigrants*; Baker, *Ambivalent Americans*; W. Darrell Overdyke, *The Know-Nothing Party in the South* (Baton Rouge, 1950); Higham, "Another Look"; Holt, "The Politics of Impatience"; Davis, "Themes of Counter-Subversion."
13. For some discussion of the attractiveness of fraternal societies to both natives and immigrants see Dale T. Knobel, "To Be an American: Ethnicity, Fraternity, and The Improved Order of Red Men," *Journal of American Ethnic History* 4 (Fall 1984), 62–87.
14. See, for example, "Know-Nothingism in Georgia," *Augusta Daily Constitutionalist*, April 10, 1854; *Jackson Mississippian*, December 5, 1854; *Remarks on the Majority and Minority Reports of the Select Committee on Secret Societies of the House of Delegates of Maryland* (New York, 1856), 29; *Scioto* (Ohio) *Gazette*, July 25, 1844.
15. "A Calm Discussion of the Know Nothing Question," *Southern Literary Messenger* 20 (September, 1854), 540; Greeley, *Recollections of a Busy Life*, 290.
16. John Higham sums up these prejudices in *Strangers*, 3–11.
17. Fredrickson, *Black Image*, 99; Gossett, *Race*, 97.
18. Higham, *Strangers*, 9–11; Baker, *Ambivalent Americans*, 38–39.
19. "Abolition and Sectarian Mobs," *United States Review* 34 (August 1854), 113; Godwin, "Secret Societies," 95–97; *Baltimore Metropolitan* 4

(December 1856), 652; "Dastardly Conduct," *The Liberator*, September 15, 1837; "Brutal and Bloody Riot," *The Liberator*, June 14, 1837.

20. "Editorial Remarks," *Western Monthly Magazine* 5 (January 1836), 2–3; "The War on the Catholics," *Cincinnati Daily Gazette*, January 12, 1837, and January 23, 1837; "Philadelphia Riots," *New York Herald*, May 11, 1844.

21. "Relations of the Old and the New Worlds," *DeBow's Review* 20 (May 1856), 531; *National Intelligencer*, August 11, 1855. Democrats attacked the Know-Nothings on just these grounds in their 1852 national platform. See Porter and Johnson, eds., *National Party Platforms*, 16–18.

22. Billington, *Protestant Crusade*, 445–82.

23. See Appendix B for the procedure followed in sampling nativist literature.

24. See Table 5.1, p. 232.

25. Evaluative assertion analysis reveals both the unfavorability and evaluative homogeneity of the nativist stereotype. See Table 5.2, p. 233.

26. Robert J. Breckinridge, "Memoranda of Foreign Travel," *The Baltimore Literary and Religious Magazine* 2 (August 1836), 288.

27. Before 1845, 9% of all unit-perceptions of the Irish in ordinary "conversation" drew attention to Category 7, "Conflict/Hostility." Between 1845 and 1852 this increased to 15%. In nativist rhetoric the proportion of unit-perceptions that fell into this category decreased from 15% to 11% over the same lapse of time.

28. See Table 5.3, p. 233.

29. *The Republic* 1 (January 1851), 44; Higham, *Strangers*, 4.

30. For varying expressions of concern for American "national character" see "Know Nothing Convention in Philadelphia," *New York Times*, June 9, 1855; Anna Ella Carroll, *The Great American Battle; or, the Contest Between Christianity and Political Romanism* (New York, 1856), 100; 1856 American party platform in Porter and Johnson, eds., *National Party Platforms*, 22–23.

31. The proper attitude toward the words of George Washington, a nativist speaker admonished, was to "cherish them, and teach your children to revere them, as you cherish and revere the memory of Washington himself." "Know-Nothing Ritual," *New York Times*, April 30, 1855; Jefferson, *Notes*, 93; Henry Cabot Lodge, ed., *The Works of Alexander Hamilton*, 12 vols. (New York, 1904), 8:288, 8:217.

32. Sanderson, *Republican Landmarks*, 44; William M'Gavin, *The Protestant: Essays on the Principal Points of Controversy Between the Church of Rome and the Reformed*, 2 vols. (Hartford, 1833), 2:735; M. W. Cluskey, *The Political Text-Book or Encyclopedia* (Philadelphia, 1858), 55.

33. George Bancroft, *History of the United States*, 7 vols. (Boston, 1858), 7:21–22. For an example of nativist usage of this theme see "An Oration Delivered by the Hon. William W. Campbell," *The Republic* 4 (September 1852), 9.

34. *Mass Meeting of the Citizens of Washington*, September 27, 1854 (Washington, n.d.), 12.

35. "Our Country," *The Republic* 2 (September 1851), 110–11; U.S. Congress, House, Speech of Cong. Henry Winter Davis, *Congressional Globe*, 34th Cong., 1st sess., 1855–1856, XXV, 730.

TABLE 5.1: *Two Languages of Ethnic Description*

Category	Characteristic	1820–1844 Non-nativist "conversation"	1820–1844 Nativist rhetoric	1845–1852 Non-nativist "conversation"	1845–1852 Nativist rhetoric	1853–1860 Non-nativist "conversation"	1853–1860 Nativist rhetoric
1	Positive Relational	12%	0%	13%	0%	11%	1%
2	Positive Intellectual	4	0	2	3	2	0
3	Positive Moral	5	0	2	0	1	0
4	Negative Relational	13	9	7	18	9	22
5	Negative Intellectual	11	22	6	30	10	11
6	Negative Moral	5	13	15	7	4	14
7	Conflict/Hostility	9	15	2	11	9	13
8	Substantial	2	1	7	3	2	0
9	Insubstantial	9	0	11	1	9	2
10	Emotional	9	1	2	4	12	2
11	Political/Religious	4	16	5	8	5	2
12	Economic	3	6	2	4	2	6
13	Aesthetic/Cultural	3	1	2	4	4	6
14	Physical	9	12	14	5	19	16
15	Group Subjective	5	4	4	4	2	2
	Observations	N = 598	N = 72	N = 520	N = 77	N = 474	N = 94

TABLE 5.2: *Evaluative Character of Two Languages of Ethnic Description*

Stereotype and measure	1820–1844	1845–1852	1853–1860
Non-Nativist "Conversation":			
Mean EAA Score	−4.8	−3.7	−4.8
Standard Deviation	2.8	3.9	3.1
Nativist Rhetoric:			
Mean EAA Score	−8.4	−7.2	−7.2
Standard Deviation	0.9	0.6	0.6

TABLE 5.3: *Emphases of Two Languages of Ethnic Description*

Type	1820–1844		1845–1852		1853–1860	
	Non-nativist	Nativist	Non-nativist	Nativist	Non-nativist	Nativist
Positive Intrinsic (Cats. 1, 2, 3)	19%	0%	17%	3%	14%	1%
Negative Intrinsic (Cats. 4, 5, 6, 15)	34	48	23	59	25	59
All Intrinsic (Cats. 1–6, 15)	53	48	40	62	39	60
All Extrinsic (Cats. 7–14)	47	52	60	38	61	40
Observations	N = 598	N = 72	N = 520	N = 77	N = 474	N = 94

36. Noah Webster, *An American Dictionary of the English Language,* ed. Chauncey A. Goodrich (Springfield, Mass., 1850), 744; "Oration . . . by the Hon. William W. Campbell," 9, 15.

37. "Dangers and Safeguards of the Union," *American Whig Review* 9 (February 1849), 111.

38. See, for example, "The American Drama," *The Republic* 1 (March 1851), 133.

39. Samuel F. B. Morse, *Imminent Dangers to the Free Institutions of the United States Through Foreign Immigration* (New York, 1835), 19.

40. "Unity of government" seems to have been an expression borrowed from George Washington's Farewell Address in which the President lauded "the unity of government which constitutes you one people." See David Everett Wheeler, *A Discourse Delivered at the Request of the Order of United Americans, New York City, February 22, 1851* (New York, 1851), 34.

41. "Speech of William Cost Johnson of Maryland in the House of Representatives, February 1838," *New York Review* 10 (1842), 180; Thomas R.

Whitney, *A Defense of the American Policy as Opposed to the Encroach-ments of Foreign Influence* (New York, 1856), 33.

42. Frederick Rinehart Anspach, *The Sons of the Sires: A History of the Rise, Progress, and Destiny of the American Party* (Philadelphia, 1855), 116, 72.

43. M'Gavin, *The Protestant*, 2:766; *Declaration of Principles of the Native American Convention, Assembled at Philadelphia, July 4, 1845* (Philadelphia, n.d.), 4–7.

44. Frederick Saunders and Thomas B. Thorpe, *The Progress and Prospects of America; or, the Model Republic, its Glory or its Fall* (New York, 1855), 108; Morse, *Foreign Conspiracy*, 78.

45. Charlotte Elizabeth Tonna, *Letters from Ireland* (New York, 1844), 379. Tonna was an Anglo-Irish woman whose anti-Catholic works were republished and widely distributed in the United States; Beecher, *A Plea for the West*, 77; Rev. W. C. Brownlee, *Letters in the Roman Catholic Controversy* (New York, 1834), 181.

46. Carroll, *The Great American Battle*, 166, 168.

47. Anspach, *Sons of the Sires*, 65–73, 115–17, 173–74; Breckinridge, "Memoranda of Foreign Travel," 288.

48. Saunders and Thorpe, *The Progress and Prospects of America*, 208.

49. See "Know-Nothing Ritual" and "Know Nothing Convention in Philadelphia." The latter reported the speech of New York delegate E. T. Andrews: "So it was with every man that was joined with a nation; if he did not become a part of its very organism, he was but a dead branch."

50. Saunders and Thorpe, *The Progress and Prospects of America*, 230.

51. Nicholas Murray, *Romanism at Home* (New York, 1852), 194, 199.

52. Whitney, *Defense of the American Policy*, 165; A. Blaisdell, *Principles and Objects of the American Party* (New York, 1855), 11; Robert J. Breckinridge, *Papism in the Nineteenth Century in the United States* (Baltimore, 1841), 25.

53. Whitney, *Defense of the American Policy*, 129; *American Protestant* 3 (January 1848), Appendix:10; John Hancock Lee, *The Origin and Progress of the American Party in Politics* (Philadelphia, 1855), 243.

54. Blaisdell, *Principles and Objects*, 27.

55. Brownlee, *Letters*, 178; "Chapter Rooms," *The Republic* 3 (January 1852), 51; "Mass Meeting of the Citizens of Washington," 14; Anspach, *Sons of the Sires*, 106–07.

56. "The Second Irish Generation in America," *The Republic* 3 (May 1852), 255.

57. Scisco, *Political Nativism*, 207, 141; "The City Since Election," *New York Times*, November 9, 1855; "Know Nothing National Council," *New York Times*, June 5, 1856; *New York Times*, August 8, 1855.

58. "The Brooklyn Riot"; "American Principles," *Harper's Monthly* 14 (1857), 410–11; Anspach, *Sons of the Sires*, 105–06.

59. Samuel Busey, *Immigration: Its Evils and Consequences* (New York, 1856), 39, 88; Morse, *Foreign Conspiracy*, xvi.

60. "The Irish American and the Proposed War with England," *The Republic* 4 (October 1852), 210; "Editorial," *The Republic* 3 (May 1852), 209; "Advance Backwards," *The Republic* 4 (September 1852), 160–61.

61. Morse, *Imminent Dangers*, 24; *New York Journal of Commerce*, November 4, 1843; Whitney, *Defense of the American Policy*, 140.

62. For a discussion of the appeal of nativism to anti-abolitionist Whigs in New York State, home of the Order of United Americans and the Order of the Star-Spangled Banner, see Dale T. Knobel, " 'Native Soil': Nativists, Colonizationists, and the Rhetoric of Nationality," *Civil War History* 27 (December, 1981), 314–18. W. Darrell Overdyke makes much of the appeal of a nativist third party to Southern Whigs. See Overdyke, *Know Nothing Party in the South,* passim.

63. "The Colored People," *The Republic* 3 (January 1852), 40.

64. "What shall we do with the colored people?" began the editorial in the January 1852 issue of *The Republic.* "This is now the great question with the pseudo-philanthropists, and the conclusion seems to be, that we must send them to Africa. To this proposition the colored people object, and, as we think, very reasonably and very naturally." Following this opening sally against the African colonization movement and its chief institutional patron, the American Colonization Society, Thomas Whitney offered an even stronger opinion: "We are utterly opposed to the proposition of a wholesale expatriation of the colored race. . . . We question very much the assumed right to remove them, or the policy of encouraging them to emigrate." For some material on the connections between nativism and colonizationism see Knobel, " 'Native Soil,' " 314–19.

65. "Relations of the Old and the New Worlds," 531; "Henry Clay: Speech to the Annual Meeting of the American Colonization Society, January 21, 1851," *African Repository* 27 (April 1851), 110; "A Memorial From the Free People of Color to the Citizens of Baltimore," *African Repository* 2 (December 1826), 295; George S. L. Starks, "Analogy Between the Anglo-American and the Liberian," *African Repository* 27 (November 1851), 345; "Slavery in the United States: Its Evils, Alleviations and Remedies," *North American Review* 73 (October 1851), 370–71.

66. Alfred Brewster Ely, *American Liberty, Its Sources, Its Dangers, and the Means of its Preservation—OUA Address, August 22, 1850* (New York, 1850), 23.

67. William Lloyd Garrison, *Thoughts on African Colonization,* 2 vols. (Boston, 1832), 1:12; *Rochester North Star,* January 26, 1849. Black abolitionists, especially, took the position that American nationality was the earned right of their race and no mere accident of birth. See Henry Highland Garnet, "Address to the Slaves of the United States of America," in Garnet, ed., *Walker's Appeal with a Brief Sketch of His Life* (New York, 1848), 94; and James M'Cune Smith, "Citizenship," *Anglo-African Magazine* 1 (May 1859), 144–50.

68. "A Real North American," *The Republic* 3 (February 1852), 105.

69. Copway's name has cropped up in bibliographies of western Great Lakes and upper Mississippi Indian history for over one hundred years, yet he remains a particularly enigmatic figure in American history. For example, Copway rates mention in Peter Jones, *History of the Ojibway Indians* (London, 1861), 189; Frederick W. Hodge, ed., *Handbook of American Indians North of Mexico,* 2 vols. (Washington, 1906), 1:347; and Frederick J. Dockstader, *Great North American Indians: Profiles in Life and Leadership* (New York, 1977), 59. For Copway's autobiography see *The Life, History and Travels of Kah-Ge-Ga-Gah-Bowh* (Philadelphia, 1847). For some of Copway's contacts with literati see Benjamin Silliman to George Copway, November 22, 1849, in George Copway, *Organization of a New Indian*

Territory East of the Missouri River (New York, 1850), 31; James Fenimore Cooper to George Copway, June 17, 1851, in James Franklin Beard, ed., *The Letters and Journals of James Fenimore Cooper*, 6 vols. (Cambridge, Mass., 1960–68), 6:274–75; Henry Wadsworth Longfellow to Ferdinand Freiligrath, July 16, 1851, in Samuel L. Longfellow, ed., *Life of Henry Wadsworth Longfellow*, 2 vols. (Boston, 1886), 2:198–99.

70. See George Copway, "The American Indians," *American Whig Review* 18 (June 1849), 631–37; George Copway, *The Life, Letters, and Speeches of Kah-Ge-Ga-Gah-Bowh* (New York, 1850); George Copway, *The Traditional History and Characteristic Sketches of the Ojibway Nation* (London, 1850), 284–98; George Copway, *Indian Life and Indian History* (Boston, 1858), 257–58; Copway, *Organization of a New Indian Territory*, 7–23; Copway, *Life, History and Travels*, 126–27.

71. Thomas L. McKenney, *Memoirs, Official and Personal; with Sketches of Travels among the Northern and Southern Indians* (New York, 1846), 247; Lewis H. Morgan, *League of the Ho-De-No-Sau-Nee or Iroquois* (New York, 1851), 444, 57; Henry Rowe Schoolcraft, *Algic Researches, Comprising Inquiries Respecting the Mental Characteristics of the North American Indians*, 2 vols. (New York, 1839), 1:18–20; H. R. Schoolcraft, comp., *Information Respecting the History, Condition, and Prospects of the Indian Tribes of North America*, 6 vols. (Philadelphia, 1851–57), 5:473. Helpful discussions of philanthropic ethnocentrism can be found in Gossett, *Race*, 245–52, and Michael C. Coleman, "Not Race, But Grace: Presbyterian Missionaries and American Indians, 1837–1893," *Journal of American History*, 67 (June 1980), 41–60.

72. Copway, *Life, Letters, and Speeches*, 169, 190, 195.

73. Copway, *Organization of a New Indian Territory*, 17; Copway, *Traditional History*, 202.

74. Copway, *Organization of a New Indian Territory*, 238; "Letter From George Copway," *New York Times*, September 8, 1856.

75. Congressman James Doty of Wisconsin was a political opportunist, sometimes a Whig, sometimes a Democrat, and eventually a Republican, but in the early 1850s he was an independent, self-described "Old Whig," which in Wisconsin as in much of the North was code for "nativist." The essentials of Copway's plan were contained in a memorial that Doty addressed to President Fillmore in January 1851 on the creation of a "state" along the Missouri that would eventually lead to citizenship for the northwestern Indians. James Duane Doty to Millard Fillmore, January 26, 1851, in Annie H. Abel, "Proposals for an Indian State, 1778–1878," *Annual Report of the American Historical Association for the Year 1907* (Washington, 1908), 103–04; Richard N. Current, *The History of Wisconsin: The Civil War Era, 1848–1873* (Madison, 1976), 209–14, 222–27; Alice Elizabeth Smith, *James Duane Doty: Frontier Promoter* (Madison, 1964), 320–21, 337, 362–63.

76. Benjamin G. Armstrong, *Early Life Among the Indians*, ed. Thomas P. Wentworth (Ashland, Wis., 1892), 26–31; Millard Fillmore, Third Annual Message to Congress, in James D. Richardson, ed., *A Compilation of the Messages and Papers of the Presidents, 1789–1897*, 10 vols. (Washington, 1900), 5:171.

77. Millard Fillmore Collection, The Penfield Library, State University of New York at Oswego.

78. See, for example, *Copway's American Indian,* July 26, August 23, and August 2, 1851.

79. U.S. Congress, Senate, "Debate on the Homestead Bill," *Congressional Globe,* 33rd Cong., 1st sess., April 19, 1854, 947–48.

80. U.S. Congress, House, "Debate on Admission of Oregon," *Congressional Globe,* 34th Cong., 1st sess., June 24, 1856, 1455; U.S. Congress, House, "Debate on Expenses of Indian Hostilities in Oregon and Washington," *Congressional Globe,* 34th Cong., 3rd sess., January 20, 1857, 387; U.S. Congress, House, "Debate on Indian Appropriations Bill," *Congressional Globe,* 34th Cong., 3rd sess., February 26, 1857, 917–18.

81. "Powhatan and His Tribe," *The Republic* 1 (May 1851), 224–25; "The Aboriginals of North America," *The Republic* 3 (January 1852), 8–10; Thomas R. Whitney, *The Ambuscade, An Historical Poem* (New York, 1845), 82.

82. "A Real North American," 105.

83. Carroll, *Great American Battle,* 86; Sanderson, *Republican Landmarks,* 217–19; Whitney, *Defense of the American Policy,* 66.

84. Saunders and Thorpe, *The Progress and Prospects of America,* 83–96, 303.

85. Ibid., 308; *Speeches of the Hon. Garrett Davis Upon His Proposition to Impose Further Restrictions Upon Foreign Immigrants: Delivered in the Convention to Revise the Constitution of Kentucky, December 15–17, 1849* (Frankfort, 1855), 7–11.

86. Sanderson, *Republican Landmarks,* 22, 20.

87. Garrison, *Thoughts,* 1:118–20.

88. Baker, *Ambivalent Americans,* 38.

89. Cluskey, *Political Text-Book,* 26.

90. Baker, *Ambivalent Americans,* 153.

91. Holt, "Politics of Impatience," 324; Benson, *The Concept of Jacksonian Democracy,* 291.

92. Fredrickson, *Black Image,* 322.

CHAPTER SIX: ETHNICITY AND NATIONALITY
IN ANTEBELLUM AMERICA

1. Noah Webster, *An American Dictionary of the English Language,* ed. Chauncey A. Goodrich (Springfield, Mass., 1864), 1295; *New York Times,* April 21, 1853.

2. *Detroit Catholic Vindicator,* January 27, 1855; Edward Pessen, *Jacksonian America: Society, Personality, and Politics* (rev. ed., Homewood, Ill., 1978), 36.

3. Higham, *Strangers in the Land,* 4–5; Handlin, *Boston's Immigrants,* 178; Handlin, "Ethnic Factor," 20.

4. Davis, "Some Themes of Counter-Subversion," 208, 213–14; David Brion Davis, "Some Ideological Functions of Prejudice in Ante-Bellum America," *American Quarterly,* 15 (Summer 1963), 116–17, 121. L. Perry Curtis, Jr. offers a remarkably similar assessment of the psychological functions of the Irish stereotype in Victorian Britain. See Curtis, *Anglo-Saxons and Celts,* 34, 90.

5. Ray Allen Billington probably best represents the position that hostility

to the Irish was more or less sustained anti-Catholicism. See Billington, *Protestant Crusade,* 36.

6. For examples of such sentiments expressed by nativists and non-nativists alike see Saunders and Thorpe, *Progress and Prospects of America,* 378–79; *The Republic* 3 (March 1852), 149; Cheever, "Elements of National Greatness, 1842," 313.

7. See, for example, Durfee, "Influence of Scientific Discovery," 62; "The Confederacy," *North American Review* 10 (September 1849), 297; Marsh, "Address, 1844," 412; George S. Hilliard, "Discourse, 1851," in Brainerd, *New England Society Orations,* 155–56.

8. Horace Bushnell, "Oration, 1849," in Brainerd, *New England Society Orations,* 90.

9. Robert H. Wiebe, *The Segmented Society: An Introduction to the Meaning of America* (New York, 1975), 31, 21.

10. Hilliard, "Discourse, 1851," 156; for examples of pessimistic reformers see Theodore Parker, "A Sermon on the Dangerous Classes in Society" (1847), in Parker, *Collected Works,* 7:60–93, or Massachusetts Commission on Lunacy, *Report on Insanity and Idiocy in Massachusetts* (Boston, 1855), 57–68. Michael B. Katz and James F. Kasson both discuss the changing outlook of mid-nineteenth century reformers. Katz argues that "hereditary pessimism" was not common until at least the late 1860s and probably after, but Kasson rightly, I think, sees reformers "dampening their avowed reform expectations" in the fifties. See Katz, *Irony,* 208 and Kasson, *Civilizing the Machine,* 106.

11. Fr. Augustus J. Thébaud, *Forty Years in the United States of America, 1839–1885* (New York, 1904), 256–57.

12. See Paul Kleppner, *The Cross of Culture: A Social Analysis of Midwestern Politics, 1850–1870* (New York, 1970), and Richard Jensen, *The Winning of the Midwest: Social and Political Conflict, 1888–1896* (Chicago, 1971).

13. Scisco, *Political Nativism,* 225.

14. See Handlin, *Boston's Immigrants,* 210, 207; Marcus Lee Hansen, *The Atlantic Migration, 1607–1860: A History of the Continuing Settlement of the United States* (Cambridge, Mass., 1940), 306; Higham, *Strangers in the Land,* 14; David Brion Davis, *The Slave Power Conspiracy and the Paranoid Style* (Baton Rouge, 1969), 84.

15. Thébaud, *Forty Years,* 256–57, 297.

16. Two of the most famous comedic songs of the Civil War era were the German dialect pieces "Corporal Schnapps," by Henry Clay Work, and F. Poole's "I Goes to Fight mit Sigel." For lyrics see Paul Glass and Louis C. Singer, eds., *Singing Soldiers: A History of the Civil War in Song* (New York, 1964), 115–19; Benjamin Apthorp Gould, *Investigations in the Military and Anthropological Statistics of American Soldiers* (New York, 1869), 29.

17. Gould, *Investigations,* 218; for a more thorough discussion of Civil War era ethnology see John S. Haller, "Civil War Anthropometry: The Making of a Racial Ideology," *Civil War History* 16 (December 1970), 309–24.

18. Jedediah H. Baxter, *Statistics, Medical and Anthropological, of the Provost Marshal General's Bureau,* 2 vols. (Washington, 1875), 1:23–56.

19. Frances Bowen, "Remarks on the Latest Form of the Development Theory," *Memoir of the American Academy of Arts and Sciences* 8 (1860), 98–107; Asa Gray, review of *The Origin of Species by Means of Natural Selection,* by Charles Darwin, *American Journal of Science* 29 (March 1860), 153–84.

20. Charles Loring Brace, *The Races of the Old World* (New York, 1863), 14.

21. Ibid., 15–16, 278–79, 511–12.

22. Charles E. Buckingham, *The Sanitary Condition of Boston* (Boston, 1875), 76. By 1875 Buckingham seems to have been among a declining number of students of population who believed that the higher mortality rate among "Celts" in the United States demonstrated the persistence of "racial" distinctions in white America; *New York Herald,* May 31, 1870; U.S. Congress, House, "Emancipation and Colonization," H. Report 148, 37th Cong., 2nd sess., 1862, 14.

23. Anders Retzius, "Present State of Ethnology in Relation to the Form of the Human Skull," ed. J. Aitken Meigs, in *Annual Report of the Board of Regents of the Smithsonian Institution for 1859* (Washington, 1860), 251.

24. John W. Draper, *Thoughts on the Future Civil Policy of America* (New York, 1865), 164–65, 86.

25. Ibid., 107, 164.

26. Baxter, *Statistics,* 1:23–56; Dr. Sanford B. Hunt, "The Negro as a Soldier," *Anthropological Review* 7 (January 1869), 42–43. John S. Haller discusses Hunt's work for the United States Sanitary Commission at length. See Haller, "Anthropometry," 315–16.

27. J. C. Nott, M.D., "Instincts of Races," *New Orleans Medical and Surgical Journal* 19 (July and September 1866), 146.

28. Ibid., 5.

29. "Sources from Which Great Empires Come," *DeBow's Review* 18 (June 1855), 704.

30. "Campaign Broadside #1: The Miscegenation Record of the Republican Party," *New York (Caucasian) Day Book,* October 1, 1864, p. 3.

31. Frances Kemble, *Journal of a Residence on a Georgia Plantation* (New York, 1863), 105.

32. For a brief discussion of the Irish-American response to Chinese immigration see Stuart Creighton Miller, *The Unwelcome Immigrant: The American Image of the Chinese, 1785–1882* (Berkeley, 1969), 199–200.

33. Tsiang, *The Question of Expatriation in America,* 86–97; Frederick Douglass to Gerrit Smith, July 3, 1874, in Foner, *Life and Writings of Frederick Douglass,* 4:306.

34. Barbara Miller Solomon, *Ancestors and Immigrants: A Changing New England Tradition* (Cambridge, Mass., 1956), 75, 79, 117; Curtis, *Anglo-Saxons and Celts,* 90.

Index

abolitionists, 15, 19–20, 125, 155
Act of Union (1801), 36, 38
adjectives, ethnic, 23–24, 27, 186–196
*Against Behavioralism: A Critique of
Behavioral Science* (Ions), xv
Agassiz, Louis, 111, 114
Ambuscade, The (Whitney), 159
American and Foreign Christian
Union, 57, 134, 136
American Brotherhood, 46
American Celt, 153
American Colonization Society, 154
*American Cyclopedia: A Popular Dic-
tionary of General Knowledge, The*
(Ripley and Dana), 89
*American Dictionary of the English
Language* (Webster), 146, 165
American Journal of Science, 115
American party, 9, 27, 131, 132
anti-Irish sentiment in, 29, 138
as culmination of nativism, 134
Fillmore nominated by, 132, 135
platform of, 136, 162, 164
American Party in Politics, The (Lee),
131
American Protestant, The, 131
American Protestant Association, 45,
152
American Protestant Reformation So-
ciety, 45
American Protestant Society, 9, 131,
151
American Quarterly Review, 58, 96–
97, 107
American Republican party, 9, 46, 153
American Whig Review, 89, 95, 125,
157
"Angel Gabriel" (evangelist), 82
Anglo-Americans:
American identity limited to, 73–
74, 89, 96–97, 99–100, 180

anti-European attitudes among, 51–
53, 64
"Celtic-American" ethnicity supported by, 180
diversity of, 95, 96
ethnicity as source of identity for,
99–100, 102, 129
ethnology and, 111, 121, 127, 129
Germans in relation to, 32–33, 99,
166
nativist view of, 160
in Philadelphia Kensington and
Southwark riots, 84–85
race issue among, 88, 90, 100–101,
102, 127
Saxon vs. Norman temperament in,
96
sense of self among, 98, 127
work ethic upheld by, 78
Anglo-Saxons, 109, 110, 121, 125,
138, 160
Celts in relation to, 175, 176, 177
physical characteristics of, 180
anthropometry, 174, 175, 177
anti-Catholicism:
anti-foreignism and, 134
ethnic attitudes and, 20
evangelical form of, 57, 67
home missionary societies and, 81
in Irish stereotype, 56, 57, 58, 66
nativism and, 9, 134, 138–139, 148,
150, 151
in political campaigns, 27, 171
publications of, 45
"trustee" controversies role in, 45
Anti-Masonic party, 20, 50
Arieli, Yehoshua, 7, 40, 129–130
Asian immigrants, 182
*Awful Disclosures of the Hotel Dieu
Nunnery of Montreal* (Monk),
45

About the Author

Born in East Cleveland, Ohio, Dale T. Knobel received his B.A. from Yale University in 1971, and his Ph.D. from Northwestern University in 1977. He has taught at Northwestern University and Texas A & M University, where he is an associate professor of history. He is one of several authors of *Prejudice,* edited by Stephan Thernstrom. His home is in Bryan, Texas.

About the Book

This book has been composed in Fairfield with Perpetua display by Yankee Typesetters of Concord, New Hampshire.

It has been printed on 50 pound Antique Cream by Maple-Vail Book Manufacturing Group of Binghamton, New York. Binding has also been done by Maple-Vail Book Manufacturing Group.

Book and jacket design is by Joyce Kachergis Book Design & Production of Bynum, North Carolina.